# Happiness

Personhood, Community, Purpose

PEDRO ALEXIS TABENSKY
*University of Pretoria, South Africa*

# ASHGATE

Published by Ashgate Publishing Limited
Gower House
Croft Road
Aldershot
Hampshire GU11 3HR
England

Ashgate Publishing Company
Suite 420
101 Cherry Street
Burlington, VT 05401-4405
USA

Ashgate website: http://www.ashgate.com

**British Library Cataloguing in Publication Data**
Tabensky, Pedro Alexis
   Happiness : personhood, community, purpose
   1. Happiness
   I. Title
   170

**Library of Congress Control Number:** 2002100835

ISBN 0 7546 0734 8

Printed and bound in Great Britain by MPG Books Ltd, Bodmin, Cornwall

# Contents

# Acknowledgements

This book, like any other book, is the product not only of its author, but also of its time. Of course, it goes without saying that one is not related to all history-builders – to all individuals – in the same manner. One relates to the totality by establishing an impressive variety of dialogical threads that weave themselves together thus forming a complex, subtle and dynamic tapestry of intertwined lives. I have the entire tapestry within which my life is nested to thank for, without such a tapestry, this book would never have come about. That said, many weavers have played particularly prominent roles in its development – many more than I could possibly mention here. But let me acknowledge a few prominent exemplars. Peta Bowden and Jeff Malpas have always shown great interest in the project, and I have gained immensely from their ongoing engagement with it. I also thank Martin McAvoy for his valuable assistance with the subtleties of ancient Greek: it is almost as if he was sent to me from the distant past. I would also like to thank the Hebrew University of Jerusalem for the much needed funding required for seeing this project through. For related reasons I would also like to thank Murdoch University and the University of Sydney. Finally, I also have my parents Judith and Romualdo to thank for breathing the right sort of life into me, and for being there no matter what.

# Abbreviations of Works by Aristotle

| | |
|---|---|
| *De Anima* | *DA* |
| *Ethica Eudemia* | *EE* |
| *Ethica Nichomachea* | *EN* |
| *Metaphysica* | *M* |
| *Physica* | *Ph* |
| *Politica* | *P* |

Let us resume our inquiry and state, in view of the fact that all knowledge and every pursuit aims at some good, what it is that we say political science aims at and what is the highest of all goods achievable by action. Verbally there is very general agreement; for both the general run of men and people of superior refinement say that it is happiness; but with regard to what happiness is they differ, and the many do not give the same account as the wise. (Aristotle, *Ethica Nichomachea* 1095a 13–22)

But this must be agreed upon beforehand, that the whole account of conduct must be given in outline and not precisely, as we said at the very beginning that the account we demand must be in accordance with the subject matter; matters concerned with the conduct and questions of what is good for us have no fixity, any more than matters of health. The general account being of this nature, the account of particular cases is yet more lacking in exactness; for they do not fall under any art of precept but the agents themselves must in each case consider what is appropriate to the occasion, as happened also in the art of medicine or of navigation. (Aristotle, *Ethica Nichomachea* 1104a 1–9)

Chapter 1

# Introduction: A Basic Topography of the Ethical Domain

## The Legacy

The primary aim of this investigation is not to elucidate complex philosophical matters for the sake of making a contribution to the philosophical tradition within which it is embedded – not at all. To be sure, the investigation will hopefully have the effect of paying respect to the venerable philosophical tradition of the West. Indeed, the manner in which I pay my respects is one that takes me back to the very origins of Western philosophy. But I have been taken so far back not primarily because of my love for the history that precedes me and on which my philosophical views depend, but because I wanted to capture the very spirit that was present when Western philosophy was born and which was largely lost during its long journey to the present. But rather than excavate its remains in the manner of an archaeologist investigating the material remains of a long dead civilization, what I want to do here is to help resuscitate the spirit of Ancient philosophy.

Socrates died for philosophy. He gave his life for what he believed. He could do this not simply because he *did* philosophy but, more importantly, because he *lived* philosophy. The case of Socrates – his sacrifice – epitomizes the way in which the Ancients understood philosophy. They did philosophy for the sake of life. One could be tempted to hold the view that Socrates' sacrifice contradicts this last claim. But no contradiction exists – on the contrary. Socrates gave his life for the sake of life, but not simply for the sake of life. He gave his life for the sake of the best sort of life – the noble life (life in its most complete form). He could have avoided death but he did not because he understood the value of dignity and personal strength. Socrates understood that his life as a whole would have been tainted if he did not choose to die in the way that he did. Philosophy formed an integral part of this life that ended as it did insofar as this life was the expression of a philosophical outlook – a philosophical way of living.

I was led back to the Ancients because, for them, philosophy was lived and not just done. This was so because philosophy was not the goal of philosophy. As mentioned already, they did philosophy for the sake of life – the best sort of life. Aristotle's distinction between *sophia* and *phronesis* – between intellectual and practical wisdom – attests to this. He was fully

1

aware of the limitations of purely intellectual pursuits in the sense that he thought that the intellect alone could not solve the problems of life, and life was ultimately what needed to be understood – both intellectually and practically.

The path I have chosen in philosophy is one that a Greek thinker would have typically chosen, and it is because of my desire to come to terms with life that I have written this book. However, I am fully aware that the task of coming to terms with life is much more complex – and interesting, I might add – than the mere task of writing a book. And it is for reasons of this sort that I think this book, like any book on the matter, can only play a limited role.

So, this investigation can be seen as an attempt to recapture the Greek spirit and to suggest that perhaps we should begin to rethink the manner in which we understand our lives, and what we do with them. Its aim is to show that we must start to understand the way in which we conduct our lives in relation to an understanding – both practical and intellectual – of the sorts of creatures that we are, and my suggestion at this point – one which this investigation attempts to substantiate – is that we are the creatures that we are in relation to the ethical ideal of living for the sake of happiness – happiness understood to a large extent as Aristotle understood *eudaimonia*. I can do no more than leave the reader to decide whether or not this investigation succeeds in achieving its goal.

This book is, at the same time, an ambitious and a humble attempt to understand our lives in relation to the fundamental goal of happiness. It is an ambitious attempt because its purpose is to set out the fundamental structure of an ethical outlook, and it is a humble attempt precisely because it recognizes that nothing more can be done here but to determine some fundamental directions for a manner of understanding our lives that is both new and old. One could say that the central goal of this book is to reconfigure the manner in which we understand the ethical and to open the floodgates in order to allow an ethical outlook that deserves much more attention to flow into the contemporary landscape of the ethical.

## Ethics Without Foundations

It would perhaps be helpful at this stage to further outline the motivational impetus behind my overall ethical project and, in so doing, I hope also to address one important objection to it. My concern to develop an ethic that flows from the very structure of our being partly stems from a view famously expressed by the Nietzschean dictum that God – understood generally as an external source of meaning – is dead. This sort of ethical outlook involves the view that there are no external grounds for meaningfully talking about the ethical. In other words, it involves holding the view that there is no hope of creating what could be characterized as a

Cartesian ethic – there is no hope of finding 'ethical axioms'. I would further like to stress here that it seems that any conception of the good not grounded on a holistic ontology of the subject will be forced to rely on some external authority as a source of ultimate justification. Traditionally, this source was a divine one, and I do not think a better one has replaced it.

I want to distance myself as far as possible from this Cartesian (foundationalist) approach to ethics, since such an approach, I believe, will always and necessarily end up attempting to explain the ethical by attempting to shift the burden of explanation from the immediate concern of explaining the ethical to the less immediate concern of making sense of the notion of an external authority. This last notion, I suggest, is a hopelessly obscure one (whether divine or not). So, if I am right, appealing to an external authority amounts to appealing to something that cannot be clarified for the sake of explaining what could conceivably be clarified – namely, the ethical. Moreover, and relatedly, an appeal to an external authority does not help us understand how a given moral principle is relevant to our lives – of how we can grasp the point, the *raison d'être*, of a given moral principle. The question is left open regarding how to fit a given moral principle into the overall pattern of a life. But if this is the case, as I think it is, then it appears that the theoretical work being done by appealing to an external authority is very limited indeed. A holistic ontology – and, I believe, *only* a holistic ontology – can explain the fit of a given moral principle into the overall pattern of a life, and in this manner make the principle relevant, and hence meaningful, to our lives.

One can only, for instance, make sense of the principle that, in general, killing should be avoided if one understands how this principle fits into the overall pattern of one's life *qua* the life of a person.[1] Put another way, one can only make sense of this principle from the vantage point of a person, and doing so amounts to understanding the principle in the light of an overall understanding of who one is. Moreover (and this is a crucial point against foundationalist approaches to ethics) it is this overall understanding that justifies the principle precisely because it is its source of intelligibility. It is only within the system that constitutes a life that the principle that killing should be avoided can be made sense of, since the system in question is its source of justification. Why this is the case is something that shall become plain as this investigation proceeds.

I have claimed that the beauty of holistic systems is that they do not need to appeal to questionable higher authorities as a source of justification. But, of course, holistic systems avoid appeal to higher authorities by being circular. While it might initially seem as though circular systems are necessarily vicious ones, I do not think this is the case at all, and I hope it will become apparent in the ensuing discussion why I take this view. One holistic system that is clearly not viciously circular is a map. A map is a holistic system because each of the elements of a map derives its significance from the system within which it belongs. More specifically, it is a system of locations, and locations are just that in relation to other such locations. Likewise, the meanings of the aspects that constitute our lives are a function of comparable, yet certainly not identical, structures.

I argue our lives are structured holistically. Moreover, this holistic organization is also a teleological one insofar as it has happiness as its ultimate source (*arche*) of meaning. Why the source in question is not a foundation in the Cartesian sense will be further elucidated as this investigation unfolds. Since happiness plays such a central role in the investigation, let us move on and attempt to shed some light on this singularly important, yet elusive, concept.

## The Plausibility of a Unitary Conception of Happiness

I never cease to wonder how it is that, for the most part (at least after giving the matter a bit of thought), we tend to agree that happiness is the fundamental goal of people's lives. Let us refer to this apparent guiding principle – that life is lived for the sake of happiness – as the '*eudaimon* principle'. On the whole, we seem to agree (though perhaps we might not express it in this way) that the desire for happiness is the fundamental justification for choosing what could generally be characterized as a particular lifestyle – a particular way of going about the business of living.[2]

I share this wonder about happiness with the Ancients, particularly with Aristotle (and also, to a lesser degree, with Plato). Aristotle's basic insight – one that is at the core of what could be characterized as his ethical ontology of the subject – is that people desire above all else to be happy. In fact, one could safely say that, for Aristotle, any ethic that did not address the issue of happiness would be inconceivable, since the very reason for theorizing about ethics is to understand the nature of happiness and the conditions within which happiness can be attained. The very purpose of working within the field of ethics, Aristotle thinks, is to increase our understanding of what it is to live a good life, and the good life is just what the happy life is, according to him. I agree with Aristotle on these matters, and I shall attempt to show why happiness and ethics are so tightly coupled.

I also think it is fairly safe to claim that, on the whole, we are able to recognize individuals who are happy (relatively speaking), and also to recognize to some extent, though not unambiguously, the degree to which specific individuals are happy. Moreover, it seems that we are able to share our individual conceptions of happiness in our conversations about the matter in a way that strongly suggests that we are talking about a specific subject matter known to us all. Indeed, if there was no such agreement, there would be no common subject matter underpinning our conversations about happiness. Happiness would be an equivocal term. For agreement about the nature of happiness to be possible we must have a pre-theoretical understanding of the nature of happiness.

Although some might legitimately protest that I am being over optimistic here, I nonetheless want to insist that there are good reasons for not being pessimistic about the existence of a common conception of happiness, since we obviously attach a great deal of importance to being happy, and we do so in a way that suggests a large degree of intersubjective agreement. For example, we are often willing to tell others that happiness is the goal of life. The very act of telling someone presupposes that one has the intention to be understood, and presumably we can only be properly understood in this instance if, when we communicate, we use 'happiness' in at least roughly the same way; alternatively, the speaker must at least believe that the meaning of his or her sentence will be understood, independently of whether or not the target audience speaks the same language (or idiolect) as he or she does. Generally, that we do seem to be talking about much the same thing when talking about happiness is evidenced by the fact that we are willing to have agreements and disagreements about the nature of happiness in a manner that is analogous to our agreements and disagreements about any other subject matter that preoccupies us on a day-to-day basis.[3]

So, we must have knowledge about what happiness is in order to be able to know what it is we are agreeing about, or indeed, disagreeing about, when talking about it. But, given that this knowledge is not readily available to the mind's eye since, if it were, then we would not have to make sense of the notion of happiness in the first place (because we would already explicitly know what it is), the knowledge at issue must to some degree, be concealed from our intellectual faculty.

I wish to emphasize here that the type of concealment at issue here is not complete concealment, but rather, as I have said, concealment from our intellectual faculty, since we are, as already mentioned above, to some extent capable of identifying individuals who are happy (relatively speaking). If we were not capable of doing this, happiness would not even be an issue (yet it clearly is). The type of distinction between the forms of knowledge at issue here is analogous to the distinction between being a competent language user and being *aware* (in an intellectual sense) of the rules of grammar, and the meaning of the words one uses. One does not need to be aware of the rules of grammar, and one does not have to know the definition of the words that one uses in order to be able to speak competently (although one certainly must know grammar and, for the most part, know the meaning of the words one uses). Likewise, one might be able to use the word 'happiness' competently while being unable to articulate accurately what 'happiness' means. Nonetheless, if one is able to use the word competently, one must, to a large extent, know what happiness is – one must be able to identify the phenomenon. I hope to show – following Aristotle in particular, but not exclusively – that there is much of substance that can be said about the nature of happiness.

Since the notion of happiness is something that is presupposed in our conversations about the matter, then the process of understanding happiness can be understood as one of unconcealment, but the unconcealment of something already familiar to us. It is an unconcealment of something which, in a sense, is known already. I hope, for this reason, that the findings of this investigation will not be completely alien to the reader but, rather, familiar and enlightening at the same time – much like the process of discovering something that, in some way, we knew all along. Moreover, it is crucial that my account of happiness is found to be familiar, since I want the reader to agree with me that the subject matter under discussion is indeed happiness and not another matter altogether.

I mentioned above that the process of understanding the nature of happiness is to *unconceal* what we already know about this subject. This claim must be qualified though, since in discovering what we already hold about happiness we are also able to find inconsistencies and fill in gaps in our original conception. So the process of fully understanding happiness will also involve *revising* our original conception. But, of course, this revision must not be too radical, since, to repeat, I want to understand what happiness is rather than end up talking about another subject altogether.[4]

I shall argue, following Aristotle, that one of the fundamental reasons for wanting to unconceal the nature of happiness is that our fundamental directedness towards happiness is what grounds an ethical life – a good life. More precisely, a good life, I shall argue, is the sort of life that is lived for the sake of happiness, and it is defined as a good life precisely because it is constitutive of happiness. To put the matter in slightly different terms, it could be claimed that the ethic I will be developing here is able to address the question 'Why be ethical rather than unethical?' by showing that the fundamental motivation for being ethical is that our happiness depends on it. I have good reasons to believe – reasons that will hopefully become plain – that Aristotle has more of interest to say than anyone else in the long history of philosophy about the crucial relationship that exists between happiness – between what Aristotle refers to as *eudaimonia* – and ethics.

I certainly do not agree with everything Aristotle has to say about the ethical, but since my inquiry is not primarily exegetical – as I intend primarily to use Aristotle's thought rather than provide a contribution to Aristotelian scholarship – I will not, for the most part, engage in detailed analysis of the parts of Aristotle's philosophy, and particularly of his *Ethics*, that do not play a substantial role in the development of a new ethic grounded on our natural desire for happiness. There is certainly much to be said against Aristotle's defence of aristocracy over democracy and also about his views regarding the status of women and slaves. But, as I hope to show below, Aristotle's controversial stance on these matters does not affect the central tenets of his ethical thought and, in fact, his views on the status of women and slaves conflict with his central views regarding what it is to be a person – they conflict, in other words, with his ontology of the subject.

In developing an ethic in the spirit of Aristotle's thought, I will use some key Aristotelian themes to develop an ethic of my own. And it is precisely because I am not primarily interested in the details of Aristotle's work that I shall take the liberty of not always following Aristotle closely and shall also be drawing from the intellectual wells of other thinkers. Aristotle, for instance, assumes that by nature we are social creatures. I believe that this is something that cannot be taken for granted and will primarily make use of the work of thinkers such as Donald Davidson, Nancy Sherman, Jeff Malpas, Martha Nussbaum and Alasdair MacIntyre, among others, to support this fundamental claim.[5]

Let me now proceed to outline the basic structure of this investigation. In the following section I illustrate what Aristotle means by *eudaimonia* by contrasting Aristotle's conception with three prevalent contemporary common-sense conceptions of what happiness is, and I argue that Aristotle's conception accords with one interpretation of one of the three common-sense conceptions of happiness. More specifically, I argue that *eudaimonia* means roughly the same as 'happiness' in the sense of living a happy, or good, life. Moreover, the sense of good that is relevant here is the ethical sense – the sense of good as in 'he or she is a good person'.

In Chapter 2 I discuss the relationship that exists between ethics, being a person, and achieving *eudaimonia*. I argue that we are defined as persons by a certain manner of operating that is constitutive of an ethical life, which is, but not without qualification, what a *eudaimon* life is. I argue, moreover, that the *eudaimon* principle – the principle that life is lived for the sake of *eudaimonia* and for the sake of nothing else – is the basic structural feature of the lives of persons. This does not mean that to be a person one must actually be living one's life for the sake of *eudaimonia*. Rather, it means that the lives of persons are defined in relation to the ethical ideal of living for the sake of *eudaimonia*. In other words, my claim is that *eudaimonia* is the *telos* – the goal or end – of the lives of persons. It is in relation to this *telos* that the teleological structure that is constitutive of personhood is determined, since our *telos* is the ultimate source (*arche*) of the meaning of our lives understood as the lives of persons (as opposed to, say, understood as the lives of creatures that belong to a certain natural kind).[6]

In the final section of Chapter 2 I establish some revealing parallels between being a person and making a work of art principally in order to set out some of the basic themes that will be dealt with throughout this investigation. I argue, among other things, that the process of forming one's life is not typically rule-governed. One of the fundamental distinctions I try to establish is the one between having a rule of conduct and having a skill. I argue that ethical action is typically skill-based rather than rule-based. Skills, moreover, are developed in a manner that is analogous to learning how to paint or learning how to play an instrument. These skills are learnt in the act of exercising them; they are mastered once one has come to develop certain *habits*. In the case of living, the habits at issue are the virtues, which are precisely that – namely, virtues – in relation to the ideal of good living. Indeed, it is by mastering the virtuous habits that one is able to form one's

life as a whole in the best possible way – in the way that is constitutive of
*eudaimonia*. I shall make special use of these findings in the last part of this
investigation in order to show how ongoing intimate (and healthy
relationships) – relationships of *philia* (roughly, friendship) – are necessary
for developing the habits that are constitutive of *eudaimonia*. Indeed, I
further argue towards the end of the investigation that good *philoi* form the
basis for a healthy community given that healthy communities are
communities constituted by virtuous individuals – individuals who have
mastered the technique of good living in the company of good friends.

In establishing the analogy between painting and living I also emphasize
the role that difference plays in our lives. I argue that, although there is much
in common between us, in the same way there is much in common between
the different ways in which paintings are produced, there is nevertheless a
huge scope for unique manifestations of the ideals that define both the
practice of painting and the practice of living.

In Chapter 3 I provide a relatively detailed critical account of Aristotelian
teleology. In this chapter, more than anywhere else in this investigation, I
engage with the details of Aristotle's ontology in order to clarify the
fundamental structure of the lives of persons. The structure at issue, I have
already claimed, is a teleological one. In this chapter I argue, among other
things, that our substantial form – that which ultimately defines us as the
sorts of creatures that we are – is *eudaimonia*. This particular interpretation
goes against the canonical view that our substantial form is, according to
Aristotle, *psyche* (soul). I argue that my interpretation is better because it
integrates more successfully the material from *Metaphysica* and *De Anima*
with the central tenets of the *Ethics*. However, my main purpose here, as
elsewhere, is not primarily to make a contribution to Aristotelian
scholarship. Rather, by arguing that *eudaimonia* is our substantial form, I am
able to clarify my own views with regard to the central structural role that
happiness plays in our lives. In this chapter I provide a relatively detailed
account of why we are defined as the creatures that we are – as persons – in
relation to the *eudaimon* ideal. This last claim amounts to saying that what
gives a life its meaning is its ideal directedness towards the *eudaimon telos*.
The different aspects that constitute our lives are ideally organized in a way
that renders each of these aspects intelligible in the light of the overall
*rational* structure that constitutes a *eudaimon* life. Indeed, I argue later (in
Chapters 4, 5 and 6 particularly) that the *eudaimon* ideal is one of rationality
– an ideal in which our propositional attitudes, and the behaviour that is
expressive of these attitudes, are organized in a way that maximizes the
rationality in our lives. In Chapter 3, among other things, I work through the
intimate relationship that exists between our *telos* and *logos* (understood
both as rational principle and complete virtue in this context).

In Chapter 4 I attempt to explain what Aristotle means by his
characterization of *eudaimonia* as activity in conformity with complete
virtue (*logos*). In order to clarify this characterization of happiness, I work

through the relationship that exists between the rational unity of a life – the teleological unity – and virtue. Amongst other things, I argue, following Aristotle that the virtues are the qualities of character from which an ideally rational life flows. This theme is, of course, thoroughly Aristotelian.

In Chapter 5 I continue exploring the rational unity that constitutes a happy life by applying what I refer to as *the method of critical introspection*. This hermeneutic method aims to show how our lives are ideally organized. I use three examples to illustrate in what sense our lives are rationally organized. By using the method of critical introspection I attempt to show that lives that were fundamentally directed towards the achievement of pleasure, the lives of gods or immortal lives would not be lives capable of achieving *eudaimonia*, since they would not be compatible with the ideal of organization that constitutes a *eudaimon* life. The method of critical introspection determines the value of a particular mode of living by establishing how the different aspects defining our lives fit together. An immortal, for example, would be incapable of having the relevant ordering required for living an ideally rational life. That is, the sorts of sacrifice that would have to be made for living an immortal life would, after close scrutiny, be far too great to be desirable. By showing how the different aspects that constitute our ideal mode of living hang together I also show that it makes sense to speak of such a thing as personhood (the being of persons), and I also establish the tight correlation between being a person and living a *eudaimon* life.

In Chapter 6 I show why there are good reasons for believing that persons are, by nature, social creatures – something that Aristotle himself takes for granted. But notwithstanding the strong intuitive appeal for holding that our sociality is an integral part of being the sorts of creatures whom we are, it is not something we can now simply take for granted. Donald Davidson's discussion regarding the sociality of thought is of particular relevance here. I also extend Davidson's argument somewhat in order to make a case for understanding the ideal social order as one that provides the conditions and fosters the expression of difference. I do this by making use of Orwell's *Nineteen Eighty-Four* in order to show how the basic conditions for rationality set out by Davidson cannot be fully implemented in a world where only one perspective prevails – Big Brother's in the case of Orwell's dystopia. The issue of our sociality is a central one, and I take it up in detail in Chapter 7.

In the final part of this investigation (Chapter 7) I focus on the relationship that exists between the *teloi* of individuals and the way in which we relate to others. I argue that the rational ideal that constitutes a *eudaimon* life can only be achieved if we are able to relate to others in ways that promote not only one's own good, but also that of the community at large within which one's life is played out. The good of others, in other words, is implicated in one's own good. First, I establish the constitutive role our bonds of love or friendship (*philia*) – enduring intimate relationships of *care* – play in making our lives ones that are blessed with *eudaimonia*. I argue that one can only develop and fully exercise the virtues – the qualities of character that are constitutive of *eudaimonia* – if one is capable of establishing enduring bonds of love with others, and particularly, with virtue friends – friends who live their lives in accordance with complete virtue (the enduring states or dispositions that are constitutive of the best sorts of characters). Friendships, I further argue, following Aristotle, do not merely play an instrumental role in the achievement of *eudaimonia* as it might initially appear. On the contrary, having friendships is a constitutive aspect of *eudaimonia*. My friends' happiness forms part of my own.

Finally, I argue that one can only achieve *eudaimonia* if the community at large, within which our lives are embedded, is what could be characterized as a *eudaimon* community – one that is informed by the ideal of what I refer to as communal justice. This is a community of the sort in which, on the whole, the individuals who constitute it express their care and concern for the community at large, and not just for those whom they share with intimately.[7] Moreover, individuals are only able to express themselves fully in ways that are constitutive of *eudaimonia* if their actions are informed by the ideal of communal justice. This ideal of justice, I further argue, is fostered primarily in the intimate company of virtue friends. In short, I argue that individual virtue and public justice – the principles that inform our ideal interactions with the community at large – form a continuum that cannot be broken without undermining both individual virtue and public justice. Individual virtue and public justice are bound up in such a way that the very reason for the existence of justice is the role that the general good plays in the achievement of *eudaimonia* by the members of a given community.

In summary, then, the structure of this investigation is as follows. The fundamental question I address is 'What is happiness?' and I argue, among other things, that happiness is the goal of life – it is the goal that defines us as persons. As such, happiness is a rational ideal. I provide a relatively detailed account of what happiness is, and I argue that individual happiness cannot be separated from the overall happiness of the community within which individuals dwell. The central goal of this investigation is to establish what happiness is and to show that one cannot live this ideal sort of life unless the social conditions, including one's relationships with *philoi*, are adequate. The happy person is the person of good character (the person who has developed the virtues) living in a community within which that individual can express his or her goodness amongst other individuals similarly disposed. In this investigation I establish what I take is the fundamental interconnection that exists between psychological well-being, the ethical, and the social.

## The Different Senses of Happiness and their Relationship to *Eudaimonia*

I mentioned above that the Aristotelian term for happiness is *eudaimonia*. However, this translation cannot be taken for granted, since, at first glance,

Aristotle's characterization of *eudaimonia* is radically different from anything we would simply and uncontroversially be prepared to call happiness. In short, for Aristotle, a *eudaimon* life is a life of an individual with practical wisdom (*phronesis*) living in a good (*eudaimon*) community or, perhaps, more generally, living in a context which is suitable for the development of *eudaimonia*. This context is, fundamentally, intersubjective and, more particularly, an intersubjective context in which individuals in general *act* in ways that are constitutive of their own individual *eudaimon* lives. Importantly, the reason why the context which makes *eudaimonia* possible must be intersubjective is that *eudaimonia* is constituted by a manner of operating amongst others. Clearly, this very schematic characterization of *eudaimonia* is not a characterization of what we would normally mean by 'happiness'. In order to establish the adequacy of the translation at issue, I shall now discuss what I take to be the three prevailing contemporary modes of understanding happiness and show that, on closer inspection, one of these modes or, more precisely, at least one of the possible interpretations of one of these modes, is very similar to Aristotle's notion of *eudaimonia*.

First, happiness can be understood as a current state of mind – a state of cheerfulness – as it is understood in the context of the sentence 'I feel happy now'. To be happy in this way is not, at first sight, dependent on the moral status of the cause of cheerfulness. It seems that one could, for example, feel happy independently of whether or not the emotion is, or is not, caused by an evil act. So, this sense of 'happiness' appears to lack an ethical dimension.

Second, happiness can be understood as being in favourable, fortunate, good or happy circumstances such as, for instance, being healthy and having more than sufficient external goods (I might be happy, for example, because I have a good job). To be in a happy situation, quite obviously, is to be in a situation that allows an individual to be happy. Now, since happiness is most commonly understood as the feeling of cheerfulness, we would most commonly consider that those circumstances that facilitate this feeling are those that we would describe as happy circumstances.[8] So, we can now see how this second sense of happiness is most commonly intimately related to the previous one. In fact, both of the senses of happiness just described can be seen as mutually dependent. One can feel happy only if one is in appropriate circumstances and, to be in appropriate circumstances, under the most common understanding of what a happy circumstance is, is just to be in the circumstances required for feeling happy. It is also important to note that the second sense of happiness also seems to lack an ethical dimension since, as we have just seen, to be in favourable circumstances is determined by the first sense of happiness, which lacks an ethical aspect.

Finally, the third sense of happiness I shall discuss – happiness as in 'living a happy life' – is the kind of happiness we attribute to a life which, taken as a whole, is a *good* one. (Or, perhaps more commonly, a life is considered to be a happy one if the segment of a life that, for example, I am currently living is, taken as a whole, good.) This last sense of happiness, unlike the previous two already discussed, is the sense of happiness we would most willingly be prepared to describe as having, in some instances, an ethical dimension. We would be prepared to describe this last sense of happiness in this way if, as no doubt is often the case, by 'good' we mean 'morally good'.

It will become clear below that happiness understood in this third sense, particularly if understood as referring to the quality of a life (understood as a whole), cannot be fully characterized in terms of the first two senses of happiness, even though, obviously, a happy life must in general be pleasant and, for a life to be pleasant, the circumstances must generally be good (good circumstances being understood here as circumstances from which a given subject takes pleasure). The fundamental reason why one cannot reduce the third sense of happiness to the first two senses is, as we shall see below, that a life is an extremely complex fabric that involves much more than simply pleasure and the circumstances for pleasure (a complexity that is, I think, commonly acknowledged by most of us). In addition, I shall argue that, to understand a good life in this manner is to understand it as an organized – structured – whole (or unity). Such a unity is constituted by a general sort of organization of circumstances, emotions, thoughts, dispositions, actions and so on.

It is important to note at this point that the three senses of happiness discussed above are considered by Aristotle when analysing the popular Athenian beliefs about *eudaimonia*, and this coincidence just gives more support to the view that *eudaimonia* is appropriately translated as 'happiness'. Aristotle, with regard to '… the highest of all goods achievable by action …',[9] argues that:

> Verbally there is very general agreement; for both the general run of men and people with superior refinement say that it is happiness, and identify living well and faring well with being happy; but with regard to what happiness is they differ, and the many do not give the same account as the wise. For the former think it is some plain and obvious thing, like pleasure, wealth, honour; they differ, however, from one another – and often even the same man identifies things, with health when he is ill, with wealth when he is poor.[10]

Aristotle argues that, on the one hand, some people identify *eudaimonia* with pleasure, and this identity is analogous with the identity some establish between happiness and pleasure. On the other hand, some people identify *eudaimonia* with wealth and honour, and these are just two types of pleasant circumstance.[11] After this basic analysis of what is normally meant by the term, Aristotle proceeds to analyse *eudaimonia* proper, and his analysis is similar to, though much more sophisticated, than my initial characterization of one of the possible interpretations of the third sense of 'happiness' – the interpretation that involves understanding 'good' in ethical terms.[12]

*Eudaimonia,* we shall see, is most properly understood as a particular interpretation of the third kind of happiness. I shall, from now on, call the third sense of happiness 'well-being', 'flourishing', or simply 'happiness'. 'Happiness' will only be used to express the other two senses of happiness when specified. The choice of expressions is not capricious since 'well-being' and 'flourishing' are also common translations of *eudaimonia.* While both these translations have their strengths and weaknesses, I consider well-being to be an appropriate translation because the notion of well-being, like the notion of a happy life, refers to a certain style of living and so *may* implicate considerations regarding not just a specific segment of a life, but a life in its totality (understood as a complex active unity across time). The sense of happiness that involves considerations regarding a life as a whole is precisely the sense of happiness that Aristotle is most interested in analysing, and it is that which he refers to as *eudaimonia.* But although 'well-being' is a good translation of *eudaimonia,* as most translations of complex terms go, it is not a perfect one. 'Well-being', I think, does not place sufficient emphasis on the fact that, for Aristotle, happiness is a particular type of complex *activity,* indeed, more specifically, he argues that happiness is activity in conformity with virtue.[13]

Finally, 'flourishing' is also a relatively good translation of *eudaimonia* because it emphasizes other central features of this fundamental concept. 'Flourishing' is primarily a botanical concept and it denotes not only activity, but also activity in a particular direction – it denotes development (in the sense, for example, that a seed develops into a healthy mature plant). Moreover, when we say that something flourishes, we do not only mean that it develops in a particular direction. We mean something stronger. We mean that there is a *peak* of development in a particular direction, and this peak is what Aristotle refers to as the *telos* of a developing thing.[14] Plants that flourish, for example, not only grow into mature specimens of their particular species, they are also *paradigmatic exemplars* of their species. Moreover, human flourishing, like the flourishing of a plant, involves the full manifestation and the exercise of the characteristic dispositions that define us as the creatures that we are.[15] Furthermore, a plant flourishes not when one part of it flourishes to the detriment of other parts (assuming this type of flourishing is available to a plant), but when the plant as a whole flourishes – when the plant as a whole reaches its peak of development, its *telos.* Analogously, the flourishing of a human life understood as a whole involves the flourishing not of one aspect of that life (say, the professional aspect) to the detriment of another or other important aspects of that very life (as so often happens with compulsive professionals who dedicate little or no time to those they claim to love).[16]

Another crucial parallel between the concepts of flourishing and *eudaimonia* is that plants flourish when external conditions are *ideal.*[17] So the notion of flourishing ties in the flourishing of a given plant with the context in which that plant is located. As we shall see in more detail below, the *eudaimonia* of a given individual likewise cannot be separated from the external conditions within which that individual's life is played out. Indeed, for an individual to achieve *eudaimonia*, the external conditions must also be ideal. To use an example made famous by Aristotle and which I shall discuss in detail below, a person does not merely require friends, without further qualification, in order to achieve *eudaimonia*. Rather, an individual needs the best sorts of friends – friends who exercise their friendship in accordance with the *ideal* of friendship. Moreover, as I shall also discuss in some detail below, the ideal circle of friends which is required for a given individual to flourish depends also on its embeddedness in an ideally constituted community.

However, although the idea of flourishing stresses some aspects of *eudaimonia*, it does not give sufficient emphasis to other central aspects of *eudaimonia*, such as to the role pleasure plays in a *eudaimon* life. Nonetheless, even though 'flourishing' is not a perfectly adequate translation of *eudaimonia*, I still think it is a useful term given that it does bring the developmental and contextual aspects of *eudaimonia* into prominence. The similarities between the ideas of flourishing and *eudaimonia* will become clearer as we shed more light on the meaning of *eudaimonia*.

So, to recapitulate, depending on what aspect of *eudaimonia* one wants to bring into prominence, it can be understood most appropriately as either happiness, well-being or flourishing. It will become even clearer why *eudaimonia* can be understood in these ways as the discussion proceeds.

I have mentioned above that a correct analysis of happiness would show us that the best way of understanding happiness is to understand it as *eudaimonia*. Yet there are reasons for doubting that such an identity can be established. Contrary to Aristotle and, for that matter, contrary to ancient ethics generally, our contemporary intuitions, and many strands of contemporary ethics, seldom relate happiness to ethics and virtue. *Eudaimonia*, on the other hand, is the central concept of Aristotle's *Ethics* (as already stated above). But, I think, a proper clarification of 'happiness' – in the sense of living a happy life – will show us that it is, in fact, fundamentally an ethical concept. The reason why we do not generally understand happiness in the way in which Aristotle understands *eudaimonia*, we have already seen, is at least partly due to the fact that we generally and simplistically, though by no means universally, identify happiness with *feeling* happy. That said, however, pleasure particularly, and the emotions generally, also have a central role to play in Aristotle's *Ethics*. In fact, Aristotle explicitly provides us with reasons to believe that the *eudaimon* life is the *pleasantest* of lives.[18]

It might be worth clarifying that the defence I will be providing for an understanding of happiness understood as *eudaimonia* should in no way be understood as involving a refutation of the other senses. One of the beauties of the concept of *eudaimonia* is that it involves all prevalent understandings of happiness. We shall see in what sense the different senses of happiness form a system. And, indeed, it is partly because *eudaimonia* implicates all prevalent senses of happiness that I will be able to establish the plausibility of the sort of conception of happiness that I am currently defending. It is my hope that, by the end of this inquiry, one will be able to claim something along the lines that what has been argued in this investigation was something known to us all along. And indeed, as already argued above, one of the fundamental requirements of an acceptable theory of happiness is that it accords with basic intuitions, since the sort of analysis in question is an analysis of a concept that in a sense is already at least partially known to us all (or at least to most of us). I might just add parenthetically that the same applies to the concept of ethics. All I do, and all Aristotle does, is clear the way of confusion so that the concepts under analysis shine in all their splendour. Their brilliance is largely established by showing how concepts known to us all to some degree fit together to form a system of mutually constitutive concepts.

## Notes

1   One sort of external authority which I have not tackled explicitly is what could be described as intrinsic authority. This is the sort of authority one would be eliciting if one wanted to claim that a given moral principle was self-justifying. I have not explicitly dealt with this sort of self-justifying external authority because I think my comments against external authority generally apply to any sort of appeal to external authorities as grounds for the ethical.

2   One should not be tempted to suppose that the present claims are taken as gospel – they are not. The claims will be substantiated in the ensuing discussion.

3   Of course, the subject matter under discussion might not be clearly defined. But, if this were the case, then one of the fundamental goals in this type of discussion would be to determine the specific nature of the subject matter under scrutiny. Also, and crucially, even though it is perhaps an obvious point, for a subject matter not to be clearly determined presupposes that it must already be determined to a certain degree. If this were not the case then, again, our (purported) discussions would, literally, be *about* nothing. Finally, what I have said above is only intended to refer to the specific type of conversational situation which has as its goal to increase the shared intellectual understanding of the participants. Clearly not all conversational situations are discussions.

4   Indeed, to be a little more precise, a revision *qua* revision cannot be too radical, since the very function of a revision is to alter one's beliefs about a specific subject matter rather than to altogether shift one's attention away from it.

5   I will argue that the very possibility of existing as a person depends on being in communication with others. For this reason, I reject ideas such as those espoused by Hobbes and Locke who presuppose the possibility of there being radically autonomous persons. Contractarian theories of justice generally are inconsistent with the communitarian view I defend, since they presuppose the view that persons as such may exist prior to the establishment of social contracts.

6   Aristotle does think of personhood as a natural kind, and for reasons that will be given below, I think he is wrong, and wrong for reasons that he himself unwittingly provides.

7   There will, of course, be variations with respect to the sort of caring involved depending on the different sorts of relationships one (directly or indirectly) engages in. Obviously,

one will not, for example, be able to engage with every member of a given community in the same manner – that is, with the same level of intimacy and intensity.

8    I shall discuss a third sense of happiness – that which we use in our discussions about the happy life – shortly. I mention this here because an account of what are to count as favourable circumstances is parasitical upon which of the other two senses of happiness one is advocating at the time. Nonetheless, given that the most common contemporary conception of happiness is happiness understood as a state of cheerfulness, the most common understanding of living in happy circumstances is as living in circumstances that facilitate our being in a cheerful state.

9    *Ethica Nichomachea (EN)*, ed. D. Ross, Oxford: Clarendon Press, 1966, 1095a 16. Although in all subsequent quotations I will continue to use Ross's translation, I will also be comparing his translation with H. Rackham's, Cambridge, MA: Harvard University Press, 1994, and with J. Ackrill's, *A New Aristotle Reader*, Oxford: Clarendon Press, 1990.

10   *EN* 1095a 16–25.

11   I count honour as a circumstance because Aristotle holds that to have honour amounts to being honoured – to be in the circumstance of being honoured (*EN* 1095b 22–27).

12   For a rough and ready characterization of *eudaimonia* see, for example, *EN* 1098a 2–19, 1099b 25–28. Generally, *EN I* is a good starting point for coming to understand *eudaimonia.*

13   *EN* 1099b 25–27 and 1102a 5–7.

14   I do not want to suggest here that the peak of development is a fixed state. Aristotle explicitly holds the view that the *telos* of life involves the active exercise of the dispositions available to the fully developed person. Likewise, a plant *qua* living organism is continually active even when it reaches its *telos,* since it must be performing the functions that keep it alive (nourishing itself, replacing dead cells, photosynthesizing, and so on).

15   The exercise of the characteristic dispositions that define us, to use Aristotle's terminology, is a form of *energeia*, or activity. Moreover, to be more precise, the exercise of the dispositions that define us is an activity in the sense of *praxis* – that is, in the sense that the characteristic function (the *ergon*) of something that flourishes is the *refinement* of an activity typical of that very thing. Aristotle explicitly contrasts *praxis* with *poiesis*. *Poiesis* is the kind of *ergon* that is not the refinement of an activity, but instead the product of an activity (for example, the *ergon* of a hammer is to drive nails into hard surfaces rather than the act of hammering itself). For an explicit distinction between *praxis,* and its counterpart, *poiesis,* see *EN* 1094a 1–5.

16   I thank Brian Mooney for his helpful comments on these matters.

17   Note that the sense of 'ideal' being used here is quite a specific one. When we speak of the ideal environmental conditions required for a given plant to flourish, we are not alluding to any absolute understanding of what is to count as an ideal. Rather, the ideal conditions are just those conditions relative to the specific sorts of needs of a particular plant species. Indeed, what might count as ideal conditions for one sort of plant may be deadly for others. This is precisely the sort of ideal Aristotle considers when he sets out to provide, in general outline, what the ideal sort of life for persons is.

18   *EN* 1175a 17–21.

# Chapter 2

# Ethics and Personhood

**Preliminary Remarks Regarding How Personhood is Fundamentally an Ethical Concept**

In general terms, ethics is the field of inquiry that deals with issues pertaining to how persons *ought* to act (towards themselves, other persons, non-human animals, ecosystems, property, and so on). Ethics, in other words, primarily deals with issues concerning the appropriate or *good* manner of operating in the world – of acting in the world. It is only natural, then, to consider – as it has been considered by the tradition, by Plato and Aristotle particularly – that ethics in its most all-encompassing sense is the study of how one in general *ought* to live. For this reason it is not surprising that ethics and social/political theory are so closely linked, since social/political theory primarily concerns itself with the principles involved in regulating the *actions* of individuals living amongst others in social groups at large. Indeed, for Plato and Aristotle, social/political theory is just one branch of a more general ethical project, and so it should be, as we shall see as this investigation unfolds.

Moreover, to live the sort of life one ought to live is quite uninformatively to live a good life, since a good life is simply defined as the sort of life one ought to live. So, the most all-encompassing question addressed by ethics is 'What is the good life?'. This is the fundamental ethical question addressed by ancient philosophy, and it is the fundamental question, or one of its formulations, that I will be addressing in this investigation, because it will emerge that the good life *qua* ethical life is, to a large extent, the happy life. And, indeed, it is precisely because of this that we will be justified in characterizing the happy life as an *ethical ideal*.[1]

One of the predominant views of the Ancients is that one cannot understand what it is to be a person unless one also understands what sort of life the good life for persons is, since, following Aristotle particularly, the good for persons – the *telos* of persons – determines what it is to be a person. I might also add that, according to Aristotle, the reason why one must understand what sort of life the good life is in order to understand what it is to be a person is that a good life is the kind of life in which the potentials that define the lives of persons have been actualized. And, moreover, it is only in relation to a grasp of the actualized expression of a potential that we are able to determine a potential as such. As already claimed above, to understand fully what I mean by a potential and by the actualization of a potential I shall have to deal in some detail with Aristotle's very sophisticated teleological ontology – an ontology, furthermore, that I endorse in general outline. It is because of his teleological account of the being of persons that Aristotle is able to argue that a good life is the end of a process of development leading to the actualization of the potentials that define the lives of persons. Indeed, more generally, development, as such, is a goal-oriented process that leads to the actualization of the potentials of that which is in development. The goal itself is the condition of having all potentials actualized. When studying Aristotle's teleology in detail below we shall see that talk of potentials presupposes talk of a *telos* – a goal of development – which, in the case of persons, is the good or *eudaimon* life. Indeed, we shall see that it is only because we have a conception, albeit a rough one, of what it is to be a fully developed person – a person who has actualized his or her potentials – that we can conceive of persons as having the potentials in the first place.

I will now briefly explain some aspects of Aristotle's teleological ontology that are involved in being able to claim that someone is healthy, or indeed, unhealthy.[2] This example is a good one for it clearly shows how teleology is central to understanding the idea of development. It is only because we already have an idea about what it is to be healthy, and moreover only because we already conceive of the state of being healthy as a *good* one – as a state persons *ought* to be in – that we can talk meaningfully about persons having the potential for being healthy in the positive sense in which we refer to health as opposed to the negative sense in which we refer to the lack of health. Talking about a state in which one ought to be is tantamount to talking about a state that is an end – a *telos*. Conversely, it is also important to note that there is a sense in which it makes little sense to hold that people are potentially unhealthy simply because a person might become unhealthy. Clearly, we do normally refer to people as having the potentiality for lacking health but we also talk about having potentialities in another sense, and that is the sense that is relevant at present – namely that which is implied when we speak of having capabilities in contexts such as 'the conditions should be created for people to develop their capabilities'. The notion of a capability implies the notion of a potential, but one that is defined as such in relation to a good. To be unhealthy is not to gain something – to actualize a capability – but, instead, it is to lose something, to lose something good (health).[3] To repeat, a specific capability is only recognized as just that if one already has an idea of the end of development for that capability, and moreover the end of development is the good of development – it is defined as an end precisely because it is a good. It is only because we are able to talk in this manner – that is, it is only because the notion of the end of a developmental process is the same as the notion of the good of a developmental process – that we can also talk about states of privation *qua* states of lack, such as the state of being unhealthy.

A fascinating feature of developmental processes generally is that, as will become clearer below, they simply cannot be understood independently of ethical or, at the very least, evaluative considerations – considerations pertaining to the good of development. I shall further argue that it makes little sense to talk about the being of persons *qua* rational creatures without simultaneously talking about the ethic that defines us as such – the ethical good of human development. The end – the good – of the development of persons, is the condition in which one has achieved *eudaimonia*. So, I shall continue, *eudaimonia* is fundamentally an ethical notion – an ethical ideal.

Moreover, because our *telos* is our best condition, we shall see that it is the condition that ultimately defines us as the creatures that we are. So it is for this reason that the ethic I defend is indeed an ontology of the subject. Our *telos* defines us in this way because we are creatures who exist as such for the sake of *eudaimonia*. Additionally, I claimed above that each and every stage of the development of a person is defined as such with reference to our *telos* – with reference to our *ideal* condition, which is the condition of living a good life. The sort of ideal at issue here is that which is intimately tied up with the specific sorts of creatures that we are – creatures with specific potentials. We are not, by contrast, talking here about absolute ideals such as divine ideals (for example, of immortality and omnipotence). Ideals of this latter sort are defined as such without reference to, or at times in frank opposition to, the defining features of persons.

An important consequence follows from the acceptance of Aristotle's teleology. Since *eudaimonia* is the end of the process of development of individual persons, then it follows that a *eudaimon* individual is the sort of individual who has become a person in the fullest sense. Aristotle holds this much and I agree with him. Now, it is just because a *eudaimon* life is the sort of life that is lived by a person who exemplifies the *telos* of persons that the ethical life will be determined in the process of determining the being of persons.

Asking oneself about the being of persons involves asking oneself about the fundamental conditions that constitute the *lives* of persons, since to be a person is fundamentally to live a certain kind of life – that is, a certain way of living or a certain activity. Again, I am coming from within an Aristotelian framework when making this claim. Aristotle believes that we are defined as persons, by our *energeia* (activity) – that is, by a certain complex pattern of activities.[4] This claim seems very plausible if one considers that to be a person is not merely or even to be a certain biological organism.[5] Rather, a person is primarily defined as such because he or she is a *rational creature* – a creature that *operates* rationally.[6] *Eudaimonia,* then, is a characteristic manner of operating in the world.

## The *Eudaimon* Principle and its Relationship to the Shape of a Life

Aristotle commences his inquiry into the what-it-is of happiness by asking about the function – *ergon* – of persons, and quickly reaches the conclusion that *eudaimonia* is the *ergon* of persons.[7] Additionally, *eudaimonia*, Aristotle argues, is activity in conformity with virtue.[8] From these two characterizations of *eudaimonia*, it follows that the natural function of persons is to act in conformity with virtue. Moreover, if we assume with Aristotle, as we have done all along, that a basic feature of persons as such is their ideal directedness toward the *eudaimon telos*, it follows that we are defined as creatures whose *telos* is life lived in accordance with virtue.

Given this wide-ranging conception of happiness it is clear that we cannot expect to have a satisfactory account of *eudaimonia* until the very end of our inquiry into the nature of persons.[9] But, we can, like Aristotle, start by providing a few very rough guidelines so as to leave little scope for doubting that Aristotle's conception of happiness is both different and much richer than the prevalent contemporary understanding of this notion. By the end of this investigation the reader should be persuaded that the possibility of living the best possible life depends on holding an Aristotelian conception of happiness.

In establishing that life is ideally lived for the sake of happiness – that we would strive to live in accordance with our *telos* if we had a correct understanding of it – we establish the basic organizational principle of life.[10] Moreover, when claiming that life is ideally lived for happiness, I mean that happiness is the only *telos* of the lives of persons which is self-justifying and, also, that it is the ultimate justification for choosing all other *teloi* that compose a life. The *telos* of achieving happiness is self-justifying in the sense that the desire for happiness is ideally desired for its own sake and for the sake of nothing else. In establishing this basic principle we are able to wed the structure of desire to the ethical life, since the ethical life is, at the very least, the life guided by the basic desire for happiness. The desire for happiness forms the ethical life in the sense that it is the basic ideal organizational principle of our desires and of our lives generally. By 'basic' here I mean that the desire for happiness is the ultimate desire, the desire that, on the whole, ideally justifies our other desires.

The reason why happiness is the *telos* of the lives of persons is, we have seen, that happiness is the *ergon* – the ideal function or activity – of persons.[11] Additionally, our ideal function – *eudaimonia* – is only something we achieve once a process of development has been completed. To recapitulate, the function – the endpoint of development – of the lives of persons is a kind of activity, a manner of operating in the world. And, the manner of operating at issue is *eudaimonia*.

In apparent contradiction with what I have been claiming thus far, Aristotle argues that the proper relationship between the *ergon* and the *telos* of persons is not one of equivalence (it has always been clear that these terms are not identical in meaning). Aristotle illustrates this distinction as follows: the *ergon* of a lyre-player *qua* lyre-player is to play the lyre, but, on the other hand, the *telos* of a lyre-player *qua* lyre-player is to play the lyre in accordance with the excellence – *arete* – of lyre-playing.[12] Analogously, the *ergon* of persons *qua* persons is to act in ways that are typical of persons and, on the other hand, the *telos* of persons *qua* persons is to achieve happiness (to act in accordance with the *arete* of persons).[13] In general, then, the *ergon* of a particular kind is the characteristic function of that kind and the *telos* of a particular kind is the *ergon* in its most perfect form.[14] So, the characterization of *ergon* as the mere function of something, rather than the function of something when it is functioning at its best (as I have been characterizing it thus far), widens the scope of the term, and it is precisely for this reason that the apparent contradiction has emerged. I have been using *ergon* in the narrow sense that identifies the *ergon* of something with that thing's *telos*. I shall continue to use '*ergon*' in this manner, unless otherwise specified. The reason I shall stick to the original usage is that the function of something when it is at its best is its primary function in the sense that all other senses are derived from the primary sense in so far as they are defined in relation to the primary sense.

To recapitulate, we have seen that the *ergon* of something whose *telos* is the perfecting of its characteristic function is not necessarily its *telos*. Instead *telos* is the most perfect expression of its *ergon*. This ideal sense of *ergon*, moreover, is the primary sense, given that it is only in relation to this ideal sense that we are able to form a conception of the other, more general, sense of *ergon*.[15] Let us see why this is the case. We say, for instance, that an imperfect lyre-player is just that sort of lyre-player because we already have a conception – rough or otherwise – of what it would be like to be a perfect lyre-player. We bring our paradigmatic conception of lyre-playing to bear in order to provide a qualified account of the *ergon* of an imperfect lyre-player, namely, that he or she is a lyre-player who has *not fully* mastered the relevant art. To say that a lyre-player has not fully mastered the art of lyre-playing is just to say that there is something *lacking* in his or her performance of this instrument. The lack here is determined by comparing it with a conception of what a flawless – complete – performance would be like.

But why not argue that to say that a lyre-player is perfect is also to have a qualified account of what it is to be a lyre-player? Why not claim, for instance, that it is only in relation to a conception of what an imperfect lyre-player would be like that we are able to determine what a perfect performer would have to be like? The reason for not holding this account of perfection as a kind of qualification is that one must be able to recognize these as such and to recognize states of lack as just those sorts of states amounts to recognizing that, in the case of an imperfect performer, he or she is found wanting with regard to the art of lyre-playing. Conversely, to recognize someone as being a virtuoso is to recognize that person as not lacking anything that *defines* a lyre-player as such. A virtuoso lyre-player is just that sort of lyre-player because he or she is an embodiment of all that defines a lyre-player as such. It is for this reason that a virtuoso lyre-player is a lyre-player without qualification – a lyre-player in the fullest, most complete, sense.

Analogously, it is clear that not all persons are happy in the sense that, clearly, not all persons are living good lives. In other words, not all persons are performing their proper or ideal function. This is a crucial point since, even though it seems clear that most of us are not living happy lives, our what-it-is is nevertheless still defined in relation to the ideal of achieving happiness – in relation to our *telos*. A novice lyre-player, after all, is nonetheless a lyre-player insofar as he or she is defined as such in relation to the *telos* of lyre-playing. It will become apparent as this investigation unfolds how happiness is achieved once we have perfected the skill of living as persons, which just is the skill of living in accordance with our defining ideal. Happiness, finally, must be understood here as the condition in which we become persons who embody their most excellent condition. One could say that a happy person is one who has mastered the art of living. He or she is a virtuoso performer of the delicate art of plucking the chords of life.

It is important to stress here that not all persons fully embody the *eudaimon* ideal, but insofar as someone counts as being a person, he or she has this *telos* – a *telos* which could also be characterized as personhood as such (the fullest expression of our what-it-is).[16]

In further discussing Aristotle's teleological ontology of persons, I will need to explain his basic principles of development: matter (*hyle*), form (*eidos*), potentiality (*dynamis*) and actuality (*energeia* and *entelecheia*). *Dynamis* will be particularly useful for understanding how one is able to talk about the what-it-is of persons existing implicitly – potentially – rather than explicitly in persons. Take the following example as an preliminary explanation which will be supplemented at a later stage:[17] suppose, for the sake of argument, that a particular individual – a child – is not yet capable of thinking, and suppose, also for the sake of argument, that individuals are essentially thinking creatures. How are we able to tell that a child who does *not yet* think is in fact a person? We are able to tell because a child has the *capacity* to become a thinking creature. A child, in other words, is *potentially* a thinking creature, even though the nature – understood as the what-it-is – of this individual is only *manifested* as a lack – that is, as a state of *privation* (a state of *steresis*). But, for a particular feature of an individual to manifest itself in this negative manner is for it to manifest itself in a given way – to manifest itself potentially. We are not, after all, entitled to attribute the possibility of thought to anything, and this shows that to exist potentially is, after all, a kind of manifestation of a corresponding *telos*.

But how are we able to identify states of potentiality as such? Given what I have argued above regarding what a potential is, it is clear that we can only identify these states if we already have an idea – understood as an ideal – of what a thing is when fully actualized. This ideal, we know already, is a *telos*. The justification for holding fast to the idea that things have *teloi* is that, as argued above, the possibility of recognizing something (or someone) as not yet fully developed presupposes that we already have a conception of the relevant *telos*. Furthermore, to be able to recognize something as fully developed presupposes being able to recognize the condition in which something is at its best, since to be able to recognize something as fully developed presupposes recognizing it as having reached the condition for the sake of which the previous stages of development have their existence – the condition of completion. What is implicit in this *teleological* structure of developmental processes is that the final stage of development is the *best* stage. I shall return to these issues later on.

In studying Aristotle's teleology in more detail we shall see that it makes a great deal of sense to speak of a distinction between an account of how people actually are and an account of what it is to be a person. This distinction shall perhaps become more plausible if one considers the widespread intuition that it is always possible and desirable to become a fuller – more complete – person. And it is also worth noting that the possibility of becoming a better person presupposes that one is already a person to start with, but in a qualified sense – like an imperfect lyre-player.

The *eudaimon* principle is central to Aristotle's ethic insofar as he considers it to be the basic organizing principle of our lives. And, as we have seen, its plausibility depends on being able to make sense of Aristotle's teleology. I will show how the possibility of well-being involves being a good – virtuous – person, and being a virtuous person is fundamentally to have a life that is organized in a certain manner. One of the basic organizational aspects of being a virtuous person involves relating to others in ways that are constitutive of our *telos*. Being with others in relevant ways amounts to organizing one's life in the company of others or, more specifically, organizing one's life in such a way that it is embedded in the relevant matrix of social interactions. We shall see that this manner of relating to others forms the basis for the development of a comprehensive theory of social organization. I shall argue in detail below that a good life is the sort of life that cannot be separated from the relevant matrix of social interactions.

## Matters Pertaining to Teleology and the Unity of a Life

Having argued that our potentials are defined by our *telos*, I now add something that has already been suggested above: namely, that once our potentials are actualized – once we have reached our *telos* – our lives will have reached an ideal unity. More precisely, our *telos* is defined as such, I shall argue below, insofar as it is the state in which the different components of our lives fit together – cohere – in the best possible manner (this sort of characterization of our *telos* accords with the basic intuition that a good life is a harmonious one). In fact, we shall see, following

Martha Nussbaum particularly,[18] but also Donald Davidson[19] and Jeff Malpas,[20] that the procedure for determining personhood – for determining our *telos* – fundamentally involves establishing the ideal organization of a life. The organization at issue, we shall see, flows from the fact that our lives are structured holistically. I might also point out that the sort of organization that is constitutive of the sorts of creatures that we are, and from which our *telos* flows, is one that is also discussed by the hermeneutic tradition (by Husserl, Gadamer, Ricoeur, Dreyfus and, of course, Heidegger to mention some of the main proponents), and I shall have something to say about this tradition below.[21]

In discussing the procedure required for unveiling the structure of the psychological I shall show, as paradigm cases, that the desire for immortality, or indeed the desire to live a life of pleasure and devoid of reason, is incompatible with the overall (mostly implicit) conception we already have of ourselves. Indeed, to put this slightly differently, it is this procedure for determining the correct fit between the different aspects of personhood that will reveal the nature of persons, and it will do just this because the different aspects of personhood hang together in relationships of mutual constitution, such that, for example, one could not both live in accordance with the defining ideal of persons and be immortal. For this procedure to work, it is clear that, before setting out to establish an explicit and relatively complete account of personhood, one must in some sense already have a good idea of the different aspects that constitute a person (since, as we have already seen, this initial account of personhood is a precondition for recognizing people as such).

Also, as stated above, I shall argue, following Davidson particularly,[22] that one can only be a person if one forms part of a community of communicators. I will show that the desire an individual might have for living the life of a radical hermit (let us call a paradigmatic exemplar of this sort of individual Cacus, after the son of Vulcan), a radically autonomous creature, is incompatible with the overall conception we already have about the type of creatures that we are. One might initially – and prior to further analysis of how an understanding of the sort of life under scrutiny would fit not just with an understanding of this or that aspect of personhood, but with an overall conception of personhood – believe that one could desire to live like Cacus. But this initial appreciation of what sorts of lives are available to us is based on a misunderstanding of the adequate criteria for choosing one life option over others. We shall see that the criteria at issue are based on an understanding of the overall, largely implicit, conception we already have about who we are – a conception embodied by our unique mode of operation. A corollary of this fundamental methodological thesis is that the choices we make regarding the direction of our lives ought to be based on an overall understanding of who we are, since in this manner we would be able to fit, say, the new choices we make into the overall pattern of our lives in ways that are constitutive of *eudaimonia*.

I shall have much to say about how an understanding of our rational nature involves understanding how we ideally relate to others. Additionally, I shall argue that healthy intimate bonds of care and concern (bonds of *philia*) form the foundation for all other healthy social engagements. Paradigm cases of bonds of *philia* are bonds of friendships. I will argue that persons as such need friends and that, moreover, not any kind of relationship can count as a relationship of friendship. A friend, we shall see, is paradigmatically an individual whom one respects and cares for independently of the obvious immediate gains one gets from the engagement. So, in conclusion, I shall argue that we require relationships of friendship in order to reach our *telos*, and to engage with others in this manner involves respecting what we could call an ethic of friendship – a manner of comportment that defines friendships as such.

I will further argue that communities are fundamentally constituted by (healthy or unhealthy) webs of interlocking bonds of *philia* and the health of individual bonds are dependent on the overall health of what could be characterized as the overarching web of care. Once this issue has been discussed, it will follow that it is in our best interest not only to care for the specific individuals who are closest to us, but also to care for the overall framework which makes caring possible.[23] In this manner I will establish that, because *philoi* are necessary for *eudaimonia*, to be a maximally happy person involves forming part of what could be characterized as a *eudaimon* community.

It is also important to realize at this point that the ideal of personhood I am advocating here is not an ideal that should be understood as constraining the life options that persons might choose – not at all. Instead, I am more interested in establishing the conditions for the possibility of diverse instantiations of personhood. To be sure, constraints on our life options that are imposed by the mere fact that we are persons will no doubt exist but, given an understanding of what it is to be a person, these constraints are of the sort that we would, on final analysis, gladly choose to have because the very possibility of being a person presupposes that we must be constrained in these ways. That we must be constrained in certain ways is demonstrated by the simple and straightforward fact that a person cannot be anything.

Clearly, for an argument of the sort just schematically presented to work, I must also be able to show that, on final analysis, an individual desires to be a person, since if this were not the case, then I would be unable to argue that choosing a life option that did not accord with the type of creatures that we are would necessarily be undesirable. That we do, on final analysis, desire to be persons will not be hard to see once I have shown how the different aspects that define us as persons are interlinked.[24] Let me add here that it will become evident, as the discussion proceeds, that the ultimate criteria for desirability flow from the system that constitutes us as persons and not, by contrast, from a point outside this system.

The good life is the sort of life that is *truly* desired rather than the sort of life that is simply desired, because the desire I am talking about here is the desire a given person would have only if that person had an understanding of how life should be lived.[25] Additionally, and as we have seen, an understanding of this sort requires us to possess an appropriate account – one that is able to inform action – of what it is to be a person. Indeed, it is possible to be mistaken about our nature – to hold a partially inadequate pattern of beliefs (including implicit and explicit beliefs) that form an account of personhood – and moreover this mistake would affect our system of desires in such a way that we would end up having mistaken or inappropriate desires. It must be appropriate to speak of desires in this way, since experience teaches us well that one can be *deceived* about what one actually should desire.

It is also important to acknowledge that the possibility of being deceived about certain aspects of personhood implies, as argued above, that one must already have a reasonably good idea of what it is to be a person to start with. Generally, one must have knowledge (conscious or unconscious) about the object one is being deceived about.[26] It follows that, on the whole, we know what it is to be a person, as we have already concluded above.

The claim regarding our self-knowledge provides us with insights connected with the procedure for developing an explicit account of personhood. Such an account, I will argue, is determined by applying what could be characterized as *the method of critical introspection*, which is a procedure that involves studying the beliefs we already have about what it is to be a person, correcting inconsistencies one might find in the pattern of beliefs that constitutes our understanding of personhood and, finally, drawing conclusions from these initial findings. Once the effectiveness of this procedure is determined, and once the conclusions that flow from this critical procedure have been established, we will be better placed to understand why to believe that one can be deceived about what one ought to desire is to believe one has desires that, in fact, conflict with one's overall pattern of beliefs and desires.

The issue of coherence and its relation to having a good life is something about which I shall have much to say, since one of the fundamental aspects of the lives of persons is that they are organized in characteristic ways – they are organized rationally. And, more specifically, the good life is constituted by a particular variety of the more general organizational principle. The most excellent form of the organizational principle that constitutes the lives of persons defines the good life. As stated above and following Aristotle, I will argue that a good life is the sort of life that is lived in accordance with its fundamental organizational principle.[27]

## Parallels Between Living and Painting

*Preliminary Remarks*

The sort of ethical outlook I am presently developing is one that does not give primacy to rules, which is not surprising given that it is concerned primarily with life understood as a dynamic whole. I do not think that, on the whole, nor even primarily, being ethical can be reduced to a conglomerate of activities that accord with rules, and I hope it will become apparent in the ensuing discussion why I believe this is the case. I will defend my case by means of an analogy between the practice of painting and the practice of living. I think this is a very informative analogy, given that it is relatively easy to make sense of the claim that painting is not typically an activity that accords with rules, but nonetheless constraints exist which determine the quality of the results. The practice of painting, like the practice of living, primarily involves having a skill. The contrast between acting in accordance with a rule- and skill-based action will be explored below. Further, in what sense skill-based activities are teleologically structured shall also become evident by studying this analogy.

Let me clarify what I mean by my claim that being ethical is not primarily a rule-based activity. I do think that, at times, we do act in ways that accord with certain rules in the sense that a rule can be elicited to describe a particular move. However, notwithstanding the fact that, in some instances, appropriate action can be characterized as action that accords with a rule, the goodness and meaning of a given move are not determined by the rule itself. Instead, goodness and meaning are determined by the fit of a given move within the context of a life. Consider the case of rape. There seem to be very good reasons for claiming that rape is never acceptable such that the rule 'do not rape' should always inform action. What I hope will become apparent as the discussion progresses is that maxims such as 'do not rape' are not good in and of themselves in the sense that they are good independently of any contextual considerations. Instead, universal maxims are universal precisely because they apply across context – that is, they derive their meaning, their identity, within the context of our dynamic and ever-changing lives. Typically, our lives shift and move, and the story of how one should comport oneself in the ongoing task of living resists being characterized in terms of an ossified set of rules. And indeed, even if in some instances appropriate action does accord with a given rule, choosing to perform actions of these sorts still involves having a skill as opposed to a set of exhaustively specifiable procedures – procedures that accord with rules. More generally, I will argue that living is a skill-based activity as opposed to a rule-based one and, moreover, that it is a skill-based activity that is teleologically structured.

Given that the goodness and meaning of a given move in life is determined by the manner in which the move is integrated into a given life, then it is clear that the sort of ethic I am developing is one that is sensitive to contextual variations. In other words, it is one of attachment as opposed to detachment. Moreover, it is precisely because ethical activities are typically context-bound that I will be developing an account which shows that the moral worth of a given action cannot typically be fixed once and for all, and may be subject to revision in the light of further evidence, such that one cannot typically know for sure whether a given move one might make is actually appropriate (although it will certainly make sense to speak in terms of degrees of certainty).

It is also important to understand at this point that, given the inherent indeterminacy with regard to our practical moves in life, one cannot expect the practical skill at issue to guarantee that one will *always* act appropriately. One, after all, can only act in accordance with one's practical understanding of a given situation, and this understanding is never complete.

*Living and Painting*

Let us now turn to the fundamental distinction between having a rule and having a skill. As mentioned already, this distinction shall be explained by drawing parallels between the practices of living – the fine art of living one could say – and the fine art of painting.[28]

When one has mastered the art of painting, one does not come to possess a set of rules that one simply applies endlessly. Rather, one acquires a certain skill, a certain manner of approaching the canvas (for example), which will allow one to have the capacity to produce an indefinite number of distinct works. Indeed, every canvas is a new challenge, which the appropriately skilled artist will know how to complete successfully (though, of course, even the best artists may sometimes fail). The person who has mastered the art of painting knows that, typically, prior to the act of painting itself, there is no exhaustive plan which determines every detail of the completed successful work; in fact, if such a plan existed, as it often does in the minds of novice artists, the painting would inevitably end up being uninteresting, predictable and lacking in subtlety. Typically, the completed form of a successful work of art, as opposed to a work produced by an inexperienced novice, is determined, not prior to its making, but in the making itself.

To a great extent, the act of painting is an act of balancing the different elements that make up a painting with the purpose of establishing a coherent whole – a whole, moreover, that expresses certain very general standards of adequacy in a unique manner.[29] But, typically, the whole is never fully determined prior to a painting's completion. So, how is a skilled artist able to integrate the distinct parts of a given work in progress? To answer this question we need to examinbe more closely what painters actually do.

A skilled painter goes about producing a painting by adjusting the distinct elements that are already present at a given stage in its development.

Moreover, each time a skilled artist introduces a new element into a given work in progress, he or she will typically be able to fit it into the provisional whole and make the relevant adjustments within this system, so that this new element best coheres with the provisional totality, or best coheres with his or her present expectations regarding the development of the work in progress. But, given that a skilled artist typically does not know the exact final form of his or her work until it has been completed, he or she will never be certain (until the work is completed) that the way in which a new element is introduced into his or her work in progress will be adequate. What a skilled artist is able to do instead is work with this indeterminacy and use it to his or her advantage. Amongst other things, he or she is able to do this by adequately adjusting his or her expectations with regard to the final form of a completed work in accordance with the changing pictorial circumstances of a work in progress. Indeed, one could characterize the expectations of skilled artists as fluid. There is, of course, a less fluid aspect regarding the expectations of skilled artists, which is that, built into the capacity of a skilled artist to be fluid about his or her expectations, is the general expectation that he or she should be able to adapt to the changing circumstances of a given work in progress.

This accident-prone and inherently risky procedure of nosing one's way through a penumbra of uncertainty is typical of the skill of painting with watercolours. When a brush saturated with pigment touches the damp rough surface of a sheet of cotton-paper the pigment acquires a life of its own and spreads out through the irregular capillaries of the paper in ways that are never fully predictable. The temperature and humidity of the environment and the sometimes uneven distribution of water throughout the paper contributes to the accident-prone nature of the medium. In addition, the not so predictable changes in pigmentation, as the paint is absorbed into the cotton-paper and dries, compound this accident-proneness. The skill of watercolouring involves having control over these fluid and accident-prone aspects. Typically, having control does not involve subjecting the watercolour medium to what it is not naturally suited for. On the contrary, having control involves being able to adapt endlessly to the largely unpredictable nature of the medium.[30]

The development of a painting is also dependent on an artist having at least a rough and provisional conception of the *telos* of a particular work in progress. A crucial element in all developmental processes involving rational agency is a certain relationship, which could loosely be characterized as a dialogue between a provisional whole (in the case of persons, the whole being constituted by a coordinated manifold of projects, expectations, emotions, desires, beliefs, dispositions, past history, current circumstances and so on) and a provisional goal, such that, at the end of a developmental process of the sort under scrutiny, a relationship of identity is established between the completed whole and the final *telos* of the specific practice. One could say that the provisional totality informs the development of the provisional goal and the provisional goal informs the development of the provisional totality. And it is by means of this dialogical relationship that one is able to reach the *telos* – the final *telos* – of a given type of practice.

To be sure, an experienced painter will certainly have quite a large repertoire of technical skills, and this perhaps accounts for why one can recognize a unique identifying style in the works of a given painter. This could be used as evidence against the view I am currently developing that a skilled painter is not the sort of painter who follows a rule manual in his or her head, or elsewhere. However, this plausible objection fails once one realizes that the particular applications of the skills amassed by a competent painter vary from painting to painting (and, indeed, generally vary within a given painting, and vary in unforeseeable ways). A skilled painter, in short, does not come to possess a rule manual for painting but, rather, develops a certain manner of going about the business of painting that is expressed in his or her paintings' characteristic style.

But, although the differences between painters (differences which determine their unique styles) are definitely very important, it is also crucial to acknowledge that there is a *telos* of painting (even if not explicitly known) common to all acts of painting, and which allows us to separate out the *practice* – to use Ricoeur's notion derived from Aristotle's notion of *praxis*[31] – of painting from all other practices. The *telos* of painting is, of course, to produce fine – good – works of art. This second, more general type of *telos* must exist given that we are able to identify the practice of painting as such; and we identify this practice primarily by having an understanding of what that practice is for – what the end of the practice is. So, we have identified two senses in which we can speak about the *telos* of painting.

To recapitulate, the first sense of *telos* is the one in which each and every act of painting has its own particular *telos*, which is developed in the act of painting itself, and is actualized in the act of successfully completing a given painting. This is the sense of *telos* identified when discussing the provisional *teloi* which inform the development of specific works of art. The second sense of *telos* is the more general sense – that in which the *telos* is for the sake of which paintings as such are produced. I now add that this second type of *telos* provides the general guidelines for the development of the first type of *telos*, since the act of creating a new painting is indeed a token of the general type of practice we call painting. The play between these two types of *teloi* – the universal and the particular – allows us to explain both the unitary nature of a certain general type of practice, and also the differences between different manners of approaching, or different styles of performing, a particular type of practice. The interplay between sameness and difference can be explained teleologically.[32]

Now that we have established some basic features of the *practice* of painting, let us draw some very relevant parallels between that of painting and the practice of living. Moral experts,[33] like painters, are also individuals who have developed a certain art, a certain style of doing things. But, in this case, the style at issue is a style of living – a manner of operating in the world. Much as expert painters are unable to grasp their works in progress, moral experts (or anyone else for that matter) are unable to grasp their own individual lives in a completed form. But despite this, by the practical choices they make, moral experts are best prepared to fit adequately the new fragments of their lives into the provisional dynamic totality that constitutes their current lives. They are able to do this, amongst other things, in a way that reflects a practical understanding of the necessary indeterminacy of practical choice-making. This indeterminacy is a necessary one, given that even a moral expert is working only with a rough conception of our general *telos*, and with a practical understanding of the provisional unity which constitutes his or her particular life at a given moment.

I am assuming here that, like the act of painting, human life is structured teleologically. I do not think it is too hard to see why this might be the case. A meaningful existence is constituted by a purposive human life. But life is not merely purposive because in life we pursue goals. The criteria for choosing a particular goal over others must be drawn from an overall understanding of one's life, including an understanding of how one's life is relevantly related to the lives of others. What this means is that life can be understood as a system – an organized congregation – of goals. And, indeed, if individual goals can only be properly understood as belonging to a unified system of goals, then the unifying principle is a further goal which, I might suggest, is the sort of goal Aristotle refers to as the goal of *eudaimonia*. It is this highest goal that confers unity to life. Moreover, the unifying goal is the highest of all goals since it is only within this system of goals that constitutes the lives of persons that each goal obtains its ultimate purpose – its ultimate *raison d'être*.[34] Indeed, if human rational life did not have a unifying goal it would be difficult to consistently talk about persons *qua* rational creatures, since what ultimately defines our rational existence is our directedness towards the ideal of unity. This follows simply because the *raison d'être* of a particular project is determined by considering the overall shape of a life – by the manner in which projects intermesh with one another.

One could, of course, question the view that rational life has a single unifying purpose. It is easy to be tempted to think that projects do indeed form systems, but that the system which constitutes rational existence is not a unified one even at the best of times. Life could be conceived of as a system of conglomerates, each of which constitutes a subsystem of projects – subsystems which, taken together, do not form one unified system. While this line of argument is seductive, on final analysis it is only tempting if one does not consider the fact that what defines us as individuals – as rational subjects – is that, in an important sense, each one of us are one. Our engagements are played off one another even if only because our energy reserves are limited, and engaging in one project has repercussions on the time and energy we can invest in other projects. The source of energy, so to speak, is one entity – an individual who manages his or her energy reserves (with lesser or greater success). Yet there is another reason for holding that life is a unity, and it is that a unified life is a precondition for being able to grasp one's life as one's own – as having an author, so to speak.[35]

A moral expert is able to give form to his or her life by balancing and counterbalancing the new elements that come into his or her life with the general form of that life up to the present (and including his or her present expectations for the future). And, indeed, it is a moral expert who can best perform this compositional *tour de force* because such an individual understands that the purpose of life is defined by the *telos* of persons (the understanding at issue here, like the sort of understanding required for being an expert painter, being of the practical variety). A moral expert knows, purportedly, that we are by nature communing creatures, and moreover that, arguably, there are certain general ways of engaging with others that determine the good life. A moral expert will, for example, understand the importance that friendship plays in life, and understand that relating to others as a friend involves relating in a manner that honours the what-it-is of friendship. Acting in ways that do not pay respect to the ideal of friendship is to produce a fracture within the overall pattern of life. One could say that the practice of not acting in accordance with the ideal, or ethic, of friendship disrupts the overall unity of the composition of life in a way that is analogous to disruptions in a musical piece by a strident sound, or disruptions in the pictorial 'harmony' of a given piece of art.

The sense of harmony alluded to here should not be understood as conflict-free harmony, and this is a crucial point, since I am not advocating what could be referred to as a middle-class ideal of comfort that is impervious to the realities of life outside that select circle. In art some forms of conflict quite clearly play a central role in a given composition and may even give a work its vitality and interest. Nonetheless, this does not mean that conflict of any sort is acceptable. Just as some varieties of conflicts are a defining feature of bad art, something analogous applies to life. Life, like the process of producing art, is largely a labour of integrating new elements that, in many cases, produce disturbances in the provisional composition. The harmony in question is not typically produced simply by integrating things that do not threaten what could be characterized as the existential *status quo* of a given subject. The task of harmonizing is typically a task of adapting to new, unpredictable, and at times disruptive circumstances. And, indeed, we often consider a life in which deep conflicts have been well integrated to be an exemplary life. The capacity to overcome, which is a virtue we seem to regard very highly, can be seen as the capacity to integrate deep conflict in exemplary ways.

Earlier I claimed that the act of painting is largely an act of provisionally balancing and counterbalancing the new elements – conflicting or not – that are introduced into a painting with the integrated elements that are already there. A painter, I also claimed, has, at best, only a rough idea of where a painting in development is going – only a rough and provisional idea of the *telos* of that *specific* painting (even though the skilled painter certainly has a relatively good practical understanding of the *telos* of the act of painting in general). Analogously, like anyone else, a skilled artisan of life does not know for sure where his or her life is going. As already claimed above, this sort of individual, in contrast with one who has not developed the fine art of living, knows how to balance and counterbalance the new elements introduced into his or her life with the dynamic unity that constitutes his or her present life (including expectations for the future), such that an ideal provisional composition or organization is achieved. This ideal provisional organization, it must be stressed, is always and necessarily provisional given that one can never be sure what new elements will appear in that life, and therefore also what new organizational *tour de force* will be required of us. So, a basic feature of the skill of living is that the organization and orientation of a life is always and necessarily provisional and indefinitely subject to the contingencies of accident. But, to recapitulate, like the skilled painter, the master in the fine art of living – a *phronimos* to use the Aristotelian term – will, more often than not, know how to integrate new circumstances into the fabric of his or her already existing life. The *phronimos*, more than anyone else, is able to perform this compositional feat because he or she has developed the skill – the *techne* or the knowledge expressed in action – of good living.[36]

In addition, and fundamentally, a moral expert does not simply have an intellectual understanding of what it is to be a person in the way in which a painter may have an intellectual understanding of the basic materials and techniques of painting. A moral expert – a *phronimos* – like a painter, is also able to *apply* this understanding to his or her life. Moreover, just as it is hard to imagine in what sense a purported painter could be considered to understand the art of painting if unable to paint well, it is also hard to understand how an ethical expert could count as understanding the delicate art of living if he or she was unable to *act* ethically. The knowledge both skilled painters and moral experts have of their respective fields of expertise is intimately related to their *active capacity* – as opposed to a mere ability or an intellectual understanding – to act in a determinate way.

A person who was able to act virtuously but who never did so, would not count as a moral expert. Analogously, a person who was able to paint, but who never did so, would not count as expert in that art. The characterization of moral expertise as a kind of art is particularly fortunate in this context given that individuals who count as knowing a given art are the sorts of individuals who actually *exercise* that very art. Moreover, the reason why an expert in some art must be an individual who acts in ways that justify our referring to him or her as an expert in that very art, is that being an expert in some art amounts to being an expert in a particular type of *practice*. Indeed, knowledge of the sort that warrants us calling someone an expert in an art is knowledge that must necessarily be manifested in a particular type of doing. This said, while an expert of the relevant sort could certainly express his or her expertise in an intellectual manner, this intellectual mode of knowing would not count as good evidence that such an individual would actually possess practical knowledge of the relevant art. It might be worth adding at this point that an art is not primarily learned in an intellectual manner. An aspiring musician, to use another example, cannot theorize his or her way into developing musical expertise, although, of course, theory *might* be of assistance. In conclusion, a skill is primarily learned and manifested through practice.

## A Red Brushstroke and its Significance within the Context of a Painting

Moreover the analogy with the practice of painting also extends to the issue of the significance of particular segments of a life. Remember that the significance of a particular section of a painting (be it work in progress or a completed piece) depends on the overall context within which that section is located. This can be clarified by the following example. A thing we identify as a red brushstroke, like anything else, does not come with its interpretation attached, since individual objects (or events for that matter) can be described in countless ways. One might come to know things about the atomic composition and how the radiation emanating from the surface of the red brushstroke stimulates some of our ocular nerve endings. But, the domain of significance of the natural sciences is different from the domain of significance of aesthetic interpretation inasmuch as there are fundamental aspects of aesthetic interpretation that cannot be grasped by the vocabulary of the natural sciences. We cannot find the *aesthetic* significance of a particular red brushstroke in the physical composition of a brushstroke or in the physical effect it has on our ocular nerve endings (unless, of course, the physical composition and its effect on our nerve endings is used for aesthetic purposes).[37] The aesthetic significance of a given red brushstroke depends on the immediate pictorial context in which it is couched and also on the particular cultural–historical context in which it belongs. Indeed, the context-dependent nature of the aesthetic significance of a given red brushstroke is perhaps one reason why talk about the aesthetic significance of a particular brushstroke rings so awkwardly in our ears. A brushstroke seen in isolation from its relevant aesthetic context simply has no aesthetic significance, and the same applies to a particular sound taken out of its specific musical context or a particular gesture taken out of its theatrical context.

Given the context-dependent nature of the aesthetic significance of a given red brushstroke, it is not hard to see why token identical brushstrokes could mean radically different things to us in aesthetic terms. The significance of a given brushstroke will depend on the context in which it is located, and on the specific interpretative framework a given spectator brings to bear. The interpretative framework, moreover, is just another aspect of the context within which a particular brushstroke *qua* aesthetic object might be located. In addition, a red brushstroke of oil paint might have the same aesthetic significance as a red acrylic brushstroke, and also many things other than a red brushstroke might perform very similar, if not identical, aesthetic functions. It follows that the physicality of a red brushstroke is neither a sufficient, nor indeed a necessary, condition for its aesthetic significance.[38] What accounts for the different modes of appreciating are the specific *roles* a brushstroke might play within a particular domain of significance (such as the domain of the aesthetic).

And, indeed, it is only within a given domain of significance that a brushstroke can be just that. The brushstroke has a determinate existence as an aesthetic object if it belongs to the domain of significance of the aesthetic, and the same brushstroke has a determinate existence *qua* physical object if it belongs to the domain of significance that picks out the physicality of the physical world.[39] But, crucially, the 'object' only has a certain determinacy insofar as it is interpreted in some way.[40] The above characterization of a red brushstroke might be a bit misleading, since it might be interpreted to suggest that a brushstroke as such has a determinate nature independent of a given mode of description, but I think it is clear by now that this is not what I want to claim. When referring to a brushstroke independently of a physical or aesthetic interpretation, I have been referring to it as an object with certain qualitative features (as an object of a given colour, a general shape, and so on). This qualitative mode of appreciation is, indeed, a given mode of appreciation.[41]

A general account of being is emerging from this discussion about the nature of a red brushstroke. The world *qua* world of determinate objects (such as the red brushstroke), occurs as a relationship between interpreting or, more precisely, self-interpreting subjects and what could be described as a proto-world. This view has important consequences for it shows that the world *qua* determinate world is not something that exists independently of subjects. One could say that the world is a thoroughly human place. Although what I am briefly suggesting amounts to a divergence from our immediate topic of concern, it is important for it helps us understand how, since the bearers of meaning are moral agents, the world might be seen to have a moral dimension. If what I am saying is true, then there are few grounds for making a strong distinction between what could be described as a vocabulary that describes the world as it truly is and a vocabulary that merely projects human categories onto a morally barren reality.[42]

Let us return to our central line of argument and establish further analogies between painting and living. A segment of the life of a person can only be interpreted if one also brings to bear the context within which that segment is located and, also, if the interpreting subject has a grasp of the relevant conceptual topography within which the concept of a life is articulated.[43] A human being could most certainly be described as an organized agglomeration of distinct and highly specialized groups of relevantly interrelated cells, but this particular mode of description would certainly not help us understand certain basic traits we typically assign to persons *qua* rational creatures (traits such as having beliefs, intentions, emotions, desires, and so on). The concept of a person is *primarily* articulated not in the conceptual field of biology, but, rather, in the conceptual field of what analytic philosophers refer to as folk-psychology, or what most philosophers would recognize as the conceptual field that is expressed in the language of intentionality. So, to recapitulate, the *practice* of being a person *qua* rational creature can only be grasped from the vantage point of a particular conceptual field.

It might certainly be doubted whether, in fact, the privileged vocabulary for coming to understand personhood is provided by folk-psychology. One could plausibly hold that personhood is best described in the language of the natural sciences. Indeed, our bodies have a certain biological constitution that is typical of us humans, and these aspects of being human can only properly be described in biological terms. Nonetheless, it is only with the vocabulary of folk-psychology that we can describe persons as creatures with beliefs, thoughts, emotions, desires, expectations, intentions, intentional behaviour, and so on. Moreover, arguably, personhood is a more general class than human being, because the sort of vocabulary we bring to bear when talking about persons as rational creatures does not include a description of our specific biological nature. Personhood is a concept that pertains not to the inner working of a human body but, is more a functional concept in that it pertains to the sort of complex activity that constitutes our rational nature.[44]

A further similarity between living a life and making a painting is that the forms of both of these sorts of activities largely depends on the cultural–historical context within which they are couched. The dependency at issue here is twofold. First, a given artist develops his or her unique style within the bounds determined by a given tradition; and, second, the particular cultural situatedness of a given artist is a fundamental determining aspect of the aesthetic significance of his or her work (meaning both the skill itself of a given master and the products of the skill – the artworks themselves). Indeed, let me stress that these two sides are just two sides of one and the same coin, given that the horizons determined by a given tradition are precisely the horizons of significance that are fundamental determining factors of aesthetic significance (such horizons, of course, also include the relationship between a given tradition and how it is couched within the historical process as a whole). I have said something about this topic already, but let me retrace my steps and fill in a few gaps. The particular style developed by a given master is not only unique in the sense that it separates his or her works from the works of others, but also his or her style locates his or her works within a given cultural setting – within a given cultural tradition which has a substantial role to play with regard to the significance of the art of that master. Analogously, a given life, and indeed the uniqueness of a life, is to a large extent determined by the socio-historical context in which that very life is played out.

## Practices and Systems of Practices

Thus far, I have characterized lives and the activity of painting as types of practice, without dealing explicitly with the issue of what, in this context, I mean by a practice. A practice is, rather uninformatively, a coherent set of activities. In order to be more informative and to pick out the relevant aspects of the notion of a practice that are relevant to the present inquiry – those aspects pertaining to the issue of teleology – it might be useful to try to answer the following question: what criteria do we use to conceptually identify a coherent and distinctive set of activities which constitute a given practice from a whole range of variously interrelated activities that constitute a field of intermeshing practices? The answer is that a practice is defined by its directedness toward a *telos* – by its purpose. The purpose of painting is to create good works of art, the purpose of moving this pawn on the chessboard is to defeat my opponent and so on. So, the very possibility of recognizing a specific practice as such involves teleological considerations. In addition, every activity that is constitutive of a given practice may form part of innumerable distinct practices. This means that the significance of a given activity is determined by the embeddedness of that activity in a given practice.[45] To use Ricoeur's examples:

> ... painting is a practice, both a profession and an art, but not applying a spot of colour to a canvas. [Analogously] ... shifting the position of a pawn on the chessboard is in itself simply a gesture, but taken in the context of the practice of the game of chess, this gesture has the meaning of a move in a chess game.[46]

Analogously, a red dot on a dotted wall may simply have a decorative purpose. A red dot on a flag may have profound significance for a people who identify with the national symbol. A red dot on the chest of the figure of a saint in a Baroque painting may represent a fatal wound. Similarly, gestures of the type performed by chess-players while playing chess may have a plethora of different meanings depending on the context in which they are made – that is, depending on what practice they form part of. In short, gestures, or more generally, activities, derive their meaning from the particular system(s) of meaning within which they are couched. So, as claimed above, a practice is a coordinated set of activities, which are defined as a unity by a specific general purpose (a general *telos*), which, in turn, determines the meaningfulness of the individual actions that constitute a given practice.[47] In addition, it is only because, for example, we know the *telos* of chess-playing as such that we are able to differentiate the activities that one must perform in order to be counted as playing a game of chess from contingent activities, such as sipping a coffee or visiting the toilet, that we perform whilst playing.

The above claims that the *telos* of painting is to produce good work, and also that the *telos* of chess is to defeat one's opponent in the act of playing chess might quite legitimately be contested on the grounds that not all people who paint wish to do so in order to produce good works of art, and not all people who play chess have the intention of defeating their opponents or of playing a good game. Indeed, having possible alternative goals does not necessarily mean that one is doing something that is deficient, simply because the activities in question are not performed in accordance with the purported defining *teloi* of the respective activities. I think the concerns here are legitimate given that there are clearly cases in which persons engage in the practices of painting or of playing chess for motives that are sometimes incompatible with engaging in a practice for the sake of perfecting it and which might, nevertheless, be good motives. I am thinking here of motives such as relaxing, forgetting some painful incident, learning some basic skills that could be of use in other endeavours, or simply enjoyment. Similarly, it would be foolish to expect that a child who is engaged in the act of painting is, whether consciously or not, always engaged in that particular endeavour in order eventually to produce masterpieces. In other words, we cannot always, or indeed for the most part, explain the adequacy of children's pictorial endeavours by claiming that they are a stage in the process of becoming master painters. Moreover, it would be equally absurd to claim that a child's activities in the act of painting are somehow deficient simply because he or she is incapable of producing great art.[48] Explanations of this sort will inevitably fail because the great majority of children who paint are not on the course of becoming master painters (they are not painting for the sake of producing great works of art). Rather, in most cases, and quite legitimately, children paint for the sake of developing a whole range of skills and dispositions (motor skills, colour skills, the skill of expressing themselves pictorially, self-confidence, the skill of learning to enjoy being creative, and so on). that are useful not only to painters, but to people generally. So, it appears that there are instances of the art of painting which do not have the same goal as their 'higher' counterparts, and which nonetheless count as instances of painting. This seems to contradict my claim that painting, and practices generally, are defined by a specific *telos*. However, I think this is merely an apparent contradiction because, if we are able to recognize great art as just that (with all the fuzziness and imprecision that typifies the subject matter), by applying the same criteria, we are equally able to (correctly) recognize the work of a child as artwork and to recognize it as artwork produced by an inexperienced novice. We can do this, moreover, only if we have at least a rough conception of the defining ideal of painting, which we rightly apply both to the higher arts and to the art produced by novices. Further, we can also recognize the alternative goals of a given practice as alternative goals precisely because we have an idea of what they are an alternative of. They are an alternative to the defining ideal of painting.

I have yet to deal with the issue of how alternative goals can sometimes be considered as *teloi* – goals that allow us to claim that a specific instance of a given type of practice, which has an alternative goal, is not a corrupt practice. I think we can see how this would be possible if we consider the embeddedness of individual practices (with their individual goals) into systems of practices (defined as systems of practices, rather than, say, heaps of practices, by an overarching goal which is a unifying principle – a unifying principle, that, we already know, Aristotle names *eudaimonia*). Thus, if a given practice is embedded within a system of practices, its goodness is parasitical upon the goodness of the overall system, such that, if a given individual was to pursue the goal of becoming a master painter in such a way that this endeavour had a negative effect on the overall project of living, then this particular goal (not the *telos* of painting in general, but this particular instantiation of the pursuit of the good of painting) would not, on final analysis, be good in the sense that it would not be good for the particular person who is pursuing the goal. Conversely, if painting for reasons other than the achievement of pictorial perfection had a role to play in bettering a human life, then that alternative goal would actually be a good one.[49]

We find, then, that the goodness of a specific pursuit depends on the overall goodness of the system of pursuits which constitutes a good human life. This claim is problematic as it stands, since I have thus far been claiming that there is a *telos* of painting, which is quite independent of considerations pertaining to the lives of artists. In fact, if we could only determine the good of painting relative to the specific totality of endeavours that constitute the lives of specific subjects, then it would seem to make no sense to talk about the *telos* of painting as such, since it would vary from life to life. But we know already that there is such a *telos* of painting,[50] which means that the good of painting must, in some sense, be independent of the good of the overall system of pursuits which constitutes a specific *eudaimon* life. In this regard, we could say that the practice of painting has a certain degree of autonomy in the sense that the practice of painting does not, in any ideal sense, have to be embedded in any *specific* system of practices.[51] A serial killer could be a great artist.

The solution to the problem can be better understood if one considers that there is a distinction to be drawn between the good of painting and how the practice of painting is good for a given individual engaged in this practice. One can speak of the quality of given works of art and the abilities of their producers without having to deal with the general well-being of the producer – that is, without necessarily having to deal with how the development of his or her skill has an effect on his or her life understood as a complex unity (entwined with the lives of others). But, if our concern is not so much with mastering the art of painting, but with the role that painting might play in having a good life, then the considerations at issue vary accordingly. My attempts to become a virtuoso violinist or a virtuoso painter might have disastrous effects on my family life (think of Gauguin). Similarly, my endeavours to help a friend might have widespread negative repercussions on the lives of many people around me. Generally, we are continually forced to juggle the different demands placed on us by our different endeavours (as well as circumstances, dispositions, and so on) and in this manner, hopefully, establish an ideal balance. Such an ideal balance certainly might not have favourable consequences for all parties involved.

Not all practices have the degree of autonomy that painting has – particularly practices that could be categorized as ethical. If life does have a goal, then individual ethical acts cannot properly be understood in isolation from the specific niche they occupy within the teleological system that is constitutive of the life of a person. In other words, a given action could not properly be understood as morally praiseworthy or blameworthy in isolation from an understanding of the overall shape of a human life (with particular reference to the pattern of interactions of that life with the lives of others, if to live a human life is to live amongst others). So, ethical practices, unlike the practice of painting, cannot be separated from the totality they ideally constitute. Indeed, it seems that ethical practices are best understood in a way that is analogous to understanding particular moves in a chess game, or a particular brushstroke in a painting.

It is also important to note that, like the practice of painting, since the circumstances of a life are permanently subject to the possibility of change, it follows that the significance of a particular portion of a life is also typically subject to the possibility of reinterpretation. Thus, the meaning of a particular segment of a life is typically not fully determined for that life. Indeed, self-interpretations of a life are typically provisional. For this reason, it is fair to say that a life can never fully understand itself. It follows that a self-reflexive life is always and necessarily a life in which self-reflexion is never fully exhausted. This should not be regarded as a problem, since, among other things, this ongoing mystery – this ongoing indeterminacy – helps give life its vital impetus. Indeed, it is by continuously assessing our past in the light of the present (including our present projects for the future) and our present in the light of the past that we find the basic motivational impetus for purposive action.[52] If this is so, then it follows that since a rational life *qua* rational life is clearly purposive, then a rational life must be a dynamic one. To be a rational creature is always and necessarily to be a creature in the process of coming to terms with the world.

*Art, Life, Context*[53]

Art is a practice, and so is life. And, indeed, a practice is teleologically driven (or structured) and this amounts to saying that a practice is a project – an activity that 'projects' itself towards an end. So, rather than speaking in terms of the practice of living and the practice of painting we can speak in terms of the projects of living and painting. So far, I have focused on the teleological aspects of the projects of living and painting, but I have not focused sufficiently on the related issue regarding what happens with the objects, events and individuals who engage, or are engaged, in certain projects.

When objects come to form part of a given project they come to be grasped under a certain description. A pawn is just that insofar as it is a piece in a chess game. Its very identity as a pawn is fixed by the role it plays in the game. Also, like a piece in a chess game, a chess-player is just that insofar as he or she plays chess. His or her identity is fixed by the game of chess – by his or her specific relation to the game. Similarly, as we have seen, a red dot's significance changes in accordance with how it is used. And, indeed, art as such is appreciated as just that if one immerses oneself in the art world – if one makes oneself a spectator of art. Thus, if the *Mona Lisa* was used as a doormat, it would in an important sense, cease to be the *Mona Lisa*. Its significance – its identity as the famous painting – is determined by the manner in which it has been appropriated, and it has been appropriated as the Mona Lisa within the context of the art world – by the specific role it plays in a system of practices. Likewise, the practice of painting itself is just that insofar as it is a practice that derives its character from the particular manner in which it is taken up by the art-world at large. And, indeed, painters are just that insofar as they are producers of art, so that their very identity is determined by their relationship to the works they produce, and indeed by the specific works they produce in a specific cultural–historical context. Raphael was a man of his time but also a painter whose work defines him as the man who he was (the famous painter Raphael). And let me stress that Raphael would not be Raphael had he lived among us today, because the character of his work would be transformed accordingly, and hence the fundamental relationship to his work that makes him Raphael – the famous old master – would be transformed. He would perhaps be a postmodern painter of a certain variety painting *as if* he were one of the old masters, rather than being an old master himself.

We may conclude that specific subjects and objects are defined as such by the projects within which they are taken up – by the manner in which they appropriate or by the manner in which they are appropriated. And an appropriator of a given object is appropriated by the object he or she appropriates insofar as his or her identity is determined by the mode of appropriation – by the relationship to the object. So, if one assumes that things are defined as the very things that they are by their specific character (and this seems to be true by definition), and if one assumes that the world is, so to speak, a stage where objects – determinate entities – exist (which also seems to be true by definition, at least under one interpretation of what it is to be a world), then one can see the appeal of claiming that we are makers of worlds insofar as we are makers of projects.[54] But we are not merely makers of worlds, we are also what could be characterized as makers of self in the process of making worlds. We are, after all, agents – that is, creatures capable of making ourselves (to some degree and in some respect). Indeed, our identity is determined by the manner in which we engage and constitute things as the things they are. We embed ourselves in our all too human practices and, in the process of making worlds, we never emerge untransformed.

Moreover, it must be stressed that projects do not merely exist in isolation from one another. Projects form part of systems of projects, and the way in which projects are embedded into further systems of projects is constitutive of the specific projects themselves. Indeed, the source of intelligibility of a project is its mode of embeddedness in a matrix of such projects. The character of soccer played in the slums of Rio by destitute children with dreams of becoming soccer stars is very different from the character of German professional soccer: the soccer played by the Brazilian children, or indeed by Brazilian professionals, is appropriately described as carnivalesque, whilst the soccer of the German professionals can be described as Prussian in its general style. Culture affects the identity of the objects, subjects and activities that are constitutive of a given practice or project, and the value and meaning of projects, such as the one being discussed, cannot be drawn exclusively from inside the project itself. Soccer is a cultural event, but so are all other projects insofar as the reason for engaging in any project whatsoever is determined by the role the project plays within a dynamic matrix of such projects. Projects, in a manner of speaking, feed off each other.

These last claims might be seen to contradict my previous claims to the effect that practices, such as the practice of painting, have a certain degree of autonomy. If this is the case, one might think, then projects of this kind should not be seen as forming part of any network of projects. But this would be impossible. Art acquires its character as art insofar as it forms part of what I have been referring to as the art world, and an art world is ultimately defined by the manner in which it is embedded in a culture. The art world of the Renaissance is very different from the art world today, and consequently so are the artworks produced in that period. What I claimed above, and this is the reason no contradiction exists, is that the practice of painting has a *relative* degree of autonomy. The autonomy in question is not absolute. To use a familiar example, the character of an artist – what identifies a given artist as just that artist – might not be essential to understanding his or her art, but the cultural climate within which the artwork is made is crucial. In fact, much the same applies to persons generally. A person is, indeed, an autonomous creature but such autonomy is not absolute insofar as we are, to a large degree, creatures of our times.

Because projects form a complex, yet unified, system of variously interrelated projects one could be tempted to think that there is one overarching project which encompasses all other projects, but this thought is only partly true for there is no end to the sorts of projects one could engage in, and hence there is no specific set which encompasses all possible projects. A project, after all, could always be encompassed by further projects; it could always form part of yet another system of projects. If one takes not only this basic fact, but also the fact that the character of a project is determined by the manner in which it is embedded within a system of projects, then one can see that there is a fundamental indeterminacy that is endemic to the very task of project formation. It is this indeterminacy that is responsible for the very possibility of change – of reconfiguration. Projects are never fixed, and they always leave a door open for reconfiguration. A chess game might certainly be determined as such by a certain system of procedures, but its character is radically underdetermined by this system, and this is precisely because chess, like any other project, forms part of an open-ended, and hence dynamic, matrix of projects. I will supplement this discussion in Chapter 5.

## Concluding Remarks

Up to this point I have, for the most part, presented an outline of how ethical expertise compares with artistic expertise. But how does the expert's life differ from the novice's? To make the contrast between the expert and the novice clearer, I shall describe the life of a seriously incompetent novice, using the painting analogy. A seriously incompetent painter is the type of individual who simply has no practical understanding of what he or she is doing when painting. Additionally, he or she has little or no practical understanding that the different elements of a painting acquire their significance in the context of the composition, which constitutes the painting in its entirety. That is, he or she does not see how this particular red here or this particular figure here operates within the context of a painting understood as a unitary object. Since the incompetent novice is incapable of understanding how the different elements in a painting acquire their significance in the context of a complete painting, he or she is, in short, simply incapable of understanding – in the practical sense of understanding – the expressive value of the visual medium.

Analogously, an incompetent artisan in the delicate art of living is incapable of understanding – in the practical sense through which a *phronimos* understands – his or her life as a unitary whole (including the relationship between his or her life and the life of others). He or she does not understand that his or her life is a dynamic unity from which the distinct segments of a life acquire their signification. He or she, for instance, does not understand that the specific choices for pleasure may have widespread repercussions within the fabric of his or her life understood as an integrated totality. Lives, like paintings, are composed, and lives are not well lived when they are lived, as it were, by following a given manual. Instead, skills guide our paths through a penumbra of uncertainty that always threatens to upset – in ways that can never be fully envisaged – whatever provisional balance we might have achieved thus far. One cannot fully know in advance what sorts of surprises are looming behind the veils of darkness, but an expert in the art of living will be best equipped to integrate unforeseeable circumstances into the overall composition of his or her life.

Moreover, it is the overall composition of a life that determines its goodness, and I would like to suggest here that, if a given life is well composed then it is a happy one – a life which, to use Aristotle's expression, has achieved *eudaimonia*. The compositional principle at issue, we shall see, is the primary sense of rationality, and this means that the happy life just is the rational one, if by rationality we mean rationality in the primary sense – a sense which will be explored below. Indeed, we shall further see that the psychological domain is structured holistically and, more specifically, that the specific holistic structure at issue is a teleological one which is in turn what rationality primarily is. Finally, we shall see that a proper understanding of an individual life cannot be separated from what could be characterized as the existential context within which that life is played out. The rational unity that constitutes a life, we shall see, cannot be separated from the rational unity of the existential context. Lives are intertwined.

## Notes

1    It will initially not be obvious why a happy life is an ethical ideal rather than simply an ideal. That it is an ethical ideal will become plain once I have provided some details regarding what sort of life the happy life is. This will become most clear in Chapter 7 where I discuss what I hold to be the fundamental relationship that exists between being happy and our ethical engagements with others. For an interesting discussion regarding Aristotle's notion of the nature of persons understood as an ethical ideal see Julia Annas's, 'Aristotle: Nature and Mere Nature', *The Morality of Happiness*, New York: Oxford University Press, 1993, pp. 146–58.

2    This discussion will be supplemented in the next chapter.

3    This is the case even though, in some instances, lacking health may end up having many positive effects for an individual suffering from ill-health. Take the case of an individual who due to ill-health, suffers a near-death experience (or something of this sort) and, as a result, learns to value life in ways that many persons who have never had such an experience will never do. However, even though such things do occur, they nevertheless do not show that there are instances of ill-health that are good. Instead, what they show is that the effects of ill-health may be positive to the overall life of a given individual. Analogously, a victim of incest, in the act of having to overcome the repercussions of his or her predicament, might very well become a better person than he or she would have become were he or she not to have been sexually assaulted as a child. This, of course, does not mean that, in this instance, incest is good; it only shows that the overall – the

all things considered – effects of incest were good. Congratulating the perpetrator of incest for the overall positive effects his or her actions have had on the victim would indeed be an obscene thing to do.

4　It is worth mentioning here that the manner of operating in question is not very different from the manner in which, for the most part, we conduct our lives on a day-to-day basis. The manner of operating which constitutes our *telos* is simply a highly refined version of our system of common practices. Indeed, the distinction between the manner in which most of us conduct our lives and the manner in which a *eudaimon* does is analogous to the distinction between the artistic conducts of novice musicians and those of accomplished performers.

5　In Chapter 3 I shall take issue with Aristotle and argue that persons need not be creatures of a particular biological type.

6　The sense of rationality at issue here is not that of conscious rational thought. Rather, it is the sense that pertains to the overall organization of a life – the manner in which thoughts, emotions, desires, hopes, expectations, and so on. are related to one another and to behaviour. I shall have more to say about this sense of rationality in Chapter 4.

7　*EN* 1097b 23–1098a 18. The notion of *ergon* is equivocal in the sense that the *ergon* of persons could be an activity or a capacity. That is why *ergon* is appropriately translated as 'function' (the notion of function is equivocal in the same manner). In this context, by *ergon* Aristotle means activity (*energeia*) rather than capacity.

8　*EN* 1102a 5–6.

9　We shall see that a satisfactory account of *eudaimonia* is not an exhaustive account. One can at best only provide an extremely general, albeit informative, account of this concept.

10　The sort of understanding at issue here will have to be qualified, since I do not mean understanding just in the intellectual sense. Instead I also and fundamentally mean understanding in a practical sense. The type of understanding that is relevant here is, to use Aristotle's terminology, not primarily the sort that involves *sophia* – intellectual knowledge or wisdom – but instead is the sort that involves *phronesis* – practical knowledge or wisdom. *Phronesis* is the type of wisdom that is required in our practical, rather than in our intellectual, engagements with the world. The distinction between these two types of knowledge is central, since, clearly, having an intellectual grasp of any practical matter whatsoever does not straightforwardly translate into actions that accord with the understanding. The type of understanding that is relevant here is the type that is intimately tied up with action, such that it is primarily expressed through deeds. I will argue, following Aristotle particularly, that ethical understanding in the broadest sense is a certain skill – the skill required for good living.

11　It is worth stressing at this point that having a function is not just meant to be understood here as the possession of certain dispositions. Instead, it should primarily be understood as the exercise of those dispositions since, unlike hammers and the like, we are primarily defined by a manner of operating rather than by a power to act – *dynamis* – in certain characteristic ways. A hammer permanently lying idle on a workbench is still a hammer but a person must exercise his or her powers to be a person. Aristotle believes that to be a person, in the fullest sense – that of a person who is living his or her life in accordance with the *telos* – is to be active.

For a discussion about the different kinds of good – *teloi* – see *EN* 1094a 1–5. *Eudaimonia* is the kind of good that is an activity – a particular manner of operation. In *EN* 1176b 1–2 Aristotle explicitly says that happiness is an activity. See also *EN* 1098a 8–18 where Aristotle explains why the good – the *telos* – of humans is their natural function – their *ergon* in the sense of *energeia*.

12　*EN* 1098a 7–18.

13　We reserve the term 'happiness' only to refer to the *ergon* of persons who live in accordance with the excellence of persons. Aristotle's characterization of happiness as the *ergon* of persons is quite a counterintuitive manner of defining this notion but that is only because we do not normally understand happiness as an activity. It will become clear in the ensuing discussion why, in fact, Aristotle's understanding of happiness is indeed an adequate one.

Let me just attempt to transform current intuitions so that we can come closer to making sense of the idea that happiness is an activity. Think about the matter as follows: to be a person is not merely, nor even, to be a human being – not at all. To be a person is to do things that persons typically do – to be active in ways that warrant referring to the activities in question as being rational for the most part. To be a person is, after all, to be a rational creature. But there is more. Another way of characterizing the sort of conception of happiness under scrutiny is to characterize it as the sense used in contexts where our being is said to be a happy one – that is, in contexts of the sort where we are tempted to claim that a given person *is* happy in the sense that happiness is what defines him or her. If I am right here, we have all the ingredients for making sense of the idea that happiness can properly be understood as an activity. If being a person is to be active in certain characteristic ways, and if a person can be happy in the sense that happiness is what defines him or her, then it makes sense to say that happiness, the relevant sense, is an activity.

14  It is important to notice here that the *telos* of something is not always the most perfect expression of its *ergon* and could be something that comes as a consequence of an activity. The *telos* of medicine, to use one of Aristotle's examples, is not to perfect the art of medicine. Rather, one perfects the art of medicine for the sake of health (*EN* 1094a 1–9).

15  Indeed, it is because the ideal sense of *ergon* is the primary sense that, from now on, I will refer to it simply as *ergon*.

16  I shall argue below that there are many, and in fact potentially innumerable, modes of embodying the *eudaimon* ideal. What this means, if I am right, is that it is not possible to provide an exhaustive list of prerequisites for being a *eudaimon* subject. The most one can do, and the most one can expect to do, is to provide certain general guidelines for finding one's own particular expression of the *eudaimon* ideal. And, indeed, it is a good thing that *eudaimonia* cannot be fully specified, since this squarely places the responsibility on oneself for finding one's own expression of the *eudaimon* ideal. That an account of *eudaimonia* cannot be an exhaustive one is a good thing because, if *eudaimonia* were something that could be exhaustively specified, then all a given subject would have to do in order to actualize his or her *telos* is follow something like a rule manual for being happy, thus leaving no scope for a subject to express his or her unique qualities – qualities that separate individuals out from one another and which are constitutive of each individual's unique agency. Let this suffice as a preliminary explanation of the role of difference in the task of pursuing an understanding of happiness. A more elaborate explanation will follow in due course.

17  In Chapter 3.

18  Martha Nussbaum, 'Aristotle on Human Nature and the Foundations of Ethics', in J. E. J. Altham and R. Harrison (eds), *World, Mind, and Ethic: Essays on the Ethical Philosophy of Bernard Williams*, New York: Cambridge University Press, 1995, pp. 86–131.

19  The fundamental aspect of Davidson's philosophy that I will be considering here is his understanding of the psychological as holistically structured. This is a prevalent theme in his work and I shall cite his works as I make use of them.

20  Jeff Malpas, 'Death and the Unity of a Life', in J. Malpas and R. Solomon (eds), *Death and Philosophy*, London: Routledge, 1998, pp. 120–34; and idem, 'Self and the Space of Others', *Place and Experience: A Philosophical Topography*, Cambridge: Cambridge University Press, 1999, pp. 138–56.

21  Malpas supplements Davidsonian holism with central ideas derived from the hermeneutic tradition. I am particularly thinking of notions such as what Malpas refers to as the intentional–horizonal structure of the psychological. See his *Donald Davidson and the Mirror of Meaning: Holism, Truth, Interpretation*, Cambridge: Cambridge University Press, 1992, pp. 104–44.

22 Donald Davidson, 'Rational Animals', *Actions and Events: Perspectives on the Philosophy of Donald Davidson*, Oxford: Basil Blackwell, 1985, pp. 473–48; idem, 'Thought and Talk', *Inquiries into Truth and Interpretation*, Oxford: Clarendon Press, 1984; and idem, 'Three Varieties of Knowledge', in A. Phillips Griffiths (ed.), *A.J. Ayer: Memorial Essays*, Cambridge: Cambridge University Press, 1991, pp. 153–66.

23 I do not want to suggest here that the reasons for caring for one's community at large are primarily instrumental. Rather, it will become apparent that one should care for one's community because the caring at issue is implicated in our own happiness as opposed to being something that will function as a kind of means to an end.

24 See Chapter 5.

25 I do not want to claim here that desires have truth-values; rather, one may truly or falsely desire something because the *beliefs* expressed by a given desire are either true or false.

26 The case is analogous with that of happiness. As argued above, the possibility of being deceived about the nature of happiness, or indeed, the fact that it is possible to have agreements and disagreements about the nature of happiness, means that we must know, even if roughly, what happiness is.

27 I will return to the method of critical introspection in Chapter 5.

28 I am aware that the ensuing description of the art of painting is controversial. However, I hope that the description adequately describes a particular and widespread manner of going about the business of producing works of art. I think this limited account of the skill of painting could be seen as problematic only if one loses sight of the fact that I am not primarily interested in characterizing the skills involved in the art of painting. Rather, I am interested in bringing some key aspects of the art of living into prominence by the use of some key aspects of a common manner of approaching the skill of painting.

29 For the purposes of the present inquiry I do not need to specify these general standards of adequacy in any significant detail (and such an undertaking would far exceed the scope of our present concerns). All we have to agree to here is that such standards do exist. And, that they do exist must be the case given that, in some instances at the very least, we are able to distinguish, with varying degrees of adequacy, good works of art from mediocre ones. In making this claim, moreover, I do not need to be committed to the obviously false idea that, for any two works of art, it will always and uncontroversially be the case that competent critiques will be able to determine the better of the two. However, the more subtle idea I am committed to is that, in extreme cases, it will be quite easy to determine the gold from the straw. That we are able to do this shows that specific, albeit rough, standards of adequacy inform aesthetic judgements.

　　Let me remind the reader at this point about one of Aristotle's famous, and I think true, dictums. He claims that, to attempt to be overly precise in some modes of inquiry, particularly with regard to the subject matter of human conduct, is to be imprecise (*EN* 1104a 1–9). How, for example, could one exhaustively characterize love or friendship? Or, more generally, how could one possibly exhaustively specify the shape of personhood? The innumerable variations in character and circumstances make this task impossible, and indeed undesirable. I think it is clear that the same applies to artworks. One could not possibly exhaustively specify the ideal form of artworks, such that if one had a grasp of this form, all one would have to do is reproduce it on a canvas (or some other such material) to produce a 'perfect' work of art. Luckily, no such exhaustive ideal exists.

30 Consider Paul Klee's magnificent watercolours.

31 The use of *praxis* in the context of describing the act of painting might be misleading though, given that the act of painting, unlike the practice of living, is not a type of activity that has as its *final* goal the perfecting of that very activity. Instead, the final goal of the activity of painting is an object as opposed to the refinement of an activity. However, perfecting the art of painting is certainly *a* goal of the act of painting, but it is a subgoal in the sense that the final purpose – the final goal – of perfecting the art of painting is to produce better works of art. In other words, the goal of perfecting the art

of painting, unlike the goal of perfecting the art of living, is for the sake of a further – final – goal. The distinction being drawn here between the acts of painting and living is an important one that we should bear in mind. It is also a controversial distinction because it is not immediately obvious why the goal of living is not also a product of some description. I will have more to say about these matters below. I might just remind the reader at present that the sort of ontology of the subject currently being developed owes a lot to Aristotle, and I might remind the reader that for 'The Philosopher' the goal of living is *eudaimonia* – happiness. For Aristotle, *Eudaimonia* is the overall shape of the activity of living where the potentials that define persons as such have been actualized.

32    This sort of explanation, arguably, allows us to better understand how it is possible simultaneously to reasonably claim that we are creatures of the same kind, and also that we are individuals with unique particularities that separate each of us out from all other members of our kind.

33    In discussing the issue of moral expertise I am deliberately drawing on Hubert Dreyfus's very informative discussion regarding the different stages in the becoming of a moral expert in his 'What is Moral Maturity?: A Phenomenological Account of the Development of Ethical Expertise', presented at Murdoch University, Perth, 1996.

34    Aristotle opens his *Ethica Nichomachea* with a discussion about the teleological structure of personhood.
      I might add here that Aristotle, at times at least, seems to hold that the intellectual life – the life of contemplation – is good in and of itself in the sense that its goodness is not dependent on the system of goals that are constitutive of the best sort of life. One could reasonably argue that, on the whole, Aristotle believes that intellectual activity – the contemplative life – is, so to speak, a free-floating good. However, although there certainly is evidence for attributing this sort of thesis to Aristotle, I do not think it is the most productive possible reading, and there is also evidence against such a reading in the Aristotelian corpus. I can think of two passages in the *EN* where Aristotle is notoriously ambiguous with regard to the exact role the life of contemplation plays in the best sort of life (1177a 12–18 & 1177b 26–1178 8). Let me provide a related example to illustrate why the sort of reading I am proposing is at least one adequate reading: according to Aristotle, *eudaimonia* is good in and of itself, but this is certainly not to say that it is a free-floating good – not at all. *Eudaimonia* is the good of the lives of persons, and it is defined in this manner in relation to the sorts of creatures that we are. Analogously, if one wants to read Aristotle as holding that contemplation is the highest of goods, then it seems to me that Aristotle is best understood as claiming that the life of contemplation should not be something that is a good irrespective of what it is the good of. The intellect, under the present interpretation, and *eudaimonia* are best understood as goods in and of themselves because they are ultimate goals and, as such, they are the principles around which human life is ideally organized. And there is no contradiction in claiming that both *eudaimonia* and contemplation are the highest goals in life, since the highest goal of a life that is organized in accordance with the *eudaimon* ideal is the life of contemplation (at least according to some parts of the Aristotelian corpus – although not the parts that I prefer to focus on). A life that gathers around its contemplative aspect is, according to one reading of Aristotle, a *eudaimon* one.

35    For a very good discussion on the issue of the unity of a life see Jeff Malpas's, 'Death and the Unity of a Life', *op.cit.*, n. 20. I might also add that Alasdair MacIntyre is well known for his views on the narrative unity of life. See his *After Virtue*, Notre Dame, Indiana: University of Notre Dame Press, 1884, pp. 204–25.

36    There are, as Nussbaum very eloquently points out, particularly in Chapters 11 and 12 of *The Fragility of Goodness: Luck and Ethics in Greek Tragedy and Philosophy*, Cambridge: Cambridge University Press, 1994, limit circumstances – tragic reversals – in which even the best of us will be unable to perform the compositional feat required for good living. That said, a *phronimos* is nevertheless best equipped to deal with tragic circumstances of this extreme sort. Analogous considerations also apply to the practice

of painting (say, when the canvas rips, or when paint accidentally falls on it, although of course, in some instances, though not in all, accidents of these sorts can be very beneficial).

37   I am not, by the way, making the absurd claim that the red brushstroke *qua* aesthetic object is not a physical object. Rather, what I am suggesting is that one cannot grasp the aesthetic significance of a given brushstroke with the vocabulary of the natural sciences. The difference at issue here is not a difference in substance, but, rather, a difference in interpretative framework.

38   One might conceive of cases in which the materiality of something is tightly tied in with its aesthetic significance, but cases such as these are atypical. Consider Duchamp's works made with found objects – his ready-made.

39   The thesis I am currently defending is reminiscent of what Davidson discusses in 'Psychology as Philosophy', in *Essays on Actions and Events*, Oxford: Clarendon Press, 1980, pp. 229–44. Davidson appropriately calls this thesis 'anomalous monism'. It is also interesting to note at this point that the anomalous monism thesis is strongly reminiscent of Aristotle's claims in *EN* 1104a 1–9 (already cited above) where, in terms that are slightly different from those I use, Aristotle claims that different conceptual resources must be brought to bear in accordance with the demands of different subject matters.

40   An object proper is a determinate object – an object *qua* physical object, *qua* aesthetic object, and so on. Objects, after all, are those things we have beliefs about, and we can only have beliefs about determinate things. To have a belief, after all, is to hold true – to hold that something is the case about something.

41   This qualitative or phenomenological mode of appreciation is perhaps a necessary aspect of an aesthetic mode of appreciation, but it certainly seems of secondary relevance when it comes to describing a brushstroke in physical terms (in terms of electromagnetic radiation, its effect on nerve endings and neural processes generally).
     I might take this opportunity to thank Sally Talbot for her valuable assistance in pressing me to explain more clearly the ontological status of the red brushstroke prior to being interpreted aesthetically (or in any other way for that matter).

42   Of course, I do not want to be interpreted as holding the seemingly absurd view that any interpretation goes. I just want to highlight the fact that the world we live in is a very human place and as such, it is a place with a moral dimension.

43   It is the conceptual field within which the concept of a life is articulated that allows us to recognize a life *qua* life of a rational creature rather than, say, a life *qua* biological organism. This is just an application of the general principle that there is no perception without conception.

44   Analogously, the conceptual field we bring to bear when describing the inner workings of a clock does not allow us to understand what a clock is, since a clock is defined not by its inner workings but by its function. A clock could be constituted in many different ways. What allows us to say that the inner workings of this mechanism are the inner working of a clock is an understanding of the function, the *telos*, of a clock – namely, telling time. Similarly, no matter how thorough an account of the inner workings of our bodies one might care to provide, this account alone would not suffice for us to conclude that a human body is the body of a person, since personhood, like 'clockhood', is a functional concept – a concept that pertains not to the how-it-works of something, but rather, a concept that pertains to the what-for of something. We are defined as persons by a certain manner of operating.
     The distinction being drawn here is only partially adequate, since bodily organs are also defined functionally. This said, it still holds that no matter how complete a functional description of the system of organs that constitute a body, a description of our highest *telos* would not supervene upon it. A description of this highest *telos*, which could be characterized as personhood, would not merely help us understand the fact that human bodies are unique as a biological description of our bodies does, but it also helps

us understand that human bodies are special because they are the bodies of persons. A functional understanding of our system of organs would not yield this last sort of understanding. What this shows is that the concept of a person has a relative degree of autonomy from the concept of a human being understood here as a particular sort of natural kind.

45  In *Oneself as Another*, Chicago: University of Chicago Press, 1992, pp. 153–4, Paul Ricoeur characterizes the embeddedness of activities into systems of activities that constitute practices in terms of the *subordination* of activities into practices.

46  Ibid., p. 154.

47  Of course, a general *telos* does not exist independently of a corresponding set of activities that constitute the general *telos*. The *telos* of chess-playing, for example, is to checkmate one's opponent in the act of playing a good game of chess. In conclusion, one is only playing chess, if, in addition to all those possible contingent reasons for playing, one is also playing in accordance with the defining ideal of chess, or, more precisely, if one is informing one's game sufficiently with the defining ideal of chess. This last refinement is important, since we are also able to recognize corrupt or alternative instances of chess playing as just that.

48  There might certainly be reasons for claiming that the endeavours of a given child are deficient in some respect or other, but clearly, if such criteria existed, they would be quite different from those we use to judge the skills of a master painter.

49  Now, one might consider possible actions that are, at first sight, beneficial to someone engaged in that activity, but which are at the same time extremely harmful to others. Imagine, for example, a case in which one occupies, because one has some minor ailment, the last available hospital bed in town, which would have otherwise been occupied by someone with a life-threatening disease, and who dies as a consequence of this neglect. Cases such as these might initially seem to challenge the claim I have just made that the goodness of a given action depends on whether or not it is good to the individual who is actually performing the action. I want to hold fast to my initial claim, but must add more complexity to the picture. The complexity relates to the highly plausible fact that our lives are intertwined in such a way that goodness in general cannot be a function of purely individualistic considerations. It is highly plausible that individual goodness is at times a function of intersubjective goodness. For instance, it is highly plausible, as Aristotle famously thought, that one's goodness is a function of the goodness of those one loves. More on these matters follows below.

50  We know this because the *telos* of painting is what distinguishes the art of painting as a unique kind of practice. But, of course, it is conceivable that a non-person – a robot of some sort, for instance – could be a great producer of art, and this points to the fact that the practice of painting is only contingently embedded in specific systems of practices.

51  Although it must be embedded in some system of practices, given that a person cannot just be a painter.

52  I have said nothing yet about how even someone's completed life can never be fully interpreted by someone else, since a life is embedded in a fabric of practices which are also ongoing – never static. I think it is clear that many interesting things can be said, and no doubt have been said, about this topic but, since we are presently concerned with the topic of self-interpretation, we need not, for our present purposes, fathom the depths of this well. MacIntyre deals with this issue in his *After Virtue*, *op.cit.*, n. 35, pp. 204–25. It is also perhaps one of the key themes of Hegel's *Phenomenology of Spirit*.

53  This section is largely inspired by Jeff Malpas and G. Wickham's, 'Governance and the World: From Joe Dimaggio to Michael Foucault', *The UTS Review: Cultural Studies and New Writing*, **3** (2), November 1997, pp. 91–108; and idem, 'Governance and Failure: On the Limits of Sociology', *Journal of Sociology*, **31** (3), November 1995, pp. 37–50.

54  There is another, more fundamental, understanding of world: the world as that which underlies, as that which exists prior to our engagements with it – the realm of the indeterminate, which forms the backdrop for any interpretative project. This latter

understanding of world is an understanding of world as matter as opposed to the prior understanding, which is to understand world as form. When discussing Aristotle's hylomorphism I shall further discuss the form/matter dynamic – the *eidos/hyle* dynamic – in the context of an explanation of his teleological ontology. That said, let me point out that the understanding of the matter/form dynamic, which is central to Aristotle's ontology is somewhat transformed here, for Aristotle has a much less fluid understanding of the dynamic than is presently being discussed. Indeed, in this regard, the dynamic at issue is more closely aligned to the Heideggerian project, and the works I have primarily been drawing on in this section are largely inspired by Heideggerian holistic ontology. I am referring to the above-cited pieces by Malpas and Wickham in note 53.

# Chapter 3

# The *Eudaimon* Principle

## The Teleological Structure of the Real

My main aim in this chapter will be to justify and explain the *eudaimon* principle. I have already had much to say about this principle above, but a more complete understanding of it will require a more detailed understanding of Aristotle's teleology.[1] In this chapter, in contrast with the approach I have generally chosen to adopt throughout this investigation, I will be focusing on the Aristotelian corpus in some detail since this, I think, is the only way that one can do justice to Aristotle's teleology, which is crucial for understanding the central principle of his *Ethics* – the *eudaimon* principle. Although initially, particularly when dealing with the material of the *Metaphysica*, much of the detail might seem superfluous to the present investigation, I think it will become apparent as the chapter progresses why the level of detail has been necessary for establishing a clear set of relationships between some of the investigation's central concerns. In general, I hope that, by the end of this chapter, it will become clear, among other things, how and why Aristotle understands the ethical as he does and, more specifically, that the reader will have a better idea of the central constitutive relationships that exist between our *telos*, personhood, the virtues, and *logos*. Indeed, this chapter will set out the fundamental structure of a *eudaimon* life.

There are two further significant reasons for wanting to engage with Aristotle's thought in detail here. The first is that there are important parts of his thought which I do not think have been very clearly elaborated by Aristotle himself and which are directly relevant to our present concerns. The second reason is that my interpretation of Aristotle's account of the soul (*psyche*) differs from the canonical interpretation and this has forced me to provide a relatively detailed account of why I think my interpretation is better.[2] This second reason, I might add, is related to the first in that it is because Aristotle is not clear about aspects of his conception of *psyche* that scholars have been led astray.

Finally, it must also be noted here that, although there will be much detail with regard to exegetical matters in this chapter, I do think that a comprehensive investigation into Aristotelian teleology would have to be much more extensive than this investigation allows. Teleology is at the core of Aristotle's understanding of reality, and, for this reason, there is an important sense in which his teleology cannot be fully understood without understanding his philosophical project in its entirety.

*Happiness*

Teleology, Aristotle thinks, is to a large extent an account of what *physis* (nature) is – of how the different senses of *physis* are structured. However, I think Aristotle is wrong to think of teleology primarily as explaining what *physis* is. The primary reason I think he is wrong is that his account of *physis* is hopelessly inadequate in dealing with the possibility of artificial life, as will be evidenced as the discussion proceeds. This said, notwithstanding the fact that Aristotle's teleology is not an adequate account of *physis*, it is nevertheless one of the most beautifully elegant accounts of being – of what is said to be – ever produced in the long history of Western philosophy. Its beauty flows from the fact that it furnishes the conceptual resources for explaining the being of developmental processes. And this is just what we want to explain because, as argued above, personhood is not a natural kind concept. Instead, it is a category that pertains to moral agents – agents whose activities are defined in relationship to their ideal directedness toward the *eudaimon telos*.

For Aristotle, *physis* is primarily and paradigmatically,[3] though certainly not exclusively, understood as the form (*eidos*) – understood as substantial form – of living entities.[4] *Physis* is also understood as the matter (*hyle*) of a living thing, but, as we shall see, this last sense of *physis* is derivative – its reality is determined in relation to substantial form.[5] Aristotle thinks that what is unique about living entities, what differentiates them from all other entities, is that they have an immanent principle of change.[6] The fundamental modality of change, and the one I shall mainly be focusing on here, is development (rather than, say, changes such as those that occur when one stands up). And, indeed, development is the modality of change that is of primary importance for understanding the *eudaimon* principle. *Eudaimonia* is, after all, the *telos* of the developmental process of persons *qua* persons.

Aristotle argues that the *eidos* of a living entity is the primary sense of *physis* because it is the good – the *telos* – of a process of natural development.[7] *Eidos* is the good insofar as the good of development is achieved when a given thing or creature's *eidos* is actualized. This is just another way of saying that natural development occurs for the sake of the actualization of *eidos*.[8] A house, for instance, reaches its state of completion – its *telos* – when 'houseness' – the form of a house – has been embodied in 'these' bricks and mortar.[9] But one must be careful here because this manner of formulating what the *telos* of development is might be slightly misleading given that it suggests that actuality – *energeia* – is something over and above *eidos*. Aristotle does not think this is the case – 'actuality is the end'.[10] But, to identify *energeia* with *eidos* might also be rather misleading given that, if developmental movement is in fact a movement toward the actualization of *eidos*, then it must also be the case, Aristotle thinks, that the *eidos* of a thing is able to exist as a potential – as *dynamis*. However, and this is a crucial point, the manner in which the *eidos* of a thing exists as *dynamis* is a derivative – a secondary or relative – mode of understanding *eidos*. The sense of *eidos* at issue is secondary in that it is only in relation to the primary (or prior) sense of *eidos* that the secondary sense has a reality of its own. The secondary sense of *eidos* is the sense in which *eidos* is understood in the modality of privation – as non-being (*steresis*).[11] Indeed, we shall see that the sense in which a thing that has not actualized its *eidos* is said to have its *eidos* in the modality of non-being is what allows us to make claims regarding the potentials of a given thing.[12]

Let me illustrate these last claims with a couple of examples. A mouth does not have the potentiality for vision, but an eye certainly does (even when it is closed). Similarly, an infant, unlike a rock or a screwdriver, has the potentiality for sophisticated thought even though he or she is presently incapable of this sort of thinking. More generally, that we are able to make discriminations with regard to what has certain potentialities and what does not shows that having a potentiality is indeed a property of something – a property in the modality of non-being. But, we must not forget that non-being is only a property relative to the primary sense of *eidos* – *eidos* as *energeia* (as opposed to *dynamis*). Returning to the eye example, it is only because eyes typically have a certain actuality, namely vision, that it makes sense to claim that a given eye, which does not have this actuality at a given moment, has the potentiality for vision. An eye that has the potential for vision, but which is not exercising this potentiality, is an eye that has its *eidos* in the modality of non-being. We are able to rightly claim that an eye has the potentiality for vision if, and only if, we can recognize that its form may dwell in it as non-being. The form dwells within only in relationship to *eidos* proper in the sense that a potentiality – a power – is for the sake of the condition in which the potential is actualized. The being of a potential, so to speak, is relative to the being of an actuality. Indeed, Aristotle makes this point explicitly:

> And actuality is the end, and it is *for the sake of* [my italics] this that the potentiality is acquired; for animals do not see in order that they may have [the capacity for] sight, but have sight in order that they may see.[13]

That vision is the *eidos* of an eye is something that cannot be taken for granted and I shall return to this issue shortly. But, first, a few more things must be said with regard to the actuality/potentiality pair.

The sorts of potentiality that are of primary importance to this investigation are the sorts that are common to all members of a given species. Let us call these potentialities 'species potentialities' or simply 'potentialities'. Our species potentialities are those whose reality is relative to our common *telos* – *eudaimonia*. By contrast, the sorts of potentiality I will not primarily be focusing on are those which are determined as such in relation to what could be characterized as accidental actualities. An accidental actuality is the sort of actuality the possession of which is not *essential* for counting as a member of a given species (musical and sporting abilities are cases in point).

With regard to the issue of potentialities it is also important to note that, given that potentialities have a relative existence, it is not surprising that there are also levels of potentiality – in other words, potentialities that are more actual than others. The potentiality an infant has for knowledge,[14] for instance, is less actual than the potentiality a thinking adult has for knowledge. Indeed, the potentiality a thinking adult has for knowledge is what Aristotle refers to as a first actuality (in opposition to what we could refer to as a second actuality, which is the activity of contemplation itself).[15] A first actuality is the highest modality of potentiality given that it is the sort of potentiality that is closest to the highest modality of actuality – actuality in the primary sense. Having the first actuality for thought is the sort of capacity a thinking person has when asleep. The potentialities an infant has for knowledge, on the other hand, are further removed from the actual exercise of knowledge relative to which potentialities derive their reality. Further still from actuality is the sort of potentiality that a permanently comatose (or permanently sleeping) individual has for knowledge. A permanently comatose individual, for instance, has the potentiality for knowledge by virtue of the fact that he or she is recognized as *ideally* – in the sense of an unattainable ideal a given creature would have instantiated if circumstances had been more favourable – instantiating the sort of actuality that defines us. That we do recognize a permanently comatose individual as ideally instantiating a given actuality negatively is evidenced by our judgements regarding the tragedy of his or her situation. We recognize a permanently comatose individual as sharing an essence (*to ti en einai*) which defines him or her as human, but who is unable to partake of this essence. Our essence – our substantial form – is that which defines us as members of a given species. And we know that the actualization of our essence is the *telos* of human development, according to Aristotle.

It might seem rather counterintuitive to some that this last sort of potentiality is indeed a sort of potentiality. But, I think, it will no longer seem that way if one recognizes that all forms of potentiality, and not just the last form, are determined as such in relationship to an ideal of actuality. We recognize a child as capable of knowledge because, if all things go as they *ought*, ideally he or she will contemplate (exercise knowledge). Also a knowledgeable person will *ideally* exercise knowledge (once he or she wakes up). But he or she might never wake up – he or she might, for instance, suffer a stroke (or something of this sort). And, indeed, if it turned out that a knowledgeable person did not wake up the next morning, this would clearly not mean that he or she did not have the power to exercise knowledge after falling asleep. Generally, we do not have to observe whether a given individual in actual fact actualizes a given potential in order to be able to claim that he or she actually has a potential. Attributions of potentials are not retrospective in this manner. Instead, what does warrant our attribution of a given potential to a given individual is knowledge of the *ideal* course of development he or she ought to take by virtue of the fact that he or she is a human being. I reiterate, what warrants attributions of a given potential is an ideal conception of what a flourishing human being is like, and not, as some might think, a conception of how most individuals have developed in the past – a kind of statistical generalization. This can be clearly seen to be the case if one considers that we would still want to claim that human beings have certain potentials by virtue of the fact that they are human, even if (and, indeed, I think it is the case) that the great majority of human beings have not been able to develop properly due to lack of proper resources (including proper education). To recapitulate, we can observe, first, that a hierarchy of actuality has emerged and, second, how the reality of potentialities is determined relative to a certain ideal of actuality which is the good of development. The ideal of actuality is *eidos* in the primary sense.

Referring again to the eye example, it might seem strange to some that the actuality of an eye is vision. This might seem even stranger if one also takes into consideration that, according to Aristotle, the actuality of a thing is also its *eidos*. But Aristotle has good reasons for holding that vision is the *eidos* of an eye. I think it is fairly straightforwardly true that an eye *qua* eye just is an organ *for* vision. Moreover, there is a sense in which 'organ for vision' is the *eidos* of an eye, but it is a derivative (or secondary) sense. To claim that an eye is an organ *for* vision is just to claim that an eye is for the sake of vision. So, the *telos* of an eye, in other words, is vision rather than organ for vision – the activity (*energeia*) of the eye rather than the organ that produces vision in conjunction with vision. So, it is *ultimately* the activity of an eye that defines an eye as such. And it is precisely for this reason that vision is the highest or second actuality (*entelecheia*) of an eye.[16] That vision is the highest actuality of an eye accounts for the fact that an eye is anything that has the capacity for vision (think of the possibility of an artificial eye).

This point becomes especially clear if one notes that one cannot properly define vision as the activity of an eye because, to define vision in this manner is circular, and viciously so, given that an eye just is an organ for vision. It is in terms of vision that an eye is defined, and not the other way around. One could say, following Aristotle, that the definition of vision is *prior* in definition to the definition of eye. And, indeed, it is this primary defining role that makes vision the *entelecheia* of an eye. Finally, that the present interpretation is correct is further supported by the fact that, for Aristotle, *energeia* means both activity and actuality (and *entelecheia* is the highest modality of *energeia*). Aristotle argues that 'For activity is the end, and the actuality is the activity; hence the term "actuality" is derived from "activity," and tends to have the meaning of "complete reality".'[17] 'Complete reality' (*entelecheia*) is the highest modality of actuality – the *arche* or source of intelligibility. We may conclude that vision is the *eidos*, the *telos* and the *energeia* (or *entelecheia*) of an eye.[18]

I have thus far established that there is a hierarchy of potentialities or, to put it slightly differently, a hierarchy of levels of actuality. But, according to Aristotle, at each level of the hierarchy there are two sorts of potentiality operating. He is referring here to the agent and the patient of change. The active potentiality (the agent) is the moving cause – the source (*arche*) of motion (*kinesis*) – and the passive potentiality (the patient) is matter – *hyle*.[19] These are two of the four basic principles (or 'causes') of development that are central to Aristotle's teleology.[20] Let us see how these principles operate. Natural development, as opposed to artificial development, we already know, is a movement toward the actualization of form that is already in a natural thing potentially, as *steresis* or *dynamis*. Natural development, in other words, is a bringing out into the open something that was, in some way, already there. This movement – the movement Aristotle refers to as coming-to-be (*genesis*) – towards the actualization of *eidos*, which already resides in a developing thing, is the fundamental structuring aspect of natural development. An artisan, for example, moulds clay into a vase. It is not the clay itself that does the moulding. The clay, rather, is the patient – it allows itself to be moulded in certain ways when acted upon by the external agency of an artisan. But what makes an artisan an agent? *Prima facie*, this question might sound slightly absurd given that, clearly, a person is an agent by the mere fact that he or she is able to act in accordance with his or her (implicit or explicit) beliefs and desires. And, more specifically, an artisan is an agent *qua* artisan insofar as he or she is able to act in accordance with a conception of the form, which in this case is the form of a vase.[21] So, one could say, the reason why an artisan is an agent and not just another patient in a possible chain of causation leading to the formation of a vase, is that the artisan has the *eidos* of a vase in his or her mind and, through his or her actions, the clay comes to embody the desired *eidos*. Indeed, it is because one can locate the *eidos* of a vase in the artisan who makes it that the artisan is the primary moving cause of the vase.

There are, of course, moving causes other than those of the primary variety. One could say, and rightly so, that the hands of an artisan are a moving cause of a vase. Alternatively, one could say that the parents of the artisan in question are the moving cause of the vase. In fact, there seems to be no limit to the number of moving causes of a particular thing or event. However, there is a limit with respect to the moving causes that explain the 'why' of something – that explain why that something is just that. It would be quite uninformative, though true, to claim that the moving cause of a vase are the parents of the artisan who made it, or that the moving cause are the hands of the artisan or, indeed, that the moving cause are the atoms that constitute the artisan and so on. The *primary* moving cause is the moving cause that does the work of explaining the 'why' of the vase – namely, the artisan – although it must be noted that it is not only the moving cause which explains the why of the vase. As we know by now, Aristotle also argues that there are three other causes – matter (*hyle*), *eidos* and *telos* – that explain the why of something, but in different ways (ways which shall be further discussed shortly). The primary moving cause of a vase is the artisan who made it because the process of making a vase is, Aristotle would argue, primarily the process of embodying a particular form that exists in an artisan's mind. For this reason, explaining the why of a vase in terms of the artisan who made it is much more informative than eliciting any old moving cause. The artisan is an agent, and hence a moving cause, in the sense that he or she is the one who forms the vase.

It might be worth mentioning that the maker of the vase – the artisan – stands in a particular relationship to the vase, being constituted as the maker of the vase only in relationship to that vase. The relationship at issue here is a *for-the-sake-of* relationship. The maker of the vase *qua* maker of this vase is for the sake of the vase. Parents, hands and atoms do not stand to the vase in this way – their relationship to the vase is *incidental*. Their identities as parents, hands and atoms are not dependent on the vase. Of course, it is also the case that the identity of the artisan *qua* person is not established in relationship to the vase. But the identity of the person *qua* maker of the vase is. And it is for this reason that the maker of the vase is the primary moving cause of the vase. The artisan has a form in his or her mind that leads him or her to make the vase and, in doing so, he or she places him or herself in a relationship that binds the identity of the artisan *qua* maker of the vase to the vase itself. Their beings, so to speak, converge. Analogously, and as discussed towards the end of the previous chapter, the painter is constituted as such in relationship to the paintings he or she makes. The beings of the paintings and of the painter converge. They derive their respective existences from the specific manner in which they relate to each other.[22]

In contrast with artificial development, in natural development both the agent and the patient are one and the same entity. If one leaves a lump of clay standing there, it will not become a vase (nor will wood become a bed unless acted upon by the external powers of an agent).[23] But, by contrast, if one left a child or a seed in certain characteristic conditions they would typically develop into thriving exemplars of their species by their own impetus. Children and seeds, unlike lumps of clay, have an internal principle of change.[24] In other words, the moving cause of a given natural thing is immanent to that thing. And it is immanent because the *eidos* of a natural entity is immanent. That the *eidos* is immanent – that it is potentially in a natural developing entity – is evidenced by the fact that a natural entity in adequate conditions will, as already claimed above, typically become a thriving exemplar of its species.

We know already that the maker of a vase is just that in relation to the vase, and, more specifically, the maker *qua* maker is for the sake of the vase because the maker is the agent who acts upon the clay to form it. In other words, the agent acts on the patient – on the clay, in this case. And, indeed, it is in relationship to what is made that the maker is rendered intelligible *qua* maker. So, it is not just that the maker makes, but also that the maker is made, *qua* maker of a vase, in the making of a vase. Additionally, the patient – that which receives the form – is the matter (*hyle*) of the subject that has been formed by the artisan. *Hyle* is the recipient of *eidos*. It follows, then, that *hyle* is for the sake of *eidos*. That is, the existence of *hyle*, like the existence of the moving cause, is relative. They are both, so to speak, means for the instantiation of *eidos*; their respective realities (beings) are determined in relationship to what they are for – namely, *eidos*.

In the case of living organisms, the patient of change is the 'body' and the agent of change – the first actuality – is the soul of a living organism. I place 'body' in quotation marks here to emphasize the fact that, for Aristotle, both the agent and the patient of change constitute the body – a body, properly speaking, could not exist without a soul. That Aristotle conceives of bodies in this way should come as no real surprise if one considers that, according to Aristotle, a body is just that because it has the potentiality – understood as second actuality – for being alive. And indeed, having the potentiality for life involves having both an agent and a patient of change. I shall return to the issue of the relationship between the soul and the body shortly, but, for now, would like to conclude my general discussion on the four principles of change.

I think it is clear by now that Aristotle's use of 'cause' (*aition*) differs from our contemporary usage. For us, the cause of something is the efficient cause, which more nearly resembles the moving cause than any other of the three causes. For Aristotle, on the other hand, the four causes are just that by virtue of the fact that they explain *why* something has come-to-be. In other words, the causes of something are, for Aristotle, what we elicit to explain 'the why' (*to dia ti*) of that very thing.[25]

All aspects of natural development are intimately related to *eidos* in that, to repeat, development (natural and artificial) occurs for the sake of the actualization of *eidos*. *Eidos*, one could say, is the focal point of intelligibility precisely because all aspects involved in development as such exist only in relationship to it. Indeed, this movement towards the actualization of form is the fundamental aspect – the focal point – of development as such, precisely because the actualization of form is that for the sake of which development occurs. But one must be cautious in making these claims given that the *eidos* presently at issue is not just any *eidos*. Rather, it is substantial form – the form that allows us to identify an entity as a determinate sort of entity. The substantial form of an entity is its essence (*to ti en einai*); it is the 'whatness' of an entity – a rational animal (*zoon logon echon*) in the case of human beings.[26]

## The Gathering of Beings

I think that it is clear by now that for-the-sake-of relationships are central to Aristotelian teleology. We have seen how the different principles of change (with the exception of *eidos*) are structured (or gathered) around *eidos*, and in this structuring they are made intelligible by the manner in which they relate to *eidos*. But this is only part of the story Aristotle has to tell about teleology. Aristotle's teleology is fundamentally a theory about being – a theory about the structure of what is said *to be* (a structure that is fundamentally developmental). It is an account of how things that are said to be, so to speak, congregate around a central focal point or *arche* (source) of intelligibility, which is what renders them intelligible. The *arche* at issue is substantial form.

It must be clarified that the sense in which intelligibility is used here is not one that pertains primarily to our capacities to make sense of things. Rather, the sense at issue here is one in which things themselves provide the conditions for intellection – things themselves congregate in a way that renders them intelligible – and this congregation provides them with a determinate reality (a reality that can be understood).[27] Indeed, it is certainly the case that something can be made intelligible because it can be made intelligible by us. But also, Aristotle rightly thinks, it is equally true, and more fundamentally so, that if something can be made intelligible it is because that something allows itself to be made intelligible.[28] It is how things allow themselves to be made intelligible that is at the very core of Aristotle's concerns with teleology.

The structure of being I have been referring to here, the structure that renders beings intelligible, is mirrored by the structure of *pros hen* equivocation. The Greek *pros hen* means 'towards one', and the structure of *pros hen* equivocation is the structure of the different senses in which things are said to be – the structure that received its first developed form by Aristotle in the *Kategoriai*, and its final fully-fledged form in the *Metaphysica*. Being, Aristotle noted, is an equivocal term. But it is equivocal in a very interesting sense because it is not simply that there is a 'heap' of different senses in which things are said to be but, rather, there is, to repeat, a structure that renders the different senses of being intelligible. The structure of the different senses of being, as already claimed above, has a focal point, and it is in relationship to this focal sense of being – this primary sense of being – that all other senses are rendered intelligible. We have already seen how this occurs in the case of the four causes, which are four modes in which things are said *to be*. We have seen how *hyle*, the *arche* of *kinesis,* and *telos* are rendered intelligible in relation to *eidos.*

Before becoming involved in the details of Aristotle's hierarchy of beings it would be appropriate to compare the structure of *pros hen* equivocation with the basic structure of a human life canvassed above. This comparison will give us a better idea of where this discussion is supposed to be taking us. Remember that I have argued above that the basic structural feature of a human life is that human life is lived for the sake of *eudaimonia* – that is, our lives, understood as wholes, are fundamentally lives that derive their meaning from the fact that they are ideally directed towards the achievement of the *eudaimon telos*. So, one could say, in a manner that weds the *eudaimon* structure with the structure of *pros hen* equivocation, that *eudaimonia* is an *arche* of intelligibility which renders the lives of persons, understood as wholes, intelligible. Indeed, we are primarily defined as persons, and what defines us in this way is our substantial form, because we have a purpose in common – a common *telos*. Thus, our substantial form must be the form of a *eudaimon* life.[29] That Aristotle thinks we are defined in this way is in no way merely a consequence of an Aristotelian fancy. That we are primarily defined in relation to our *eudaimon telos* is intimately related to the structure of *pros hen* equivocation. Aristotle believes that all aspects of our being are gathered around – they are rendered intelligible in relation to – our essence, which is our substantial form. And this substantial form is the form of a *eudaimon* life – the form that constitutes us as rational animals (*zoon logon echon*). These matters shall be clarified further as the discussion proceeds.

What *physis* is for Aristotle is directly linked to the central question of *Metaphysica* VII, and the specific way in which Aristotle answers this question there. Aristotle asks 'What is it for something to be?', and he initially responds by noting that being can be spoken of in many senses that are organized in what could be characterized as the categorial structure of existents – the structure of *pros hen* equivocals.[30] There are two fundamental ways in which things can be according to Aristotle. Things can be as substances (the 'what' or the 'what it is' of an entity) or they can be as accidents (quantities, qualities, affections, and so on).[31] Substance is the primary sense of being, and it is, according to Aristotle, primary in all senses – in definition (or formula), knowledge and in time.[32] First, substance is primary in definition because the definition of substance is implicated (either implicitly or explicitly) in the definition of those things that fall within the categories other than substance. Second, substance is primary in knowledge because 'we assume that we know each particular thing most truly when we know *what* "man" or "fire" is – rather than its quality or quantity or position; because we know these points too when we know [of] *what* the quantity or quality is'.[33] We know what 'man' is not by knowing that a given individual is male or female, white or dark, short or tall, brown-eyed, is standing five feet to my right, lived in the past or is musical. Rather, we know what he or she is primarily by knowing that he or she is a person. And, third, substance is primary in time given that it is only possible to attribute a given quality, quantity, and so on, to a substance if there is a substance in the first place.

Whilst in his *Kategoriai*[34] Aristotle identifies substance (*ousia*) with the subject of predication (*hypokeimenon*), in his *Metaphysica* he identifies the 'what it is' of a thing with a thing's essence (*to ti en einai*). He identifies the essence, moreover, as we already know, with a thing's substantial form (*eidos*) – substance in its primary sense. The substantial form of a thing is that which defines a given thing as that very sort of thing – it is that which is expressed in the definition or formula of a given sort of thing. Socrates, for example, is defined as rational animal rather than a white animal, big animal, an animal living at a certain time or an animal with two feet.

Socrates would still be Socrates if his skin pigmentation changed or if he boarded a time machine and lived a good part of his life in a different historical period from his own. Yet, although Socrates is necessarily a member of the genus 'animal', his essence is not animal, given that were he to become a worm or a dog, he would cease to be Socrates. Rather than being his essence, animal is an aspect of Socrates' essence. That 'animality' is an aspect is evidenced by the fact that one cannot be a human being and yet not an animal. What Socrates cannot lose, if he is to continue to be himself, are those features that define him as a member of our species: those features that make him a rational animal – a rational creature of the genus animal.[35]

Why did Aristotle change his mind with regard to his account of substance? Answering this question will help us come to terms with his teleology. It seems that Aristotle changed his mind because of his need to accommodate his account of change, developed primarily in his *Physica*, into his account of the categorial structure. In order to account for change, amongst other things, Aristotle developed a sophisticated account of the relationship between *eidos* and *hyle*. The material aspect of a thing can no longer count as an aspect of primary substance in Aristotle's later work given that there is something prior to matter which determines the 'whatness' of a thing, and this is substantial form or essence. There is nothing over and above substantial form relative to which something acquires its determinate (self-sufficient) reality. Rather, substantial form, as claimed above, is the source of determinacy; it bestows reality on all the other modes of being that gather together to constitute a self-sufficient (autonomous) thing.[36]

Aristotle believes that our rational nature is the central defining aspect of our human nature. And, indeed, it is this aspect of our nature that most clearly distinguishes us from all other living organisms.[37] But there is a deeper and related reason for privileging the rational aspect of our nature over all other aspects, and that is because all other aspects of our being are subservient to this core aspect. Aristotle thinks that all *aspects* of our existence are gathered together for the sake of our rational existence in a way that renders each aspect intelligible in relation to our rational existence. Each of our vital organs, for example, has a role to play in keeping us alive. And, indeed, life *qua* being alive is that for the sake of which organs exist. But life *qua* being alive is only a sub-*telos* of our existence. Life in this sense is not something that exists for its own sake and for the sake of nothing else.[38] Rather, being alive is a requirement for a higher goal, and that goal is to have a rational existence. This hierarchical structure which gathers around the *arche* (core or source) of intelligibility of human life ties in very neatly with my claims that the goal of life is *eudaimonia*, and this is because, as we shall see,[39] *eudaimonia* is a rational ideal. Or more precisely, *eudaimonia* is, according to Aristotle, the *telos* of our rational existence – that is, it is the best possible rational existence.

### *Psyche* and the *Arche* of Life

That Aristotle holds that we are by nature rational animals, and that the *telos* of our rational nature is *eudaimonia*, is perhaps most clearly observed in his account of the soul (*psyche*) and its activities. How does Aristotle conceive of the soul? For him 'the soul is the first actuality of a natural body'.[40] What does Aristotle mean by 'first actuality'? As we have already learnt, he argues that actuality is spoken of in two ways, 'first as knowledge is and second as contemplation is'.[41] The distinction between knowledge and contemplation is drawn on the grounds that, in order to have knowledge, one does not have to be exercising one's knowledge (since one has knowledge even when asleep) whilst, on the other hand, contemplation is the act itself of exercising knowledge. Knowledge which is not exercised is a first actuality.[42] Analogously, the soul is actuality in the sense of first actuality, and not in the sense that contemplation is an actuality. On the other hand, the activities that flow from the capacities that constitute a soul are analogous to contemplation. So a soul is not the activity (*energeia*) of a body as such, something possessed by a body has that allows it to be active and which allows us to distinguish a sleeping body from a dead one. What a sleeping body has that a dead body lacks are powers or capacities.

One must not confuse the first actuality of living bodies with the substantial form of a living creature. Aristotle himself seems confused about these matters at times (and, indeed, the canonical interpretation of Aristotle's doctrine of the soul is that the soul is the substantial form of the body). The problem here is that the substantial form cannot be the soul, at least not according to Aristotle's most explicit account of what the soul is – namely, the first actuality of a body capable of living.[43] The first actuality of a body, to reiterate, is the capacities or powers of a body (actuality as knowledge rather than as contemplation).[44] Capacities, as we have seen, are not the highest grade of actuality; they are only actualities relative to the highest mode of actuality, which are the activities that flow from the capacities of a body (recall the eye example discussed above). Capacities, in other words, are for the sake of work – of *energeia*.[45] Conversely, substantial form does not derive its reality – its determinacy – in relation to anything else. Indeed, having a substantial form, as we have seen, is what determines that a given being has a self-sufficient (autonomous or separate) and determinate existence. The reason why substantial form has this role is precisely that it relies on nothing else for its reality and because it is the *arche* around which all other beings that constitute an entity *qua* that very entity congregate. So, we may conclude that the soul cannot consistently be the substantial form of a living entity. The soul, rather, is best understood as the form of a body – that which has the potential for living – and not of a living entity as such – the entity in action.[46]

This argument against the view that the soul is the substantial form of a living entity is given extra vigour if one considers that the soul has much the same role to play in a living body as the moving cause has to play in explaining change in general. The moving cause is the *arche* of *kinesis* rather than the *kinesis* itself – the potential or capacity for living rather than living itself. The source of movement, in other words, is the active *dynamis* of change. This is exactly the sort of role assigned to the soul by Aristotle. The soul is the active *dynamis* (the first actuality) of those things that have an immanent principle of change (the soul is the immanent principle). And if this is the case, as it seems to be, it follows that the soul cannot be the substantial form. Rather, the soul is for the sake of substantial form. To word this slightly differently, the reality of the soul is relative to substantial form. Indeed, Aristotle himself argues along these lines. He argues that:

> And the work of anything is its end; it is clear, therefore, from this that the work is better than the state; for the end is best, as being end: for we assume the best, the final stage, to be the end for the sake of which all else exists. That the work, then, is better than the state or condition is plain.[47]

The states at issue here, clearly, are the states that constitute the soul – the first actuality. The final stage – the *telos* – is the activities of the soul. A couple of paragraphs further on, Aristotle applies the general schema expressed in previous quotation to the specific issue of the soul and ties this issue in with our central concern – namely, with the issue of *eudaimonia*:

> Further, let the work of the soul be to produce living, this consisting in employment and being awake – for slumber is a sort of inactivity and rest. Therefore, since the work must be one and the same both for the soul and for its excellence, the work of the excellence of the soul would be a good life. This, then, is the complete good, which (as we saw) was happiness.[48]

So, Aristotle argues that living *qua* activity (*energeia*) is the end of the states or powers (*dynamis*) that constitute the soul. And he further argues that the work of the excellence of the soul – the activities of the soul when the soul is at its best – is *eudaimonia*.[49] This is why *eudaimonia* is best understood as the substantial form of a human being – it is that for the sake of which human life is lived out. *Eudaimonia* is the work of the soul – the highest modality of actuality of a thing, namely ourselves, that potentially has life.

By contrast, Aristotle also explicitly claims that 'the essential whatness' of a living body is its soul.[50] The problem with this account is that it conflicts with his more fundamental conception that substantial form is the highest modality of actuality, and it is in relationship to this form of actuality that capacities derive their reality. So, for the sake of consistency I shall, as already discussed above, dismiss the view that the soul is the substantial form of a body. My charitable interpretation of Aristotle's account of the soul also has the advantage, as we have briefly seen, of tying in very neatly with Aristotle's ethical theory, as well as in tying in the material of the *Metaphysica* (discussed above) regarding the structure of beings with that of both *De Anima* and the *Ethics*. We already know that, according to Aristotle, *eudaimonia* is activity (*energeia*) in conformity with virtue. The virtues are states or powers that constitute the best aspect of the soul – life, *qua* power, 'of the rational element'[51] – when the soul is at its best. In Aristotle's words:

> ... since the activity is better than the state, and the best activity than the best state, and virtue is the best state, that the activity of the virtue of the soul is the best thing. But happiness, we saw, was the best thing; therefore happiness is the activity of the good soul.[52]

The virtues, Aristotle explicitly argues, are just that only in relation to the activities that flow from them. States or powers, in general, I have already shown, are for the sake of the activities that flow from them. The activities that flow from the virtues are what constitute *eudaimonia*. Moreover, given that, according to Aristotle, all the other aspects of the soul (nutritive, reproductive, perceptive, and so on) are for the sake of the rational part of the soul, it follows that the activities that flow from the rational part of the soul are the substantial form of a human being.[53]

An objection might be raised to these last claims on the grounds that human nutritive and perceptive capacities are uniquely human in their internal organization. It is most certainly true that our nutritive and perceptive capacities are uniquely human, and they can be identified on these grounds, but not solely on these grounds. One also needs to know that the nutritive and perceptive capacities are the capacities of a rational creature. An analysis of the capacities at issue that did not at least implicitly consider our rational nature would establish that these capacities are different from those of other creatures, but one would not, by means of this sort of analysis, be able to determine that these capacities are in fact human capacities simply because these capacities are ultimately identified as human if they are seen as being for the sake of human rational existence, which is our *to ti en einai* (essence).

Analogously, one could know all the internal workings of a watch and how these internal workings cause the watch hands to move without in any way knowing that the machine under scrutiny is in fact a watch. Conversely, one might have no idea of the inner workings of a watch, as is the case with most of us watch-users, and nevertheless know that the object on one's wrist is indeed a watch. The type of knowledge required for identifying a watch as such is not of the mechanical sort but, instead, pertains to the *energeia* a watch has. In other words, the type of knowledge required for knowing what a watch is – for knowing the *eidos* of a watch – is not knowledge of 'how', but knowledge of 'what-for'. Knowledge of the 'what-for' variety is precisely the sort of knowledge that would be lacked by a creature who knew what all the inner workings of a human being were, but who did not know what a human being was. What-for knowledge is precisely knowledge of the *telos*. To repeat, I know that the nutritive and perceptive capacities are human capacities in relation to what these capacities are *ultimately* for. Nutritive and perceptive capacities are ultimately for the sake of *eidos* (understood as substantial form). We already know that our *eidos* is, according to Aristotle, *zoon logon echon* (rational animal). It might be worth noting here that what Aristotle means by rational animal is roughly what we mean by creature with a mind.[54]

Generally, an ensouled body exists for the sake of living such that it is only just that – a body – in relation to living. So, we could say that human living is a sub-*telos* of the nutritive, perceptive and rational aspects of the soul. But, merely living is not the *telos* proper of human living. The *telos* of human living is, we already know, *eudaimonia* (the best sort of human life). So it is ultimately in relationship to *eudaimonia* that a human body is just that sort of body. Another, by now familiar, way of expressing this is that *eudaimonia* is the *arche* – the source – of intelligibility of a human being. It is only in relation to the *telos* of human existence that the different aspects that constitute a human being – including the bodily aspects (with their respective capacities) – are rendered fully intelligible. It turns out that *eudaimonia* is best understood as the substantial form of human beings.

## How Teleology Helps Shed Light on the *Eudaimon* Principle

I hope that it is by now clear what role *eudaimonia* has to play in Aristotle's (revised) teleological account of human nature. *Eudaimonia*, we have seen, is best understood as the substantial form of human beings. Indeed, we have seen that life stands in a for-the-sake-of relationship to *eudaimonia*. But, one must not be led into thinking that *eudaimonia* somehow stands beyond life. On the contrary, it is just a kind of living or, more specifically, it is the living that embodies personhood as such; it is the *entelecheia* – the complete reality – of the lives of person. This activity – *eudaimonia* – is the highest modality of actuality of persons. Moreover, it is constituted by the pattern of activities that flow from virtue – from the powers of the soul or, more specifically, from the powers of the aspect of the soul that has a *logos* (rational principle) – when it is at its best.

These ideal activities that flow from virtue constitute our ideally rational life. Indeed, we have seen that *eudaimonia* is an ideal of rationality. However, we have not, as yet, seen in any detail to what extent the *eudaimon* ideal is an ideal of rationality. This is something that I hope will become evident when dealing with the method of critical introspection, which is meant to reveal the intimate relationship that exists between the ethical and the rational organization of life.[55] But we already have some idea of how rationality and the ethical are related according to Aristotle. He thinks that the ethical domain just is the domain that pertains to the virtues (most properly understood) and to the activities that flow from virtue – the activities that flow from the part of the soul that has a *logos*, and which constitute the best sort of human life. This is the sort of account of the ethical that I have chosen to adopt even though it is perhaps much wider than the contemporary conceptions of this domain. And there is a very good reason for wanting to adopt this more general account. The sense of 'ethical' with which Aristotle is mainly concerned is the sense that pertains not so much to this or that ethical action, but to the ethical life as such. In giving priority to the ethical life over specific ethical actions, Aristotle is not ignoring the fundamental relationship that exists between particular ethical actions and the ethical life in general. On the contrary, he thinks that particular ethical actions can only appropriately be comprehended within the framework of human life as such because, in this manner, we can grasp the for-the-sake-of relationship that renders ethical action intelligible. Ethical actions are for the sake of *eudaimonia*. Or, more precisely, ethical actions are just that because they flow from the rational aspect of the soul and they are for the sake of *eudaimonia*.

We already know why Aristotle holds that *eudaimonia* is the *arche* of intelligibility of human life – it is what ultimately renders human life intelligible. Indeed, this relationship between intelligibility and *eudaimonia* shows to what extent the *eudaimon* ideal is a rational one. What has been brought to the foreground here is that the *eudaimon* life just is the life of a person that is maximally intelligible. It is perhaps for this reason that one could be tempted to claim, and quite rightly so, that the fundamental virtue is intelligibility. But one must not forget that the notion of intelligibility at issue here is not primarily an epistemological one. Rather, it is, above all, an ontological notion that pertains to the gathering of beings around the *arche* of intelligibility – around the *eudaimon* peak of development. That intelligibility is directly related to the ethical structure is further evidence for the view that ethics and rationality are inseparable.

The *eudaimon* ideal is one of unity – an ideal in which the different aspects that constitute our rational/ethical existence congregate and draw their significance from this congregation. Indeed, it is for this reason that understanding the ethical involves grasping the unity that constitutes our rational existence. One cannot properly grasp the goodness of a particular action, and the powers from which this action flows, without also having an idea of how the different aspects that constitute our rational existence ideally hang together to constitute our *telos*. And having a grasp of this is just to have a grasp of the 'what it is' of human beings. Indeed, the ethical is what we are – our *eidos*. Our *eidos* is *eudaimonia* – the best sort of life.

The end of the developmental process of human beings is to become who we are by nature, given that our *physis* just is this end, *physis* being primarily substantial form (*eidos*). The developmental movement that constitutes the way toward the *telos*, our coming-to-be, is the way towards the embodiment of personhood – the ethical as such.

## Appendix: Humans and Persons

Until now, I have made little of the distinction between human beings and persons, partly because it is a distinction that Aristotle himself did not entertain, and partly because I think that this issue can only properly be addressed within an Aristotelian framework after we have developed a clear idea of Aristotle's hierarchical structure of beings. Aristotle thinks we are rational animals, and because of this, he does not consider rationality in isolation from animality. But, curiously, Aristotle's claim that we are rational animals is not entirely compatible with the defence he provides. Aristotle thinks that we are essentially rational but, in providing a defence for this view, he also (inadvertently) shows that we are only *contingently* animals. It seems to me that he only inadvertently argued for the contingency of our character as animals because he was working within the perhaps at times too rigid framework of his categorial structure of being where humans *qua* rational entities fall under the genus 'animal' and, relatedly, also because he was understandably not bewitched (as we now are) by counterfactual possibilities such as the possibility of artificial rational life. I will now proceed to show why I think Aristotle is actually inadvertently providing a defence for the view that we are by nature rational entities (persons) instead of rational animals (human beings). Person is a more inclusive category than human being.

The possibility of artificial life creates problems for Aristotle's account of *physis* in that it renders it impossible to hold that the essence of the natural is its internal principle of change. But, although this is a problem for Aristotle, it is not a real problem for us given that it makes no real difference to us whether personhood is a natural concept. What is presently of concern to us is that persons have an internal principle of change and how this internal principle is related to our *telos*.

Aristotle has provided us with sufficient resources to allow us to determine that, in principle, a person *qua* rational entity could be non-human. In a way that is analogous to the manner in which Aristotle argues that a sphere *qua* sphere exits in *some* matter (not any matter but, equally, not just in one sort of matter) or that an axe exists quite independently of its *specific* materiality, we can also argue that a person is just that if he or she is embodied in *some* matter. Indeed, the relationship Aristotle established between things such as spheres, axes and persons is referred to by Hartman as a relationship of *accidental identity*.[56] What sort of relationship is this? Spheres and axes must be instantiated in some matter, and certainly not just any matter will do, but what is important here is that matter does not *define* the spheres and axes as such: the beings of spheres and axes do not depend on their own specific materiality. Indeed, we have seen, when studying the hierarchical structure of beings, that matter is defined relative to form and not the other way around. So, it is *necessarily* the case that spheres and axes must be embodied in some matter but, on the other hand, it is only *accidentally* the case that they are embodied in the way that they happen to be embodied. In other words, the *identities* of these sorts of objects are not dependent on the specific matter they happen to be made of, although, of course, they are dependent on some matter. Analogously, human bodies are the sorts of bodies persons happen to have but, although persons must have some sort of body, the bodies do not *necessarily* have to be the sort of bodies humans actually have (although the bodies of non-human persons would probably have to be similar to the bodies of humans in some relevant respects). Of course, a person must *necessarily* have some body in order to be a person, but it is only *accidentally* the case that it is a human body. Now, it is certainly true that not any matter will do, and maybe in this universe (as opposed to other possible universes) only flesh organized in the way human flesh is organized can meet the desired requirements, but this, in principle, need not be the case. And it need not, in principle, be the case because the category of person is a functional category.

It is not the materiality of a person that defines a person as such – that determines the identity of persons *qua* persons – but, instead, it is the activities of the matter and, more specifically, the rational activities. We know already that, for Aristotle, a description of the substantial form of a human being does not include any direct allusions to a human body (even though he does claim that our substantial form is rational animal and not just rational entity or something of this sort). Aristotle certainly does think that we are embodied creatures and that we have certain basic biological functions such as reproduction, and nutrition, but these aspects of ourselves are not part of our rational nature – they are not what make us persons. On the contrary, the specific biological functions of our species are constituted as human biological functions in relation to our rational nature.

The category I will be focusing on from now on is not the category of human being, but the wider and more ethically relevant category of person.

## Notes

1  It might be worth mentioning at this point that Aristotelian teleology has fallen into disrepute since the Renaissance. For a good review of the history of teleology's demise, and for a good defence of teleology against the traditional arguments against it, see Andrew Woodfield's *Teleology*, Cambridge: Cambridge University Press, 1976, pp. 7–18. I will bypass these traditional arguments simply because they would lead us off course. Moreover, the traditional arguments will be rebutted implicitly in the ensuing discussion.

2  A proper understanding of *psyche*, we shall see, is central for understanding the *eudaimon* principle.

3  For an explicit account of Aristotle's understanding of *physis* see *Politica* (*P*), ed. D Ross, Oxford: Clarendon Press, 1966, 1252b 32–5. All subsequent quotations will be from this translation.

4  The substantial form of something is that which determines that a given substance – a given entity as opposed to a given aspect – is just that.

5    *Physica (Ph)*, ed. D. Ross, Oxford: Clarendon Press, 1970, 193a 28–193b 2, 194a 12 and
     194b 8–9.
6    *Ph* II.I.
7    *Metaphysica (M)*, ed. G. Goold, Cambridge, Massachusetts: Harvard University Press,
     1989, 983a 24–83b 27 and *Ph* 198a 24–7.
8    *Ph* 193b 13–8 and 194a 27–30.
9    A house, of course, is not something that has an internal principle of change, and hence,
     as Aristotle argues, the emergence of a house cannot count as an instance of natural
     development. In other words, the agency – not in the specific sense of subject, but in the
     general sense of active principle – is not an aspect of an emerging house. Instead, the
     active principle is the builder (the active principle, in this case, happens to be an agent).
     The active principle at issue here is what Aristotle refers to as the primary moving cause
     (the *arche* [source] of *kinesis* [movement]).
         It might be worth noting here, by way of preamble, that the notion of moving cause
     is central for understanding Aristotle's conception of *psyche* (soul), which, in turn, will
     play a fundamental role in understanding the fundamental structure of the lives of
     persons. I will argue, contrary to the canonical interpretation, that rather than being the
     *eidos* of living things, *psyche* is the moving cause of living things. This will further allow
     me to establish the isomorphism that exists between the teleological structure of the real
     discussed in the *Metaphysica* (particularly), and what could be characterized as the
     ethical structure of the lives of persons discussed in the *Ethics*. Notwithstanding its
     elegance, determining the isomorphism between these two structures does not have the
     mere purpose of establishing an elegant correlation. Instead, the fundamental purpose
     here is to use the material from the *Metaphysica* (primarily) to highlight some central
     aspects of the *Ethics*. In highlighting these aspects, I suggest, we will be in a better
     position to see not just that happiness is the *telos* of life, but also in what way our *telos*
     gives life its very meaning.
10   *M* 1050a 10.
11   *Ph* 193b 19–22.
12   In *Ph* 191b 18–29 Aristotle argues that *genesis* (coming-to-be) can be explained both in
     terms of being and non-being (form and the privation of form), and in terms of actuality
     and potentiality. For the most part, Aristotle uses the potentiality/actuality pair rather than
     describing *genesis* as the movement from non-being to being, and this perhaps explains
     why commentators, with the notable exception of St Thomas Aquinas (see, for example,
     'The Principles of Nature', *Selected Writings of St. Thomas Aquinas*, trans. R. Goodwin,
     Indianapolis: Bobs-Merrill Educational Publishing, 1984, pp. 7–14), do not generally
     discuss the concept of privation in relation to Aristotle's account of coming-to-be.
13   *M* 1050a 9–12. A fragment of this passage has already been quoted above.
14   Let us assume, for the sake of argument, that the capacity for knowledge is a species
     potentiality.
15   *De Anima (DA)*, ed. D Ross, Oxford: Clarendon Press, 1968, 412a 22–3.
16   Vision is what is actualized when the process leading to the development of an eye is
     complete.
17   *M* 1050a 21–3. See also *M* 1047a 30–33.
18   We shall soon see that vision is also the primary substance (*ousia*) and the essence (*to ti
     en einai*) of an eye. Aristotle also explicitly claims that vision is, in a sense, the soul
     (*psyche*) of an eye (*DA* 412b 18–22 [quoted below]). I think he contradicts himself here
     given that, according to his most explicit formulation, the soul is constituted by
     capacities (*DA* 412a 17–28) from which activities flow, rather than by activities as such.
     These matters will be discussed shortly.
19   It is important to note that, in the case of natural development, the moving cause and *hyle*
     are inseparable. In the section on *psyche* I will argue that the moving cause is the soul
     (*psyche*) of an organism, and the body of an organism is *hyle*. But the soul, according to
     Aristotle, is not something separable from the body but, rather, an aspect of a body.

Understanding the relationship between the moving cause and the *hyle* of an organism will help make sense of the claim that natural entities have an immanent principle of change. The clay that constitutes a body, so to speak, has the power to change itself because the moving cause is an aspect of it. The moving cause is the power. It is for reasons of this sort that I shall argue, against canonical interpretations, that the soul is not the substantial form of an organism. Rather, the soul is the first actuality of a living entity. The first actuality is the moving cause – the *arche* of *kinesis*.

20   The other two principles are *eidos* and *telos*. For an explicit formulation of the four types of causes see *Ph* 194b 23–5a 2.

21   The conception at issue need not be explicit, nor must it be completely determinate. The important point, however, is that forms that play an active role in the making of the vase are present in an artisan's mind throughout the process of making a vase, and that, at least at some point, a given artisan will possess the form of a vase in his or her mind. To be sure an artisan might, after all, start working with one idea of what he or she wants to make and later change his or her mind in the process of making what will end up being a vase. Moreover, if an artisan had no idea of what he or she was doing at any moment, then it is fair to say that his or her activities would be wholly meaningless because they would be lacking in purpose. What gives purpose is a certain *telos*. This goal of a process of development is precisely what form is.

22   Aristotle argues along these lines when discussing the distinction between moving causes of the primary sort – moving causes that are for the sake of something or *per se* causes – and incidental moving causes in *Ph* II 6. He characterizes the incidental (or what he also refers to as the 'spontaneous') coming-to-be of something as involving a moving cause that is not for the sake of whatever comes to be. Aristotle provides the following examples of incidental coming-to-be:

> We say, for example, that the horse came 'spontaneously', because, though this coming saved him, he did not come for the sake of safety. Again, the tripod fell 'of itself', because, though when it fell it stood on its feet so as to serve for a seat, it did not fall for the sake of that. (*Ph* 197b 15–18)

The cases presented here are different in one important respect to those I have been discussing, in that Aristotle is not so much interested in selecting a primary moving cause of a given thing or event from the secondary ones but, rather, in separating the primary sort of moving cause involved in natural and artificial coming-to-be from incidental coming-to-be. But what is common to the sorts of cases that interest me and those that interest Aristotle is the fundamental distinction that exists between moving causes that are *per se* or for-the-sake-of and those that are incidental. This distinction applies to both Aristotle's and to my concerns.

23   *Ph* 193a 12–17.

24   *Ph* 192b 12–18.

25   *Ph* 194b 17–20.

26   In the last section of this chapter I will argue against the view that our essence is rational animal. Instead, I shall argue that Aristotle himself provides us with good reasons for holding that our essence is rational entity. I think this is an important distinction given that there are compelling reasons – reasons Aristotle himself inadvertently provides – for establishing a distinction between person – rational entity – and human being – rational animal. It is important to hold a distinction of this sort because it allows us to entertain the very real possibility of there being artificial intelligent life or, more generally, the possibility of there being entities who are rational, but who nevertheless do not belong to our biological kind.

27   In making this claim I am following Jeff Malpas's very illuminating reading of Aristotle's categorial structure of being. See his '*Kategoriai* and the Unity of Being', *Journal of Speculative Philosophy*, **4**, 1990, pp. 13–36.

28  This mode of intelligibility is more fundamental than the other one discussed because it is a condition for the possibility of the first mode of intelligibility.

29  This fact seems to conflict with Aristotle's explicit characterization of human beings as rational animals (*zoon logon echon*). However, the conflict here is merely apparent, as we shall see below.

30  *M* 1028a 10–20.

31  In Aristotle's words, '[t]he term "being" has several senses ... It denotes first the "what", i.e. the individuality [substance]; and then the quality or quantity or any other such category' (*M* 1028a 10–14).

32  *M* 1028a 31–3.

33  *M* 1028a 37–b3.

34  *Kategoriai V* , trans. J. Ackrill, Oxford: Clarendon Aristotle Series, 1963.

35  Aristotle does not hold that all that is required for identifying Socrates as opposed to other persons is Socrates' essence. This is clearly not the case given that Socrates' essence is, according to Aristotle, identical with the essence of every other human being.

36  Self-sufficiency, in this context, should not be confused with another sense of the same term – the sense in which one needs nothing else to exist. The notion of self-sufficiency at issue here is fundamentally an ontological notion. And, more specifically, self-sufficiency in this context is a notion that pertains to the existence of something as a being *qua* entity, as opposed to a being that can be said to have a reality only in relation to a higher modality of being.

37  *EN* 1097b 30–1098a 18.

38  In some extreme circumstances it might seem reasonable to give up one's life. And indeed, if living were an end in itself, then the fact of our finiteness would be a tragedy of the greatest proportion. Although many deaths are certainly tragic, it is not death in and of itself that is tragic but the tragic circumstances surrounding particular deaths.

39  Particularly when discussing the method of critical introspection below. See Chapter 5, primarily the first sections.

40  *DA* 412a 27–8.

41  *DA* 412a 23–4.

42  And, indeed, the knowledge a person has when sleeping is knowledge in actuality. It is not merely that knowledge that is not being exercised is potentially knowledge because, if this were so, there would be no grounds for making the obvious distinction between knowledge that is not being exercised and merely having the potential for knowledge but not yet having it. I *actually* know that 1+1=2 when I am asleep. However, and this is a crucial point, the sort of knowledge I am presently discussing – the sort that contrasts with contemplation – is the potentiality for contemplation. Relative to a child who has the potentiality for knowledge, having knowledge is an actuality, but relative to the act of contemplation itself, knowledge is a potentiality. This means that first actuality – knowledge that is not being exercised in this case – is not the highest, non-relative, modality of actuality. Contemplation is, on the other hand, a modality of actuality in an absolute sense.

43  *DA* 412a 28–9.

44  *DA* 412a 22–7.

45  See, for example, *Ethica Eudemia* (*EE*), ed. D. Ross, Oxford: Clarendon Press, 1966, 1218b 37–1219a 12, where Aristotle explicitly argues that the activity or work is better than the state or capacity.

46  This conclusion conflicts with Aristotle's account of the mind (*nous*) given that the mind, or an aspect of the mind (*nous poietikos*), is pure actuality – pure form – rather than form only in a relative sense. Generally, Aristotle's account of the mind is incompatible with his overall account that form and matter are two aspects of one and the same thing, so I think it is Aristotle's account of *nous* that should be revised for the sake of overall consistency and not my present rendition of the relationship between body and soul. This is not the place to discuss Aristotle's conception of *nous*, though. For a brief but

informative critical discussion of this notion see Edwin Hartman's, *Substance, Body, and Soul: Aristotelian Investigations*, Princeton, NJ: Princeton University Press, 1977, pp. 264–69.

47  *EE* 1219a 8–12.

48  *EE* 1219a 23–9.

49  The excellence of the soul is complete virtue, so the work of the excellence of the soul is activity in conformity with virtue, which just is the definition of *eudaimonia*.

50  *DA* 412a 10–13.

51  *EN* 1098a 5–6.

52  *EE* 1219a 31–5.

53  The intimate relationship that exists between rationality and virtue is something that is central to Aristotle's psychology. Indeed, it is safe to say that, for Aristotle, rationality and virtue are inseparable. This becomes especially clear when one realizes that, for Aristotle, *logos* (standardly translated 'rational principle') means both rationality and complete virtue. In *EN* 1098a 2–18 Aristotle implicitly identifies *logos* (or more precisely, the right or highest manifestation of logos – *orthos logos*) with complete or perfect virtue (*arete teleia*). He claims that the 'function of man' is to act 'in conformity with rational principle [*logos*]', and he concludes that the function of 'man' is to act 'in conformity with excellence or virtue, or if there be several human excellences or virtues, in conformity with the best and most perfect among them'. The best and most perfect among the virtues is *arete teleia* precisely because having complete virtue (as opposed to this or that virtue) is what is required for living the best sort of life.

54  One of the fundamental difference between Aristotle's conception and ours is, of course, that we typically do not consider that a creature with a mind is necessarily an animal of our biological species.

Another of the most important differences between Aristotle's conception of mind and ours is that sometimes he privileges abstract thought over and above all other mental occurrences. But it might also be worth stressing that Aristotle only privileges abstract thought – contemplation of the forms – in some parts of his work. In *DA*, for instance, he privileges abstract thought, but in *EN*, for the most part he privileges *phronesis* – practical wisdom.

55  Chapter 5.

56  Hartman, *Substance, Body, and Soul, op.cit.*, n. 46.

# Chapter 4

# *Logos*

## Setting Out the Issues

In the preceding chapter I drew out the basic structural feature of the lives of persons. We saw that the *arche* that renders human life intelligible is *eudaimonia*. *Eudaimonia* is, in other words, the source of intelligibility in our lives – it is what ultimately bestows purpose and meaning on life. Indeed, it is precisely because *eudaimonia* is this fundamental *arche* that with an understanding of it – a practical understanding primarily – we should be able to decide what in our lives is relevant and what not; we should be able to understand our lives and organize the different components of our lives, including the emotional aspect. In short, a relatively sophisticated understanding of *eudaimonia* should determine a direction for our lives understood as wholes (the whole is determined as such in relationship to the common *telos*). This, at any rate, is what follows from an Aristotelian account of the structure of our lives such as the one presently being developed.

We already know that Aristotle holds that a life that is ideally organized is lived out in accordance with *logos*, understood both as rational principle and as complete virtue. A virtue just is a state or quality of character that allows a subject to be disposed to act in accordance with the *eudaimon* ideal. And, complete virtue is the totality (a totality which is indeterminate as we shall see) of qualities of character that determine a good character – that is, a character that is constitutive of the *eudaimon* ideal. Additionally, as we know, the *eudaimon* ideal is an ideal of rationality – an ideal of purposive unity between the different aspects that compose our existence as persons. My present task will be to show to what extent the two senses of *logos* specified above are related to one another. Indeed, it is not surprising that an intimate relationship should exist if one considers that, as discussed above, *eudaimonia* is the highest modality of actuality of our rational existence.

If in fact our essence – our substantial form – is that of rational creatures, and indeed if our lives are ideally guided by a system of virtues, then the relationship between rationality and virtue must be a very intimate one. The virtues, after all, are character dispositions required for living in accordance with the good of persons, and the good in question is a rational good. What this means in effect is that the system of virtues – complete virtue – must mirror our ideally rational lives, and hence it must be a rational system itself, since, as stated above, they are the dispositions for good living. One could, of course, object to the starting point of the present discussion on the grounds that our lives are not, in essence, rational. One could be particularly suspicious of the present understanding of our lives in light of the fact that, as we have seen, our substantial form can also be characterized as *eudaimonia*.

One might also take issue with the present discussion as it stands on the grounds that the virtues cannot play such a central role in our rational lives, since, arguably, we are for the most part rational (in some sense of 'rational') but not for the most part virtuous. Indeed it seems that most of us are rational creatures even though most of us are not particularly virtuous but, equally, it also seems that most of us are only rational in an imperfect sense. Moreover, it is also true that when claiming that most of us are not virtuous, we fail to consider our typical day-to-day dealings with one another, which are to a large extent informed by varying degrees of trust, friendship, care, and so on. (something that will become especially clear once we deal in some detail with the issue of friendship and the ethic implicit in the very possibility of its existence). Indeed, it seems clear that if we did not act in accordance with virtue, even if imperfectly, the social fabric would not merely be imperfect as it currently is, but would collapse altogether. So, to state that most of us are not virtuous is untrue. Most of us, it appears, are virtuous to the same extent that we are rational – namely, imperfectly. I would like to suggest here – and this suggestion will be further discussed shortly and also in the next chapter – that a virtuous life is achieved by perfecting the pattern of activities and dispositions that constitutes us as rational creatures – the pattern that constitutes us a meaning-bearing creatures. Showing this, moreover, will tie in very neatly with what has already been discussed with regard to the relationship between the intelligibility of a life and happiness.

## Rationality

Aristotle claims that 'we state the function of man to be a certain kind of life, and this to be an activity or action of the soul implying a rational principle'.[1] What he is implying here is that *eudaimonia* is a life implying a 'rational principle'. We know that Aristotle is, in fact, discussing *eudaimonia* here because we have already seen that *eudaimonia* is the excellent functioning – the *energeia* – of the lives of persons (it is the ideal mode of operation of the lives of persons). But what is this rational principle? 'Rational principle', we know already, is a common translation of the Greek '*logos*'. Unless it is properly qualified, however, this translation could prove to be rather misleading not only or even fundamentally because it is not clear what 'rationality' means, but also because rationality is most commonly associated with conscious thought. We already know that this limited understanding of rationality cannot be what Aristotle has in mind given that his ideal moral subject is not only, nor even primarily, a conscious thinker. Rather, his ideal moral subject is a doer – an individual with a certain skill, a certain know-how, for living. Indeed, we know already that the sort of skill at issue is the skill that defines a *phronimos* as such. Aristotle characterizes practical wisdom thus: 'Practical wisdom [*phronesis*], then, must be a reasoned and true state or *capacity to act* [my italics] with regard to goods.'[2] We know that the goods at issue here are the goods of persons, and that these goods are defined as such because they are constitutive of *eudaimonia*. So we know that practical wisdom, according to Aristotle, is the capacity to act in ways that are constitutive of *eudaimonia*. We further know that a *eudaimon* life is an activity that implies *logos*.

But what sort of skill is the skill of acting in accordance with, or in ways that imply, *logos*? We already know in outline what the answer to this question is: to act in accordance with *logos* just is to act in accordance with complete virtue – to act in accordance with the qualities of character (a form of *dynamis*) that define a *eudaimon* subject.[3] So, rather than being rational in the sense of conscious rational thought, *logos* just is the pattern of qualities of character from which appropriate actions ideally flow – those qualities that allow a given subject to act in ways that are constitutive of the good of people.

In light of our contemporary prevalent understanding of rationality one might appropriately ask, if this is what *logos* means (in the present context), why then would it standardly be translated 'rational principle'? To answer this question we will have to pause and reflect a little more deeply on the concept of rationality itself. More specifically, we should reflect on what we mean when we refer to a creature as *being* rational (or, indeed, as being irrational). We would have grounds for claiming that a given creature was irrational if we were able to pick out inconsistencies in their behaviour, or inconsistencies between their behaviour and their propositional attitudes, or if we were able to pick out inconsistencies within their individual networks of propositional attitudes. I might, for instance, rightly accuse someone of being irrational because he or she honestly claims to want to do one thing – all things considered – and then proceeds to do quite the opposite (this is a case of *akrasia* – of weakness of the will). To use another, more striking, example, I might also rightly accuse someone of being irrational if, say, he or she was playing soccer as usual, but suddenly started running in circles in the middle of a field uttering incomprehensible nonsense at the top of his or her voice, and for no good reason whatsoever. Generally one is behaving irrationally (or having irrational attitudes) if one's behaviour (or attitudes) somehow deviates from certain basic logical norms. Something can only count as deviant if it diverges from something that is fundamentally not deviant. Radical deviance – to use an expression that mirrors Davidson's famous claim against the possibility of radical incoherence – is not possible. More specifically, it is only possible for someone to count as irrational if we are also entitled to claim that this individual is rational in essence – that is, rational in the sense of possessing a logically coherent system of attitudes and behaviour expressive of these attitudes.

Indeed, the more a given creature seems to behave irrationally, the more difficult attributions of rationality seem to become – the more it appears as if the category of rationality does not properly apply to the creature, even if negatively. Of course, a given individual of the 'species' person could behave in ways that do not warrant us referring to him or her as being rational (or irrational for that matter), but who is nevertheless a person – a rational creature. I am thinking here of those individuals who are severely brain damaged. Such an individual is a rational one in relationship to the rational *telos* that defines us all, and we diagnose that his or her condition is lamentable by comparing the common *telos*.

Let us attempt to further elucidate rational coherence. I have no doubt that there are many ways of speaking about coherence that do not properly qualify as rational; consider, for example, the coherent whole constituted by a well-accomplished work of art or the coherence of a musical piece. But what is unique about the coherent system we describe as being rational? In 'Rational Animals',[4] Davidson argues that to be rational just is to have propositional attitudes. This claim is closely related to his holism, which will be discussed in more detail in Chapter 6. But, first, let me say a few words about Davidson's views in order to further elucidate the sense of rationality that is presently relevant. Davidson thinks that to be rational just is to have propositional attitudes (and behaviour expressive of these attitudes) because individual attitudes (and behaviour) are defined by the position they occupy in what could be characterized as a *logical* network of such attitudes (and behaviour). Indeed Davidson's conception of coherence is at least primarily that of logical coherence, and this view may quite legitimately be seen as problematic, since it seems clear that other understandings of coherence must also be brought to bear in the task of attempting to understand the psychological domain. That said, let me attempt to present Davidson's views in the most favourable possible light – a light they no doubt deserve. In Davidson's words:

> Since the identity of a thought cannot be divorced from its place in the logical network of other thoughts, it cannot be relocated in the network without becoming a different thought. Radical incoherence in belief is therefore impossible. To have a single propositional attitude is to have a largely correct logic, in the sense of having a pattern of beliefs that logically cohere. This is one reason why to have propositional attitudes is to be a rational creature. The point extends to intentional action. Intentional action is action that can be explained in terms of beliefs and desires whose propositional contents rationalize the action. Similarly, an emotion like being pleased that one has stopped smoking must be an emotion that is rational in the light of beliefs and values one has.[5]

That the primary variety of coherence, which constitutes a rational life, is logical coherence might *prima facie* seem unlikely simply because the category of logical coherence applies only to beliefs (and statements or propositions) and, clearly the psychological domain is not constituted solely by beliefs. But what must be considered is that propositional attitudes and rational behaviour generally are judged rational in light of the system of beliefs they are expressive of (or, in the case of beliefs, the system of beliefs they constitute). To be sure, logical contradiction might not be directly involved, say, in the conflict between someone's promiscuous sexual desires and his or her desire to have a stable sexual relationship. Analogously, the conflict between someone's desire to help those in need and that person's profoundly selfish pursuits need not be a logical one, although it could be. But what is important here is that attitudes of the sort just described are not irrational simply because they are in conflict. Conflict is a more general category than irrationality. The above attitudes would be irrational if a description of them reveals contradictions.

Where there are conflicts there may be contradictions, but not all conflicts involve contradictions. I might have many mixed conflicting feelings because I have harmed that criminal without there necessarily being any contradictions involved. I might feel torn between the hell I have thrown those I love into as a consequence of my going to jail for my act, and what I perceive is the legitimate pursuit of justice. Conflicts of this sort might not be considered as ones that disrupt coherence, but I think they do insofar as they upset the balance in my life. This said, I do not think actions such as these should necessarily be categorized as incoherent because, in some instances, the converse of coherence may not be incoherence, and in turn this points to important differences in the uses of 'coherence'. The converse of logical coherence is certainly incoherence, but conflicts of the non-logical variety do not qualify as incoherent and hence do not qualify as irrational. A pictorial composition may be categorized as harmonious and coherent insofar as it is harmonious, but if a pictorial composition happened to lack harmony it would not necessarily be appropriate to refer to it as being incoherent.

One such form of coherence that cannot properly be categorized as logical, and which is directly relevant to this investigation is what could be characterized as narrative coherence. Our lives are to a large extent structured narratively,[6] and the sort of coherence which bestows unity upon a narrative is not primarily of the logical sort. This claim is true, but it does not obviously contradict Davidson's conception of rationality, since narrative coherence also ultimately rests on logical coherence. That this is so is evidenced by the straightforward fact that narratives are just that insofar as they are expressive of beliefs, which are constituted as such within a field of logically related beliefs.

I must insist that I am not claiming here that all conflict among beliefs can be reduced to logical conflict – not at all. I may have conflicting beliefs towards a friend because there are certain things in him or her that I like, and others that I dislike and for sound reasons – reasons that, among other things, mirror a conflict in my friend's soul. I might, say, appreciate his or her overall kindness and generosity, but I might dislike his or her attitude towards money. There is no obvious reason why this sort of conflict is always and necessarily best fleshed out in term of contradictory beliefs. Contradiction certainly might be underlying my friend's attitudes insofar as his or her specific monetary pursuits could be logically incompatible with the ideal of generosity that informs his or her attitudes towards his or her friends, but this need not be the case. This said, insofar as my friend is a rational creature, his or her overall pattern of beliefs is a rational one, and it is just that if his or her beliefs, on the whole, logically cohere with one another. My friend's beliefs about him or herself, which include the beliefs that constitute his or her narrative understanding of him or herself, must, on the whole, logically cohere with one another, since this sort of coherence is a necessary condition for having beliefs in the first place, and hence for counting as a creature with a psychological life of the sort that defines persons as such.[7]

One might quite legitimately wonder what this understanding of rationality has to do with virtue. One could attempt to dissolve the problem by attempting to show that Aristotle's use of '*logos*' is equivocal, but I do not think that it is. Light will dawn on our current concerns when we realize to what extent the ethical is constitutive of our rational lives. It will become apparent as the discussion proceeds that there is a sense in which one could say that the greatest of all virtues is rationality simply because the rational organisation of our lives is the source of meaning of the ethical. Indeed, this claim seems to follow quite naturally from the account of rationality just provided. If Davidson's account of rationality is adequate, then it follows that ethical concepts are defined within the logical space that constitutes our rational lives.

Let me just conclude this brief discussion on rationality by recapitulating. There are at least as many senses of coherence as those canvassed above, and all play a role in defining our lives. But there is one sense that plays a primary role in defining us as rational creatures – the logical sense.

## Virtue

I will now proceed to shed more light on the issue of virtue, and in doing so we will be in a better position to integrate the two senses of *logos* that are presently of interest to us. The virtues, we shall see, play a fundamental epistemic role in our lives in the sense that they are what constitute our embodied understanding – our embodied knowledge – of the human situation, and as such they motivate us to respond to the concrete situations we are thrown into in accordance with a proper understanding of who we are. In other words, a virtue is a disposition of the sort that reflects an understanding of the world; for this reason, a virtue can be nothing more than a propositional attitude and, as such, it forms an integral part of the rational fabric that defines our lives (if Davidson's account of rationality is an appropriate one).

We know already that, for Aristotle, the maximum expression of the good for persons arises when an individual lives in accordance with the *eudaimon* ideal. Further, Aristotle understands this ideal as involving the active capacity to act in conformity with *complete virtue* – not just with this or that virtue, but with virtue in its most complete form. Lesser expressions of the good, on the other hand, are activities that are expressive of this or that virtue, such that an individual who only informed his or her life with a limited understanding of the virtues would be unable to live as a *eudaimon* individual.

One might certainly be able to speak of temperance, courage and so forth independently of speaking about *eudaimonia*. But, crucially, temperance, courage and the like are only virtues insofar as they have a role to play in the constitution of a *eudaimon* life. It is because the virtues are defined as such by the role they play within the organized assembly (of dispositions, beliefs, desires, emotions, behaviour, and so on), which constitutes a *eudaimon* life, that the virtues can most properly be understood only within the context of this ideal rational functional totality. Given this account of the virtues, it follows that one cannot properly understand the virtues either in isolation from one another or in isolation from a relatively complete theory of the good life, understood as the highest manifestation of the rational life. To repeat, individual virtues are understood as such within the context of an understanding of what it is to live a good life, understood as an organized assembly and, more specifically, in relation to complete virtue – that is, in relation to what could be characterized as a system of virtues within which individual virtues are embedded. Indeed, it is within this system that the concept itself of virtue is defined. This follows from holism.

If particular virtues are qualities an individual must possess in order to achieve *eudaimonia*, and the virtues are defined in relation to the role they play in constituting a *eudaimon* life, then complete virtue can only be the most complete manifestation of virtue, such that if an individual were virtuous in this way, he or she would possess all that is required of virtue in order to live in accordance with the *telos* of persons. So, we know that individual virtues can only be fully understood as forming part of a system of virtues that are constitutive of *eudaimonia*, and from this it follows that one can only properly understand individual virtues within the framework of complete virtue and the role complete virtue plays within the system that constitutes a *eudaimon* life. Yet, conversely, one cannot understand the issue of complete virtue without understanding how complete virtue is constituted, and it is constituted by the individual virtues.

This last claim puts us in a rather awkward position since it appears that there is no hope of understanding either what an individual virtue is or, indeed, what acting in accordance with complete virtue amounts to.

However, we have forgotten, or simply never considered, a third option – the option implicit in Aristotle's account of the virtues. I might add that the account at issue is a holistic one, and this suggests that an understanding of complete virtue might be closely related to the above characterization of rationality. One can only properly understand individual virtues as already embedded within the fabric of the type of lives we humans live, and we can only understand this totality, within which activity in conformity with complete virtue is embedded, by considering the individual aspects that constitute the lives of humans and the manner in which these individual aspects are articulated within a life. What I am claiming here will be more easily understood if we consider our previous analogy between the practice of painting and the practice of living. A painting's different aspects constitute it, but its different aspects only have aesthetic significance within the coherent set of aspects that constitutes a given painting, not in isolation from one another. It follows, then, that the fabric of virtues must be present prior to analysis. This claim should not surprise us given that one must know the subject matter of one's engagements prior to engaging with them.

But, more specifically, what is a virtue? From the discussion in Chapter 2 regarding the issue of rule-following, we know that virtues cannot properly be understood primarily as rules in the head. So, what is involved in the issue of acting in conformity with virtue if having a virtue cannot be understood primarily as possessing a given rule (or set of rules)? The answer to this question can also be found in the above discussion on the analogy between the practice of living and the practice of painting. In acting in conformity with virtue, one acts in ways that are expressive of a certain know-how. Having knowledge in this practical sense involves having developed a certain skill – a certain art. This skill, furthermore, is the skill of having a good character – a determinate fabric of qualities from which a good life *qua* activity flows. These qualities, as already briefly discussed, and as I will discuss in more detail towards the end of this investigation, are those that determine our emotional responsiveness – our involved responsiveness – towards the situations we encounter throughout the course of our lives. The emotional responsiveness at issue, I might add, is what allows us to perceive the ethical in all its seriousness and can be characterized as a form of perception or sensitivity (and hence as a form of knowing).[8]

One does not develop a good character simply by internalizing certain rules. This procedure would be far too mechanical and disengaged for Aristotle. The ideal Aristotelian moral subject is the sort of individual who has a sufficient degree of flexibility to adapt and respond to ever-new ethical circumstances in ways that reflect his or her affective perception – affective understanding – of the specific circumstances he or she is thrown into. It is these affective responses that allow a given moral subject to become deeply and caringly engaged in the practice of good living, and this caring engagement, it must be stressed, comes as a consequence of a kind of understanding. Further, if the emotions inform in this manner, then they must form part of our rational fabric. Emotions, or at any rate the emotions that permit us to be deeply and caringly involved with the practice of living, must be rational.

One way of coming to a more complete understanding of what Aristotle means by virtue would be to find out what counts as sufficient evidence for the possession of a virtue. It is very tempting to hold that one is able to determine that a particular action is carried out in accordance with virtue merely by observing specific activities of a given subject. This is something Aristotle does not hold, and for good reasons. Observations of virtuous actions might allow us to determine that the actions observed are of the sort a virtuous individual would typically perform in comparable circumstances, but this is not the same as saying that the actions in question are performed in accordance with virtue. According to Aristotle, one could act in ways in which a virtuous subject would act without actually acting in ways that flow from virtue. That is, although acting virtuously is a necessary criterion for acting in accordance with virtue, it is not a sufficient one. Indeed, Aristotle refers to those subjects who act in ways in which a virtuous subject would act, but whose actions do not flow from virtue, as self-controlled subjects – as subjects who, rather than acting with practical wisdom (*phronesis*) act with self-control (*enkrateia*).[9] A subject of the self-controlled variety is one who, like a *phronimos*, acts because he or she believes a particular course of action is the course one ought to take. But, unlike the *phronimos*, the virtues have not become part of the individual in the sense that he or she has not acquired the appropriate affective responsiveness that flows from a deep, sincere and committed understanding of the ethical.

John McDowell illuminatingly characterizes virtue as a kind of reliable sensitivity – the sort of sensitivity which the self-controlled person lacks (and, I might add, which the incontinent person also lacks, but for different reasons).[10] It is this sensitivity, moreover, that determines that someone acts in accordance with the good, so long as the activity is not impaired by constraining external circumstances.

The problem that now arises with this characterization relates to the fact that a person lacking this sensitivity – namely, a self-controlled subject – acts in ways that do not flow from this form of sensitivity. The problem is compounded if, like McDowell (who follows Plato here), one characterizes this form of sensitivity as a kind of knowledge – a knowledge of how to act.[11] What, one could ask, is a self-controlled person lacking that makes him or her ignorant as a consequence of this insensitivity? The problem is that, to repeat what I have already said in slightly different terms, both self-control and virtue issue in right action (to use McDowell's elegant turn of phrase), so that there are apparently no grounds for distinguishing virtue from self-control with regard to the epistemic role they play in motivating action. I think McDowell's solution, based on Aristotle's, is a good one. He argues along the lines that a person who acts virtuously, but who does not posses virtue, acts with a 'clouded' understanding of the good. So, the problem with the self-controlled subject is that he or she is ignorant – relatively speaking.

Let us consider the following example: a friend *qua* friend is not someone who merely acts as a friend would act – not at all. A friend *qua* friend is also one who has the right sorts of accompanying affects. Indeed, it would be most peculiar to call someone a friend who acted as a friend and yet felt nothing like the sorts of things friends typically feel for each other. This peculiarity is a consequence of the fact that actions and affects are tightly bound together such that the character itself of a given action is parasitical on the affects that precipitate and accompany it. Consequently, one can justifiably claim that the actions of a self-controlled friend are not truly actions that issue from a proper understanding of friendship. The characters of actions that flow from self-control are not the same as the characters of comparable actions that flow from virtue. The issue is analogous to our previous example of a move in a chess game and how such a move is a move in a chess game only within the context of a game of chess. Analogously, my emotional responsiveness is a constitutive element of the 'game' of friendship, such that, if I did not adequately respond, I would not count as properly understand the game, or indeed, I would not understanding the game at all.

Although one might be tempted to think that the tight correlation between affects and actions in the case of friendship is unique to friendship relationships, that it is not the case is evidenced by the fact that the values we assign to the projects we engage in throughout our lives are directly related to our emotive investments in the projects in question (the investments are a mark of their importance to us).[12] Indeed, I might further add, that even the project of a self-controlled subject to act in ways that resemble actions that issue from virtue, is one which involves an investment of the emotive sort. The problem with the self-controlled subject is that the emotive investment is on acting *as if* his or her actions issued from virtue (perhaps with the hope that some day his or her actions do issue from virtue). This investment is misplaced.

## Integrating the Two Senses of *Logos*

By now we have a good idea of why the psychological is fundamentally a rational system, and we know in broad outline what rationality means in the present context. Since the virtues are the fundamental dispositions that are constitutive of the ideal of rational living – the best lives for persons – they too must form a rational system, since they are the capacities from which the best sort of rational life flows. *A virtue, then, is a propositional attitude that is the moving cause of rational living.* We now have a better idea of the sort of roles the virtues play in rational living. The virtues are the capacities that are constitutive of the ability to become fully engaged with the sorts of lives that define rational creatures. Central to these capacities is the capacity to have the right sorts of affects. Indeed, that the virtues do form a rational structure is evidenced by the methodology used for picking out the structure of personhood – *the method of critical introspection*, which will be explored in detail in the next chapter. The method in question is one that reveals the holistic structure of the psychological and, in so doing, also reveals the structure of virtue, since, as I have argued, the virtues just are the dispositions for living the best sorts of lives available to persons – rational lives. But it must be clarified that the best possible lives available to us are not merely rational, they are maximally rational. The methodology I will be exploring in the next chapter is not just for describing how rational lives are actually lived out, but, instead, is a critical method insofar as it helps us construct a picture of the maximally rational life. Indeed, because our lives are structured teleologically, a life can only properly be described in relationship to an ethical ideal. So, let me slightly adjust my claims. The method of critical introspection is precisely the sort of methodology that is required for describing a rational life insofar as it is the method for describing the ideally rational life – the *telos*.

I shall devote the next chapter to establishing the basic procedure for determining the essential features of the being of persons. By applying the method of critical introspection we shall determine how different aspects of our rational existence hang together in constitutive relations, and this will help us see more clearly how the virtues derive their meaning and purpose within the rational fabric that constitutes our ideally rational lives. These constitutive relations, moreover, guarantee that deviations in the concept of personhood amongst different individuals cannot be all that great, thus guaranteeing the existence of a general intersubjective concept of personhood, and the ethic that flows from this concept. Moreover, as we already know that *eudaimonia* is the most refined version of the organization that constitutes our rational/ethical existence, we also know that the method of critical introspection is one that reveals the structure of happiness.

Because the method of critical introspection is the method for revealing the maximally consistent life, it is the method for revealing the maximally intelligible life – the maximally meaningful life. The dispositions for living the maximally meaningful lives are the virtues and, because they play such a role, they form an integral part of the rational pattern of our lives.

## Notes

1    *EN* 1098a 13–15.
2    *EN* 1140b 20–21.
3    I do not want to suggest here that a *eudaimon* individual just is a *phronimos*. Rather, a
     *eudaimon* individual must be a *phronimos*, but a *phronimos* need not be a *eudaimon*
     individual. A *phronimos* is the sort of individual who has the capacity to act, and acts, in
     accordance with complete virtue – with the sum total of states of character that define a

*eudaimon* individual. *Eudaimonia,* on the other hand, is the pattern of activities that *freely* flows from virtue (from the states that define a *phronimos*) and which constitute the best sort of life. The activities of a *phronimos* would not freely flow from virtue if the external conditions were bad enough, such that one was unable to exercise complete virtue in a manner that was unimpaired (or relatively unimpaired). If one's capacity to act in accordance with virtue were impaired to a significant extent then one would not count as a *eudaimon* individual, but one *could* count as a *phronimos*. Given the present characterizations of *phronesis* and *eudaimonia* we can see that the distinction between these two notions is drawn not so much by considering the dispositions of the sorts of individuals who embody these ideals (for, in this respect, *phronesis* and *eudaimonia* are at the very least very similar), but rather, primarily by considering the distinct sorts of minimally required external circumstances surrounding the lives of the sorts of individuals who embody these ideals. Indeed, Aristotle presupposes the distinction between *phronesis* and *eudaimonia* I have attempted to draw here in the following passage, which is presented as a question for rhetorical reasons only:

> Why then should we not say that he is happy who is active in accordance with complete virtue and is sufficiently equipped with external goods, not through some chance period but throughout a complete life? (*EN* 1101a 14–17)

The first condition for *eudaimonia* that Aristotle presents here is the condition which, taken in isolation, makes it seem as if *eudaimonia* and *phronesis* were coextensive concepts. On the other hand, the second condition establishes the relevant distinction. For an excellent discussion on this topic see Martha Nussbaum's, *The Fragility of Goodness: Luck and Ethics in Greek Tragedy and Philosophy*, Cambridge: Cambridge University Press, 1994, pp. 318–42 in which she presents us with a convincing argument regarding the importance of external goods for good living.

4    Donald Davidson, 'Rational Animals', in E. LePore and B. McLaughlin (eds), *Action and Event: Perspectives on the Philosophy of Donald Davidson*, Oxford: Basil Blackwell, 1985, pp. 475–6.

5    Ibid.

6    An explanation and defence of this claim will be provided at the beginning of Chapter 7.

7    Davidson's account of rationality is not one that is free from controversy. I shall take issue with some important contenders – Fodor and LePore particularly – in Chapter 6.

8    See, for example, John McDowell's, 'Virtue and Reason', in N. Sherman (ed.), *Aristotle's Ethics: Critical Essays*, Lanham, Maryland: Rowman & Littlefield Publishers, Inc., 1999, pp. 121–43; in the same book see also Martha Nussbaum, 'The Discernment of Perception: An Aristotelian Conception of Private and Public Rationality', pp. 145–81.

9    Elizabeth Telfer discusses this crucial distinction in her 'The Unity of Moral Virtues', *Proceedings From the Aristotelian Society*, **90** (1), 1989–90, pp. 35–48. It might be worth noting that *enkrateia* is also translated as 'continence'.

10   McDowell, 'Virtue and Reason', *op.cit.*, n. 8, pp. 121–43.

11   McDowell defends the Socratic thesis that virtue is knowledge, and that all non-virtuous acts come as a consequence of ignorance. I might add that if, indeed, virtue is knowledge, and I see no good reason why this ought not to be the case, then, as I have concluded above, it must also be that the virtues form part of the rational fabric that ideally constitutes us. In 'Virtue and Reason', *op.cit.*, n. 8, McDowell convincingly defends the view that virtue is knowledge.

12   A qualification is warranted here. It is clear that sometimes we engage in projects we are passionate about only later to realize that such projects were not truly important to us. Think of a passionate love affair that dies away as quickly as it starts leaving one to wonder why such an affair started in the first place. The sort of emotive investment that

is presently relevant is one that is constant, as opposed to tempestuous and short-lived. Indeed, tempestuousness might very well be a feature of constant emotive investments, but it is only a feature of such investments if it is adequately integrated into a given project. An aid-worker could be very angry about a particular incident that stops him or her from carrying out his or her project, and such tempestuousness, in this context, is a mark of a stable emotive commitment.

# Chapter 5

# The Method of Critical Introspection

## The Method of Critical Introspection Unveiled

The system that constitutes the psychological is a holistic one, and one guided by one fundamental organizational ideal – the *eudaimon* ideal. So, the holistic system at issue is also a teleological one. In this chapter I shall describe a commonsensical procedure for revealing the holistic/teleological structure of the psychological. In establishing the methodology that unveils the structure of the psychological we will also establish the procedure for determining the being of persons, since to be a person just is to have a psychological life as understood here – a rational life.

Nussbaum offers us a very enlightening discussion, based on Aristotle, regarding the role the concept of personhood plays in grounding ethics.[1] Starting with Nussbaum's discussion, I shall argue that it is by refining our already existing (largely implicit) conception of what it is to be a person that we will be better placed to come to possess the relevant understanding of how to live a good life.[2] The methodology for refining our already existing conception of what it is to be a person is what I refer to as the *method of critical introspection*.

Indeed, it is because the starting point is already a system of beliefs – beliefs about who we are – that the critical procedure in question can be characterized as hermeneutical.[3] This procedure might be seen by some to be highly problematic, since it does not seek to find external grounds – grounds that exist quite independently of our systems of interpretation – for determining personhood. This is, of course, the sort of criticism a Cartesian epistemologist would frame, since a Cartesian believes that knowledge must be founded on a source that is indubitable, and such a source cannot be found within the system of beliefs one currently has. The source, holds the Cartesian epistemologist, must be external – objective, so to speak. This sort of understanding of objectivity is rather misguided for the reasons already provided when discussing holism. There is no hope of finding independent external grounds of the sort in demand in Cartesian circles. To use a Quinean metaphor, beliefs face the tribunal of experience as a corporate body and, because of this, we cannot grasp reality independently of a system of interpretation. This claim might leave some with a sour taste in their mouths, since it appears that we are trapped within the realm of interpretation with no hope whatsoever of intimating with untainted pure reality (whatever that might be). Indeed, if one advocates holism then one is left with no reasonable alternative but to confess that all knowledge is bound up with what could be characterized as our conceptual historicity – our specific, historically sensitive, system of interpretation. The world we live in – understood as a place we are familiar with – is a thoroughly human domain. Notions such as objectivity, truth, and so on. are defined within the system of beliefs that gives us a sense of world and of our meandering within it.[4] We are, so to speak, framed within what has been suggestively characterized as a hermeneutic circle by the phenomenological tradition. But this circle should not be seen as a prison – as a place where no intellectual movement is possible. We can certainly move a lot, and this movement is something that the hermeneutic technique fosters. We continually attempt to shed light on systems of meaning by studying them from the inside and working towards making them more consistent (and complete). No one has come to this world with totally new ideas. There is always a starting point which is given, and from which new knowledge is anchored (in fact, our conceptions about the subject matters that preoccupy us are a precondition for our preoccupations about them).[5]

The method of critical introspection, I have said, is precisely the hermeneutical method applied to our understanding of who we are. As such, it is the method applied when studying our common understandings of who we are, and understanding this involves primarily studying the fit between the different beliefs that we already have about who we are. Studying ourselves in this manner, I might add, is critical, as opposed to merely descriptive, insofar as applying this procedure leads us to discover that certain aspects of our conceptions of ourselves are not adequate and need to be revised in light of who we already think we are. Some may view this method for finding out about ourselves as rather obscurantist, since all it has the power to do is to hone our self-conceptions; it can do nothing to completely alter our conceptions. In fact, this is not wholly true given that if, after analysis, one was shown that a given specific conception one happens to have was radically incoherent either because it was internally incoherent, or because it was incoherent in light of our overall conception of the world, then one would discard the conception in question. Notwithstanding these considerations, the problem with discarding some conceptions is that they are so central to our overall understanding of the world that discarding them would amount to obliterating knowledge altogether. Such is the case with the concept of a person, and such is the reason why behaviourism, or indeed eliminative materialism, to use a more contemporary example of a comparable movement, were always destined to fail. They were destined to fail because advocating such views would amount to denying the very conditions for holding such views. To be an eliminitavist about the concept of a person amounts to being an eliminativist about knowledge altogether for knowledge does not exist without a knower, and the specific entity that knows is a person.

I might point out that the method of critical introspection is a very important one not only because it will help us get a grip on the concept of personhood, but also because by getting a grip on this all-important concept, we will be able to improve our manner of living. It is important to stress, however, that I do not think that an adequate intellectual understanding of what it is to be a person will translate directly into action (including our affective responses). Rather, what I do think is that an explicit understanding of what it is to be a person will inform us with regard to how we ought to live our lives. But, and this is a crucial point, simply to have an intellectual understanding will not be sufficient to inform appropriate actions (including affective responses). One must internalize or come to embody this understanding. Of course, insofar as we already are persons, we already embody the concept of personhood, but we typically do so only imperfectly. The sort of concept we ought to embody is the most perfect manifestation of the concept of personhood, and this is the one that is revealed by the method of critical introspection. The revised concept of personhood, one could say, must become part of ourselves for it to have any substantial practical effects on our lives. For this concept to become part of ourselves – for us to embody this concept – we must develop the appropriate *habits* – the virtues, here understood in the most general sense of the term. That is, they must be understood as dispositions for acting in accordance with the good of persons – the good that is revealed by the method of critical introspection.

Let me just mention something that I will argue for more fully below. It must not be thought that the concept of a person is a fully determinate one. It is not as if one ever has a completely determinate conception of self. The task of self-interpretation is always and necessarily ongoing, and endlessly subject to reinterpretation. So, embodying the concept of personhood cannot amount to coming to possess a full account of self. What we have instead, when we come to embody the most perfect conception of personhood, is a maximally adequate understanding of self, and this is different from having what could be characterized as a perfect conception. A crucial aspect of properly embodying the concept of personhood is that one is able to be sensitive to largely unpredictable changes in circumstances, and revise one's own conception of who one is in the process. Such revisions, of course, include revising one's understanding of the virtues. The concept of a virtue, like the concept of personhood, is an indeterminate one, and such an indeterminacy allows for individual and, indeed, cultural differences with regard to the embodiment of the good. Concepts, and particularly the sorts of concepts that interest us at present, are more like thick fog than perfectly cut crystals. The indeterminacy that is inherent to any concept will be discussed more fully below.

The method of critical introspection is the method of thinking through our already existing conceptions of what it is to be a person in order to make our understanding explicit and more complete. In making this understanding explicit we will be in a better position to determine any inconsistencies we might find on the way and thus adjust our conception in order to maximize its consistency and clarity. However, it must be pointed out that the consistency at issue here is not solely logical consistency, although logical consistency is central. Rather, it is, roughly, the sense of consistency that is expressed in claims such as 'She is a consistent, integral person' or 'She has a consistent character that is reflected in her actions'. The relevant sense of consistency here, I might add, is not incompatible with having some logical conflicts. On the contrary, one could say that acknowledging one's conflicts and having the capacity to integrate them as best as possible into the general pattern of our lives is a mark of a consistent character. Integration of conflict cannot be equated with its dissolution.

It is uncontroversially the case, for instance, that life presents us with circumstances in which we are forced to make extremely difficult decisions. Such difficulties arise because of the inevitable sacrifices we must make, or the sacrifices we must put others through, in carrying out these decisions. Consider a case in which there are equally (or almost equally) good reasons for leaving a given relationship of love than there are for not doing so. One might be, and many no doubt are, torn between the love felt, the belief that the relationship has no future, the belief that things might get better if one stays, the desire to be alone, the desire not to be alone, the appearance of someone else on the scene, the desire not to hurt the person one has loved and the simultaneous understanding that staying will only prolong the agony, the belief that one's children should be brought up by both parents, the belief that it is perhaps better for the children not to be brought up by both parents if the parents are not getting on, and so on. After considering and weighing up all factors that one perceives are relevant to the given situation, one is typically able to reach a decision and act accordingly. But it must be emphasized that reaching a decision and acting upon it does not mean that the conflicts have been fully resolved. Sometimes conflicts are never fully resolved and the pain caused by one's decisions lingers on indefinitely. Typically, conflicts of this sort slowly dissolve until they become spectres that only come to haunt us sporadically. Coming to terms does not mean eliminating all conflict; rather, it usually means learning to accept and understand that one could not have acted in a better way at the time, and that one must move on and continue with one's life. It is also important to realize that in cases of this sort there is not always one best solution. There might be many ways of coping with conflicts that are equally worthy of merit and, indeed, the diversity of ways in which conflicts of this sort are best resolved are also a reflection of the diversity of possible characters that *eudaimon* individuals might have – characters, moreover, which are constituted by the unique fashions in which the ideal of complete virtue can be instantiated. Additionally, there are many ways of coping with conflicts of this sort that are very destructive. To recapitulate, one could say that maximizing consistency cannot be equated with perfecting consistency.

It is also worth stressing here that it is by appropriating – by coming to embody – an adequate conception of what it is to be a person that one appropriates the qualities of character – qualities which constitute *logos* or complete virtue – from which good actions flow. Indeed, given that the appropriation at issue is a practical one, I do not think there is a distinction to be drawn here between having an adequate practical conception of what it is to be a person and having a good character. I say this with some confidence simply because the practical appropriation of a given conception is just the sort of appropriation that is expressed by the activities of an individual who has appropriated the conception. The work done by the practical conception of what it is to be a person is identical with the work done by complete virtue, and hence it seems to me that there are no grounds for establishing a distinction between the states of character – the habits of character – and the practical conception at issue. To live in accordance with complete virtue is to live in accordance with an understanding of what it is to be a person. A happy person most fully understands what it is to be a person by virtue of the fact that he or she understands most perfectly the ideal that defines us as persons. I argued along similar lines in the previous chapter in which I showed why having a virtue can properly be understood as a form of knowing.

Moreover, life is a dynamic totality – a narrative totality. This means that the task of self-interpretation is ongoing such that one cannot reach self-understanding once and for all. This amounts to saying that complete virtue cannot, so to speak, be understood in structuralist terms – as a structure that is fully determinate. In other words, the system of capacities that one has must be an adaptive one and, as I said, this follows simply from the fact that life has a narrative structure – a structure that is sensitive to ongoing and largely unpredictable change. These ongoing changes, moreover, are not just added onto a life, with no effect on the significance of the past and of future projections – not at all. The past, present and future are permanently playing off each other in terms of their significance. These matters will be explored further below.

Let us now proceed to engage head-on with the method of critical introspection, beginning with a discussion of Nussbaum's views on the matter. She quotes Aristotle:[6]

> Being is a good thing for the good person, and each person wishes good things for himself. But nobody would choose to have everything on condition of becoming other.... He will wish to have the good while continuing to be whatever he is.[7]

The limits for personal improvement, Aristotle argues, are determined by the sorts of creatures that we are – by our kind membership.[8] I could not, for instance, choose to be a stone in the sense of choosing to be a stone whilst expecting to continue to be myself, since in ceasing to be a person I would also cease to be the individual that I am. By contrast, I could choose, in the same sense of choice just specified, to be more optimistic or to develop a certain craft, since these changes do not undermine the possibility of my continued existence. Nussbaum notes that the above quoted passage restricts, 'ethical aspirations by bringing in considerations of personal identity and kind membership'.[9] Indeed, considerations of personal identity cannot be separated from considerations pertaining to kind membership, since one can only hope to have an identity, or indeed to preserve one's specific identity – the identity that distinguishes one from all other members of one's kind – if one preserves one's kind membership, namely one's identity as a person. Additionally, considerations of kind membership cannot be separated from ethical aspirations given that we are defined as the creatures that we are by an ethical ideal – by our *telos*. So, the ethical aspirations of persons are already determined by, and built into, the fabric that constitutes our very nature. Further, it is precisely because we are persons that we have ethical aspirations at all.

Nussbaum sketches Aristotle's views thus:

> When I imagine a picture of the good and valuable life, and think of wishing it for myself and for another, I ought to get clear about the relationship between that valuable life and the conditions of my (my friends') continued existence. I ought, that is, to ask closely whether this imagined life is a life that could be lived by a being such as I am – by a being, that is, who shares with me all those characteristics that I consider to be truly constitutive of my (my friends') identity ... So our views about who we essentially are and what changes we can endure while remaining ourselves set limits of a kind upon what we can wish, on what our ethical theories can commend....[10]

So, according to Nussbaum's interpretation of Aristotle, establishing the good and valuable life for oneself involves answering the question 'What sort of creature am I?' given that what is valuable and important in a life depends on what sort of life that life is. Moreover, establishing what sort of life we are talking about amounts to establishing what is essential to that life. By 'essential' Nussbaum means both what is essential to a particular individual and also what is essential to a given type of individual. Nussbaum's fundamental concern, however, is not so much with the particularities of a given individual, but rather with the defining particularities of a given type of individual. And indeed, this fundamental concern reflects Aristotle's.

I think it is not difficult to see that the method of critical introspection applies also at the level of individual particularities. The only difference will be that the method will have to be applied at the level of individual histories, and not just at the level of generality required for revealing features of our lives that are common to us all (those features that place a limit on what sorts of lives ought to be desired by creatures of our kind). 'I' have pursued the path of philosophy, and not the path of carpentry, because, ideally, this pursuit best coheres with who I am specifically. For instance, I was born with analytical capacities, but without manual dexterity; because I was born with analytical capacities, and because tragedy hit me at an early stage in my development, I was naturally driven to analyse my situation philosophically. That philosophical approach led me to discover the beauty of philosophical labour. If, because of certain prevalent fancies, and because of peer pressure or something of this sort, I was led to pursue the path of carpentry, perhaps my entire being would have imploded, and I would have become embittered and generally twisted as a consequence (even though many are propelled toward the craft of carpentry given their unique existential footing on Earth). It is a common feature of well-to-do families that have a multigenerational tradition in some socially acceptable field such as medicine, to use another example, to place great pressure on sons – typically sons – to continue such a tradition even if their individual callings do not accord with the path of medicine. Such pressure could lead someone to become very embittered precisely because the pursuit of a medical career does not fit well with the overall pattern of a specific life. Of course, none of the cases presented here are cases in which one's unique existence as a person is undermined by a particular life option, or by a particular event, that another human being could endure, or even embrace, but there are cases of psychological collapse which do threaten our personal existence. Psychoanalysis is perhaps best equipped to explain the causes – the particular orderings that must obtain – in order for a specific individual to collapse (where others perhaps would not). A good literary example is that of Winston and Julia's fictitious lives in Orwell's *Nineteen Eighty-Four*. Their torturers targeted their particular individualities – their particular fears – in order to (almost) completely obliterate their identities (to the point in which they developed something like a morbid love for Big Brother).[11]

Since the type of beings we are concerned with here are persons, the question 'What sort of creature am I?' involves answering the fundamental question 'What is a person?' Answering this question, in turn, will involve determining the defining limits of who we are. Nussbaum's method for determining the limits of personhood involves imagining different modes of being and asking whether or not those modes of being are compatible with the being of persons. The method is essentially introspective in that it involves one's own judgement as to whether a given mode of being is acceptable to *oneself* (on final analysis). Of course, the method of critical introspection does not necessarily involve comparing our lives with those of possible others, but making use of counterfactual modes of existence is a very effective procedure for revealing at least some of the central constraints that define us. The effectiveness of this particular mode of applying the method of critical introspection shall become plain with the examples offered below.

Nussbaum asks us to consider whether a particular conception about who we might want to be coheres with the overall conception we already have about ourselves. The latter conception, I might add, is one that allows us to recognize others and ourselves as belonging to the same kind. Indeed, given that, for the most part, we are quite good at distinguishing persons from nonpersons, we must possess a common – intersubjective – conception of personhood. Let us study a few counterfactual sorts of lives a person *purportedly* could live and see whether, in actual fact, these modes of existence are available to persons.

## Radical Hedonism

Nussbaum illustrates her argument with a discussion of Plato's *Philebus*. Protarchus initially holds a radical hedonistic account of the ideal life, which asserts that happiness can be reduced to pleasure. Nussbaum characterizes Socrates' argument with Protarchus as follows:

> Socrates now asks Protarchus to join him in a thought experiment. Let us imagine he says, you, Protarchus, living a life full of large pleasures, but altogether bereft of reason and intellect. (Socrates stresses that the test will be carried out 'in you'; it is important that Protarchus should try to see *himself* living the life.) This looks appealing to Protarchus at first glance, sympathetic as he is to the claims of hedonism. He says he would gladly accept such a life, and he would think himself lacking in nothing if he had it (21A). Even if all reasoning and thinking were omitted, 'I would have everything having pleasure' (21B2). Socrates now reminds him that, by omitting reasoning, they are also committed to omitting from Protarchus' life such things as the belief that he is enjoying himself, the memory of pleasure, the ability to calculate for future pleasure (21B6–C6). In fact, Socrates now suggests, what Protarchus has left on his hands is 'not the life of a human being, but one belonging to some jellyfish or some one of the living creatures in the sea with bony bodies' (21E6–8). He now asks Protarchus 'A life of this kind isn't choiceworthy for us, is it?' (21D3). Protarchus replies, 'Socrates, this argument has left me altogether speechless.'[12]

By making use of the method of critical introspection Socrates shows Protarchus that the sacrifices he would have to make to be able to live a life for pleasure and bereft of reason are far too great and may ultimately undermine even the less ambitious goal of living a merely pleasant life. In fact, once Socrates shows Protarchus the consequences of adopting what he takes to be an ideal life, Protarchus realizes that he does not truly desire to live a life lacking in reason. But what makes the sacrifice too great? Nussbaum argues that the sacrifice is too great because it threatens to undermine the very conception Protarchus (implicitly) has of himself. Protarchus realizes that a life without reason is a life that could not be lived by him or, indeed, by any other person. Furthermore, he realizes that sacrificing his identity in such a way would be something undesirable given that the desirability itself of adopting a particular mode of being rests on the conception one already has about oneself and, more relevant to the present discussion, a conception one has of oneself *qua* person. The very character of the hedonistic life desired by Protarchus, even though Protarchus did not initially realize this, thus depends on being a person. Protarchus' conception of living a life for pleasure, Socrates shows him, would involve being able to *know* that he is having or has had pleasure, and, being able to plan for future pleasure. By merely showing him how his hedonistic conception of the good cannot function without reason, Socrates has effectively *altered* Protarchus' theoretical conception of the good life (that is, Protarchus' conception of the *telos* of life). Protarchus did not initially comprehend the wide ramifications a hedonistic lifestyle would have on his life as a whole. He did not realize that the life he was choosing for himself was more like the life of a jellyfish than of a person, and such a life would indeed not be his life at all.

The above case exemplifies the more general thesis that our attitudinal system is a system of internally dependent and mutually constitutive attitudes. Our attitudinal system proscribes options in life such as the option Protarchus initially advocated, since living a life for pleasure and devoid of reason is not one in which personhood can be expressed. I am not saying here not that it is impossible for people to desire a hedonistic life (Protarchus is a person after all), but that a life lived for pleasure and without reason is not the life of a person and, for this reason, desiring actually to live for pleasure and nothing more is an incoherent desire and consequently an undesirable one. The desire is *incoherent* because the very justification for desiring actually to live in a particular way is the implicit conception we have of what it is to be a person – a conception that informs those activities that define us as persons. Another way of making much the same point is to claim that one appropriately ceases to desire actually to live a given lifestyle when one realizes that one's desire was not *authentic* – that is, when one realizes that one's desire does not accord with who one really is. 'I' want to live this life rather than that life because of who I am. And, indeed, the reasons I give myself for wanting this life and not that one involve considerations regarding a conception of who I am.

Some clarification is warranted here. I do not want to suggest that it is not important for us to desire things that are unattainable, and even positively crazy, at times. Indeed, fantasy sometimes helps us survive in conditions of extreme difficulty – consider, for example, individuals imprisoned in concentration camps who may at times find no better recourse for survival than to transport themselves into a realm of fantasy where unattainable desires are fictitiously fulfilled, a realm, perhaps, where all hedonistic desires can be fulfilled without obstruction. So, the desirability of a desire is not necessarily a function of its attainability (nor must a desire necessarily accord with the 'what-it-is' of persons). However, these observations in no way affect the force of Socrates' argument, since the sort of desire he is trying to undermine is one that, were we to attempt seriously to fulfil it we would be eroding the very conditions for its attainability. And, indeed, in pursuing the spectre of a radically hedonistic lifestyle we would, as a consequence, be eroding the very foundations for the desirability of such a lifestyle. I could certainly fantasize about a life full of large pleasures and nothing more, and no doubt many fantasies of this sort would be very beneficial for improving my life on Earth, but what Protarchus was seriously considering, was abandoning reason altogether, and that would spell his demise as a person.[13]

Aristotle also produces an argument of his own to show that a life that only contained pleasure would be undesirable.[14] Eudoxus, Aristotle argues, believed that, since all living creatures desire pleasure and avoid pain, pleasure is the good – the *telos* – of life.[15] Aristotle points out that, paradoxically, although Eudoxus explicitly advocated hedonism, he lived a life of virtue. Eudoxus' views were mistaken because, according to Aristotle, he simply did not look closely enough at his own life to realize that his explicit conception of himself was incompatible with his own way of being.

### The Possibility of Being a God

In employing the method of critical introspection in order to show the limits of our being as persons, Nussbaum, following Aristotle,[16] also invites us to imagine the lives of Homeric gods, Cyclopes, and Erinyes.[17] The study of these anthropomorphs is meant to shed light on the conditions for the possibility of being a person. Let us start by considering the lives of the Homeric gods. These lives are described as similar to the lives of persons, with the notable exceptions that the gods are more powerful and are also immortal.[18] The questions we must answer now are: 'Would we on final analysis want to live like immortals?' and 'What sacrifices would have to be made for having such lives?' Both these questions are intimately related to one another because the answer to the former question depends on the answer to the second – on our assessment of what we stand to lose if we had the possibility of sacrificing our mortality.

Nussbaum suggests that the desire for perfect completeness – which is a defining feature of the lives of gods of the sort being considered at present – and immortality is incompatible with the type of creatures that we are.[19] Following Aristotle, she argues that a 'complete' creature would have no reason to move from place to place or worry about self-change. They need not worry about self-change because their characters are static. Indeed, such creatures might not even have a self-identity at all. She concludes from this that our limits, which are determined by our *telos*, play a constitutive role in making us persons: we cannot desire simply to be anything and hope to continue being persons. For example, Nussbaum argues that 'Aristotle attaches himself explicitly to the tradition [the Homeric tradition] when he speculates … about whether gods could have human virtues, and concludes that characteristics such as moderation would have no place in the context of such a life'.[20]

In *Ethica Nichomachea X*,[21] the passage Nussbaum refers to above, Aristotle explicitly argues that what is best for persons is defined in relation to what makes us persons. Indeed, we already know why the good for persons is our substantial form. For this reason the life of a god, which by definition is more perfect than the life of a person, cannot be the good life for persons.[22] Conversely, the good life of a person cannot be the good life of a god, since gods and persons have different natures – they are defined in relation to different *teloi*. Aristotle himself argues that the attribution of certain acts such as just acts and acts of courage to the gods would be absurd on the grounds that a god is not a person. In his words:

> We assume the gods to be above all other beings blessed and happy; but what sort of actions must we assign to them? Acts of justice? Will not the gods seem absurd if they make contracts and return deposits, and so on? Acts of a brave man, then, confronting dangers and running risks because it is noble to do so? Or liberal acts? To whom will they give? It will be strange if they are really to have money or anything of the kind. And what would their temperate acts be? Is not such praise tasteless, since they have no bad appetites? If we were to run through them all, the circumstances of action would be found trivial and unworthy of gods.[23]

In the above passage Aristotle is arguing that we cannot expect gods to act in ways that define persons as such, since these activities are incompatible with what it is to live the lives of gods. Gods are just too different from us. It would be absurd, for example, to attribute bravery to a god given that gods, as conceived here, cannot be harmed – they have no notion of personal risk. More generally, to expect a god to have the human virtues would be to expect gods not to be gods, but to be persons.

Nussbaum states what she takes to be two defining features of the gods: '… gods have no *need* either of social bonds or of the practical use of reason in planning a life.'[24] Both Nussbaum and Aristotle believe that we are essentially political creatures – that is, that our lives are defined by our need to establish social bonds. In saying that our lives are defined by our social interactions Nussbaum and Aristotle are not simply saying that we can only exist as persons if we actually belong to a social group at every moment of our lives. This would clearly be wrong, since it is possible to live as, for example, Robinson Crusoe or Philoctetes.[25] Rather, what these authors are claiming is that life as we know it depends on sharing with others.[26] A radical Robinson Crusoe, or a radical Philoctetes – a creature like us, but who has never had a political life – would be very far from living in accordance with the *telos* of persons.[27]

In the above quotation Nussbaum also states that the gods have no need for practical reason. She concludes, from this conception of what it is to be a god, that a person could not be a god. She implicitly argues that, because the gods are perfect, they have no need to make choices to make their lives better. Also, since gods are not political creatures, they do not have to engage with others (social engagements demand the use of practical reason). And, finally, since there is no risk in their lives because they are immortal and impervious to pain and suffering, they do not have to apply practical reason to avoid risk. In short, it appears that there is no place at all in the lives of gods where practical reason is required. Indeed, arguably, a god could be capable of practical reason, but the mere fact that they are not required to use it makes their lives radically different from ours, since it is clear that our lives would be senseless if we did not have to make use of practical reason.

Gods do not suffer from hunger or thirst. They do not suffer pain. They have no need for shelter. Nothing can affect them. Indeed, they do not need anything for they are fully self-sufficient. Since they are self-sufficient (in this extreme sense), and they cannot be harmed, the gods have no need to deliberate over practical matters or have friends. Indeed, the very distinction between having *phronesis* (practical wisdom or understanding) and the lack thereof is of no relevance to the gods, since the practicality of an endeavour depends, among other things, on whether or not it enhances the quality of life, and the lives of gods cannot be enhanced simply because their lives are already perfect, and because their lives are unchanging.

Indeed, I might add that gods have fixed characters, which means that they do not to work their way through life. Learning and growing is not something that these gods do. They simply go through their eternal lives doing much the same sort of things they always do. They have nothing new to hope for, given that they are impervious to change. It is for this reason that it is hard to see in what sense these gods are agents at all. Indeed, it starts to become apparent why the concept of a god as conceived here is oxymoronic on final analysis. Gods of the sort being considered could hardly be asked to be responsible for what they do. Indeed, it is hard to imagine how creatures of this sort could even be said to be able to reflect on what they do and who they are as there is no sense in which who they are and what they do can be called into question. They are more like automatons than persons. They lack the plasticity and capacity for self-change that seems to be so central to the 'what it is to be' of persons. Persons, by contrast, have vulnerable identities – identities capable of being damaged or even destroyed. Indeed, our identities are intimately tied up with our fragility – with the fact that we must work on ourselves in order to continue being whom we are (and also for improving ourselves). The fact that circumstances do affect us and force us to change either for the better or for the worse defines our lives. Indeed, the radical self-sufficiency attributed to the Greek gods is completely alien and incompatible with what appear to be central defining features of whom we are.

## Immortality

I turn now to what it would be like for a person to be immortal, and show that mortality is a condition for the possibility of living in accordance with our defining *telos*. But, first, it is important to clarify that I am not interested so much in demonstrating that mortality is a precondition for living in accordance with our *telos*. Rather, I will now consider the possibility of having an immortal life primarily in order to establish some fundamental features of the basic procedure for determining what it is to be a person. And since we already have a good idea of why persons are defined as such by the *eudaimon* ideal, we also know that, in establishing this basic procedure for determining what it is to be a person, we will have simultaneously determined the procedure for determining the nature of *eudaimonia*.

Jorge Luis Borges, in his magnificent short story 'The Immortal',[28] deals (in a literary rather than an argumentative fashion) with the effects that immortality would have on the lives of persons. His story illustrates how a life of immortality would not be a life for us. In his famous story the main character, Joseph Cartaphilus, who at one point gains the power to live as an immortal, is characterized as a man whose life has lost all purpose and satisfaction.

Borges's story helps us visualize, or at least suggests one plausible way of visualizing, the life of creatures without the 'gift of finiteness'. He argues that, for an immortal, '[n]o one is anyone, one single immortal man is all men. Like Cornelius Agrippa, I am a god, I am a hero, I am a philosopher, I am a demon and I am the world, which is a tedious way of saying that I do not exist.'[29] Through his story Borges suggests that the possibility of being immortal is incompatible with having an identity and a sense of purpose, given that an immortal creature would live the life of many individuals – of many persons. But, of course, to live the life of many is not to live a life at all, since to live the life of individuals like us just is, quite trivially, to live one life and not many. Indeed, to use Borges's words, saying that I have lived the lives of many 'is a tedious way of saying that I do not exist'. An immortal creature would not live the life of a creature that embodies the relevant unity that is constitutive of an identity because, more likely than not, such a creature would have to live through infinite changes in circumstances motivating him or herself to adapt endlessly to ever-changing circumstances – unless, of course, an immortal deliberately chose to make his or her environment static (assuming this were possible). We shall soon see that living in such an environment would not accord with our nature.

I will argue that, if someone were to become an immortal creature, he or she would lose, or perhaps simply never develop, the sense that his or her life is that of a unitary creature – a creature with an identity. As it stands, this sketch of an argument might seem to be rather unpersuasive given that it is not clear how much change, and indeed what types of change, is necessary for undermining identity. Lives of mortals like ourselves, after all, also undergo massive, though certainly not endless, changes in circumstances throughout life. Therefore we need to be more specific about how the changes that affect an immortal life are incompatible with our *telos*.

If one became immortal, one would eventually lose one's sense of purpose. An immortal would feel no *urgency* in answering the questions we typically ask ourselves (or which at least are implicit in the manner in which we conduct our lives) and which help give purpose to our lives – questions such as 'Who am I?', 'What do I want out of life?', 'Where do I want to go from here?' and 'What kind of life do I want to live?'. An immortal creature would not, assuming, of course, that an immortal was aware of its condition, see the urgent need to address these questions since, by definition, he or she has all the time in the world to try as many life options as are available to him or her.[30] This is, of course, not to say that an immortal would, in fact, try all available options. My point concerns only the urgency experienced by mortals in contrast to the relative lack of urgency facing an immortal creature with regard to such questions. If an immortal were able seriously to choose one life option over a whole array of other available life options, this immortal, like us mortals, would have to base his or her decision on an (implicit or explicit) understanding of his or her life, taken as a whole. The problem our fictitious immortal 'subject' faces here is, it seems to me, that an essential reason for *seriously* choosing one direction in life rather than another is that one chooses, in cases of this sort, because this is the life one wants for oneself, and one has no time to toy with innumerable other possible life options. The temptation to toy is certainly there, but the mere fact that we know that life has an end prevents us from succumbing to such a temptation. Here, we start to get an idea of how a mortal's options in life are limited by the fact that he or she has limited time at his or her disposal.[31]

The issue of urgency cannot be overstated. It is precisely because our time is limited that we *must*, because of the urgency brought about by the (implicit or explicit) knowledge that 'life is short', embrace one life option rather than another through the choices we make. It is also important to consider that there would be other constraints, related to the particular history of a given immortal, which would motivate him or her to choose specific directions at particular times. But if we remember that the immortal has infinite time at his or her disposal, it seems that there will inevitably be a moment in which an immortal will be left with no reasons (or, more generally, motivations) for choosing one life option rather than a bewildering array of other possibilities.

At this point in the kaleidoscopic history of an immortal's life, this creature could (perhaps out of desperation) attempt to constrain his or her life options by artificially limiting his or her life in such a way as to create the conditions for the possibility for the continuity and consistency of his or her life – a continuity and consistency that is typified by the lives of persons (and which defines the identity of a person). The problem with this sort of situation – or one of the problems at any rate – is that the purported choices an immortal could make at this point, which would allow him or her to preserve the general continuity of his or her life, would be rather contrived, because, among other things, at any given time there would be any number of equally appealing life options to try out. If one were in a situation of this sort, one would have to take a third-person vantage point and forcefully adopt, for no particular reason (except, of course, for the very good reason that one aspires to continue to live a meaningful existence), one life option rather than other equally appealing ones in order to avoid becoming, quite literally, no one.

But more can be said about the life of an immortal that adopted the semblance of a finite life. An immortal in this situation would permanently and forcefully have to monitor its life so that its life did not lose its basic organization. A given immortal would have to think through the different moves available to him or her, consider the character he or she has adopted, and imagine him or herself deliberating as if, in fact, the adopted character was who this immortal was in actuality, as opposed to a kind of puppet under his or her control.

If an immortal was going to have a structured life, he or she would be forced to look at the purported identity he or she has adopted from the position of a voyeur – that is, from a third-person perspective.[32] Mortals, by contrast, do not choose to adopt a self as actors adopt the characters they represent. The case of an immortal puppeteer just proposed is analogous to that of an actor taking on a particular role in a play in the sense that an actor, like an immortal inspired by the idea of having an identity, typically has to *imagine* him or herself as being a particular character rather than actually being that character.

Inevitably, if he or she is to preserve some sense of unity and purpose, an immortal would have to fight against ever-changing circumstances which threaten to disperse his or her unity. One way, perhaps the only way, an immortal might attempt to fight against change, I have already suggested, is to create a relatively stable and unchanging environment within which to dwell. I think it is quite clear that a static environment of this sort would be quite unbearable since it would offer nothing new to look forward to or do and would be unbearably tedious as a consequence.[33] Most importantly, to preserve his or her identity an immortal choosing to live in an environment of this sort (for the sake of preserving a purported identity and having a sense of purpose) would have to avoid engaging in any important new projects, since major projects are transformative. The immortal would have to linger on doing nothing of interest and hoping for nothing – a kind of living death.[34] A life of the sort just described is not only a life that is not suitable for persons because it is infinitely tedious, but also, and most importantly, it is infinitely tedious because it would be a life which lacked certain basic features that seem to define the lives of persons as such.

One of the fundamental problems with the static world option is that it appears that our lives *qua* rational creatures depend on having projects – on pointing our lives in particular directions by the goals we pursue (consciously or unconsciously) – and this is not something an immortal subject living in a static environment can properly do. If, say, I chose the project of becoming a doctor or of becoming a political activist, then the actions I would perform, such as enrolling in a university and studying hard or, alternatively, going out of my way to help others, would have as their purpose my becoming a doctor or my becoming a political activist (independently of whether or not in actuality I become a doctor or a political activist). It is precisely the overarching purpose – the *telos* – of becoming a doctor or of becoming a political activist that gives purpose to the activities involved in becoming those things, such that if I did all the activities involved in the sorts of practices being described, but with no goal in mind whatsoever, my actions would lack purpose. Alternatively, if I engaged in all these activities, but only with a shallow or morally perverse goal in mind, the value of my activities would be tainted accordingly. I could, for instance, help others for the sake of prestige. Or, like our immortal, I could engage in a project in order to preserve my identity. My endeavours are, so to speak, tainted by the existential framework within which they are couched.

It might also be worth stressing at this point that what gives purpose to a set of coordinated activities is not that there is a goal of which one is necessarily conscious. Rather, all that is required is that one's activities have a goal. Someone, say, might have decided to become a political activist because he or she was bored and disillusioned with life, and thought that he or she might as well give his or her life away. As a consequence of becoming involved in politics as a means of forgetting him or herself in the task of working for others, he or she might discover, with great surprise, that life was indeed worth living. In this last example there is no sense in which the person was aware that the project undertaken would change his or her life – would invest his or her life with purpose. And, moreover, I am also willing to entertain the possibility that this person might never consciously discover, and may well have no interest in consciously discovering, that his or her life has a purpose.

More generally, as we have already seen, the meaning (and value) of a given activity is determined by the role it plays within the framework of a life as a whole with its unifying *telos*, which is the achievement of the *eudaimon* ideal. This unifying *telos* is what gives meaning to the different segments of a rationally organized life. Wanting to become a doctor, or wanting to work for charity, are not the *ultimate* goals that bestow purpose on the tasks of learning medicine or working for charity respectively. This is evidenced by the simple fact that one is not able to justify one's interest in medicine, or one's interest in working for charity, as opposed to a whole array of other possible endeavours, by claiming that one wants to become a doctor or that one wants to work for charity, simply because that is what one wants. For the endeavours of studying medicine or working for charity to have a purpose one must be able to frame those projects within a system of projects in a way that is amenable to rational investigation. If, for instance, one came to realize that one's desire to become a doctor did not cohere with one's overall expectations in life, or one changed one's overall expectations because of a change in circumstances, then one would abandon one's medical endeavour (or at least would perceive the endeavour in a different light – the project would acquire a different character). As we have seen in a previous chapter, projects are embedded in systems of projects, and it is within these systems that projects derive their purpose. But it is also important to realize that the systems at issue are not static; instead, they are dynamic. As already claimed, changing circumstances might, and very often do, force us to adapt in ways that cannot be fully predicted. And, indeed, the dynamic unifying nature of a system of projects is constitutive of the purposiveness of a given project – projects become meaningful within this dynamic framework.

Moreover, it is in reacting to the world in the task of project formation – a world that presents itself to us in ways that are never fully under our control – that meaning is shed on these projects. Indeed, if one's environment were fully under one's control then one would be like an automaton, precisely because all possible moves, or all possible major moves, would be predetermined. In fact, the immortal that formed for itself a formidably stable environment did so in order not to lose control – in order for all major moves to be predetermined. What makes a given project meaningful is not just the fact that there is a goal, but that the goal is relevant to our lives understood here as unified dynamic systems of projects in which actual and possible projects are played off against each other in a realm of ever-changing circumstances. There will certainly be projects that endure more than others, but their characters will shift and move in accordance with changes in circumstances.

That circumstances ought to be, and are, ever-changing is evidenced by the fact that we have a history. And, indeed, the central role change plays in our lives is evidenced by the fact that lives are best described in terms of histories. Of course, some histories are monotonous but, notwithstanding the monotony, they are not static insofar as the characters of past, present, and future are mutually constitutive. That is, events in one's life acquire significance in light of an understanding of how these events are embedded in the pattern that constitutes one's evolving life history. Moreover, that circumstances are never static insofar as they form part of an evolving history highlights the artificiality of an immortal living in a static environment. On final analysis, he or she will never be able to preserve the fixity of his or her environment, since each segment of a life acquires new meaning in light of the evolving history that constitutes the immortal's life. Endless repetition sheds new meaning over the segments that constitute an unfolding life. Meaning is shed, paradoxically, insofar as the endless repetition brings with it the dissolution of meaning. What was at one stage a move to preserve meaning by attempting to do the impossible – by attempting to create the conditions in which history is frozen – ends up being a move to dissolve meaning altogether. Immortals cannot win.

Malpas argues along parallel lines.[35] He argues that a constitutive aspect of projects is that they 'possess a certain internal dynamic of anticipation and frustration or satisfaction'.[36] The idea here is that part of the very motivation for engaging in a project involves knowing that a given project might not be realized. If, by contrast, we knew that every one of our projects would succeed, as is the case with the particular sort of immortal life under scrutiny, then there would be little motivation for pursuing a given project. It is the permanent possibility of failure and frustration that leads us to press forward in order to achieve our aims. So the purposiveness of a given endeavour is inherently bound up with the dynamic of 'anticipation and frustration or satisfaction'. I might also add here that a given immortal living in a not so stable environment might very well fail in a given pursuit, but the failure would never be a final one, since all it would have to do is try again and again and again, if necessary. And, of course, if one always has another chance, then one of the basic motivations for labouring for success would be lost. To express this slightly differently, we live purposive lives insofar as we are frail, and vulnerable, insofar as it all might very well come to an end at any given moment. This last claim must not be taken to its absurd extreme, since typically we are sufficiently confident that we will have time to complete at least some of our major projects. Indeed, if no such confidence typically existed, then, again, a fundamental motivation for pursuing a given course of events would be lost. The possibility of frustration must typically exist, but so must the possibility of success (typically).

Let me diverge slightly from the central line of argument in order to establish fundamental interrelationships between the issues of failure (or frustration) discussed here, what was discussed towards the end of Chapter 2 regarding the issue of project formation and, finally, what will be discussed in the Appendix to this chapter and in the next chapter regarding the issue of pluralism. Remember that I argued, following Malpas and Wickham,[37] that projects acquire their identities within systems of projects, and we have seen that these systems are necessarily unstable and dynamic (being largely outside our control). Consequently, the natures of the objects themselves are unstable given that their characters emerge from the particular manner in which they are subsumed within specific projects (much the same considerations apply also to the identities of subjects). Further, the same considerations that apply to projects generally apply also to what Malpas and Wickham refer to as projects of governance.[38] If one understands the social domain as an unstable system, and consequently as a dynamic system of intertwined projects, and if one recalls the above discussion regarding the reification that occurs as a consequence of the orderings established by projects, and, finally, if one further adds that objects emerge as concrete entities not merely by being subsumed within this or that project, but more generally through their insertion within a matrix of projects that constitutes the social domain, then it follows that it is only in such a system that one can be a subject with a sense of world – understood as a realm constituted by a field of objects *qua* determinate entities. Indeed, if objects *qua* determinate entities only emerged within an inherently unstable and open-ended matrix of interpretative/projective activities (projects) then it follows that one can only have a proper sense of world within a pluralistic domain. By contrast, totalitarian regimes – regimes that attempt to subsume all or many of our central projects within the framework of one overarching project – are regimes that would, if they succeeded, limit our grasp of the concept of a world. And if one has a limited grasp of this concept, then it is hard to see how one can have an adequate grasp of self given that a self is defined as indeed a self *vis-à-vis* the domain within which we conceive of ourselves as selves – namely, the world. The overall impoverishment that occurs is adequately described as a form of alienation – a form of loss of self – precisely because one looses one's sense of self with the loss of a sense of world. We may tentatively conclude that persons flourish within regimes of difference – within pluralistic regimes. And, indeed, the governing powers of a pluralistic community *qua* pluralistic community are, in a manner of speaking, dispersed throughout the community. Moreover it is because governmental powers are so dispersed in a pluralistic community that communities of that sort could also be described as fundamentally *anarchic*. These issues will be further explored in the following chapter.

Let us now return to the central line of argument. But first let me re-emphasize that, given what has just been discussed, it is clear that an immortal subject living in a static environment would not be able to live a purposive life insofar as the relevant orderings required for project formation could not be established in such a narrowly defined environment.

Yet, contrary to what I have maintained thus far, it could be argued that some activities, such as helping those in need, may be sustained indefinitely in a way that would render an immortal life meaningful.[39] An immortal Mother Teresa or an immortal Gandhi would arguably be leading very meaningful eternal existences. The dynamic of anticipation and frustration or satisfaction, to use Malpas's terminology once again, would purportedly obtain given that there would always be new meaningful challenges to meet in this suffering-infected world. However, it seems to me that cases of these sorts fall prey to the very same reason provided above against static immortal lives in general. The problem is that tediousness would inevitably set in as a consequence of a failure to obtain the right sorts of orderings. The dynamic of anticipation and frustration or satisfaction would perhaps obtain, but only weakly, since there is only a finite range of modes of suffering. One's activities would end up becoming automatic – like the activities of an automaton. One's levels of engagement would inevitably dwindle as a consequence, and one would inevitably become, almost paradoxically, detached from one's engagements once the idea clearly set into one's mind that there is no end to the sorts of activities one is engaged in. In an important sense, one would become blind to human suffering as a consequence of realizing that one is eternally locked into a narrowly defined mode of being.

### The Method of Critical Introspection and How the Application of this Method has Revealed Some Fundamental Aspects of Personhood

We have seen how the method of critical introspection operates – how it reveals certain fundamental aspects of our being as persons. One could be tempted to claim that these fundamental aspects are *foundational* in a sense that is comparable to the way in which Descartes considered the *cogito*. Instead, what I do think is that a whole system of beliefs – a system of beliefs that contains the belief that we are by nature thinking creatures – is a condition for the possibility of holding any fundamental beliefs about who we are. Indeed, it appears that we could take any belief within the system of beliefs that constitutes our conception of what it is to be a person, and work our way into the system from that point. This is so simply because beliefs about our identity are constituted as the specific beliefs that they are only within this system, such that one given belief implicates a whole range of further beliefs. Indeed, it is precisely because our beliefs are so constituted that the method of critical introspection is so effective – it critically studies the fit between our beliefs.

The claims just made might seem to contradict the general procedure I have applied in this investigation. I have, after all, commenced my inquiry by assuming that the *telos* of life is happiness, and that a belief of this sort is what most of us hold. It could plausibly be claimed that this view regarding our *telos* is foundational since it is from this basic belief that the present inquiry has commenced. But, I think these claims miss the point because they fail to take into consideration that I also maintain (following Aristotle) that my initial claims regarding the position happiness occupies in our lives are relatively uninformative. My initial claim in and of itself holds very little weight (although it most certainly does aim us in a particular direction). Remember also that I have argued, following Aristotle, that although most of us hold that happiness is our *telos*, we disagree about what happiness actually is. And, as I have already discussed, the fundamental reason why we generally agree that happiness is important in our lives is because we already have a conception, albeit for the most part an implicit one, of what it is to be a person, and it is precisely this conception, which includes the belief that happiness is the *telos* of life, that informs our belief regarding the role happiness plays in our lives. My initial claims, and indeed Aristotle's, have as their primary function to open a door into a conceptual field that already informs the manner in which we conduct our lives – the conceptual field that allows us to perceive the role happiness plays in our lives in the first place.

These last claims might be rather misleading in that they might be seen to underestimate the importance of the starting point of the present investigation. The belief that happiness is the *telos* of life is extremely important in that it sets the parameters for an understanding of the organization of a life as a whole. By contrast, I could perhaps have commenced my inquiry by, say, studying the issue of pain (of what aspects of who we are congregate directly around pain) and then worked my way through the conceptual fabric at issue. I could, say, have commenced by inquiring about the relationship between pain and reason and, from the concept of rationality I could have worked my way through the maze by establishing links between the issue of pain and other fundamental aspects of the rational fabric of our lives. However, the problem with having the issue of pain, or for that matter with any other issue of this sort, as a starting point is that by commencing in this way one would not immediately grasp the basic structural features of our rational existence – structural features upon which all other aspects of our rational existence hang. One would be blind with regard to how the issue of pain fits into the general fabric of our lives.

The reason the *eudaimon* principle is so central and is the most important guiding principle of our lives, is that all basic aspects of our rational existence are directly related to it because it is the basic organizational principle. And it is precisely because so many things hang directly on this principle that it is self-justifying. Moreover, it is self-justifying in the sense that its denial would cause a total collapse in the manner in which persons understand their lives. To be sure, one might not be initially aware of the relevance of this principle, but its relevance can be demonstrated by showing how it determines the fundamental shape of a life.

I will try to clarify the present discussion with an analogy. Let us call it the Sydney Harbour Bridge analogy. The reason why we can best work our way through the maze that constitutes our rational existence from the vantage point of the *eudaimon* principle, and not from an analysis of the role pain plays in our lives (or from some other such vantage point), is that attempting to start from this second point is analogous to comprehending the Sydney Harbour Bridge by standing two inches away from its base and staring straight into the concrete. To get a good idea of what people are talking about when they talk about the Sydney Harbour Bridge one should ideally stand at a distance in order to grasp its general structure. Of course, by scrutinizing the bridge from a distance one will overlook important details. Nevertheless, by first having an overarching view of the bridge one is better placed to appreciate its details insofar as one is able to fit the details within the overarching structure that one has already grasped. Arguably I could attempt to build this overarching picture of the bridge by studying the details first and then patiently fitting them together in order to get an idea of the overall structure. But adopting this procedure would, amongst other things, be very time-consuming and, most importantly, one might never end up with an overarching view of the bridge simply because the details that constitute it are endless. Even more important than the sheer waste of time this would constitute is the fact that, by building a mental picture by adding details, one would not initially be in a position to judge what is important and what is not – one would have no grounds for discriminating degrees of importance in one's detailed, albeit partial, grasp of the bridge. It is only when I have an adequate conception of the totality of the bridge that I am able to fit details into a hierarchical system which allows me adequately to appreciate those details. And, indeed, given that the details are endless, one really has no choice but to determine which details are salient prior to the process of selecting them. This might seem to be paradoxical, for how can I grasp what is salient prior to grasping the details? However, this is only paradoxical if one is bewitched by a particular epistemology which is unable to explain what actually happens.

The totality that I grasp initially and from a distance is an indeterminate one. One of the basic technical skills one learns when learning how to draw is to grasp the overall form of one's subject first. One learns how to make a sketch. And it is fascinating that one must learn how to sketch, since one grasps things in schematic form all the time. This fact is revealing because it shows that we have to make an effort to grasp something that is known to us prior to one's efforts to make one's understanding explicit. And indeed, as I have claimed before, the sort of task I have set myself to accomplish in this investigation – an investigation which could be understood as a sketch – is to make explicit what is known to us all along, and which is expressed in our mode of operation. If a sketch of a bridge is successful, then, amongst other things, by looking at the drawing one will be able to have a grasp of the subject matter without getting bogged down with details. In fact, adding details indefinitely sometimes confuses things. For example, one does not paint every leaf on a tree in order to paint a tree; instead, one communicates a general impression. Grasping the general shape of a given figure is something the Impressionists were particularly good at doing, and their paintings are notorious for lacking detail. In conclusion, one grasps a bridge not by grasping all its details, but instead by grasping its most salient features. And moreover, knowing all the details does not amount to knowing the bridge any better since one might know many details without having a sense of their relevance. And because the details of a bridge are innumerable, grasping a bridge will always amount to determining salient, rather than all its features.

Of course there might be room for dispute with regard to the importance of some, or indeed many, details, and I think this applies equally to our common conception of happiness. But what we must understand here is that there is only room for dispute about what details of the bridge, or what details of an account of a happy life, are important if we share an overall conception of what we are talking about (if we know the subject matter of our agreements and disagreements). I might think that the rusting patterns of rivets are worthier of my attention than, say, the base that supports the bridge, whereas you might hold precisely the opposite view. But what is crucial is that we can only have disagreements of this sort if we consider our diverging views within the bounds of a common framework – within the bounds, in this case, of an overall grasp of the Sydney Harbour Bridge (or of happiness).

To recapitulate, although there are no foundational beliefs in our system of beliefs, there are certain ways of approaching our critical analysis that reveal the general structure of the system under scrutiny. I have claimed that the best way of approaching the conceptual fabric that constitutes our understanding of what it is to be a person (and hence of the ethical ideal of personhood) is through the fundamental structural principle of the lives of persons – namely, the ideal that life is lived for the sake of happiness.

In a very important sense, then, the desire for happiness is the ultimate justification for engaging in the projects that we typically engage in. But, in light of my anti-foundationalist stance, one must be careful not to confuse justifications with foundations for beliefs. My stance might initially seem paradoxical given that it seems that if something is an ultimate justification then it must be a foundation. Appearances at times deceive. Happiness, we have seen, is not something over and above the ideally organized aspects that constitute our ideally rational existence. So, it is not as if the desire for happiness alone, in isolation from all those aspects that constitute an ideal life, is the foundation for all other aspects of our ideally rational existence. If it did stand in isolation, in the same way as, according to Descartes, the *cogito* does, it would most certainly be a justifier and a foundation. Rather, the fundamental desire for happiness justifies in a different and more subtle manner. It justifies by pointing to the fact that a happy life is an ideally unified one, such that a given action (or a given emotion, desire, belief, and so on) is justified within the context of the totality within which it belongs.

Someone might quite legitimately want to insist that it is simply not possible for a given belief to be an ultimate justification and not a foundational belief on the grounds that an anti-foundational system is unavoidably circular, and viciously so. I agree that the system at issue is circular (and unavoidably so), but this circularity is by no means a vicious one. The anti-foundationalism at issue is circular in the sense that what justifies the belief that the desire for happiness is the ultimate justification for the ethical life is the system of beliefs (attitudes, behaviour, and so on) that it justifies. That the circularity at issue here is not vicious, however, is evidenced by the fact that it is an informative one. Indeed, we have seen that, by critically unpacking what we mean by happiness, a great deal has been revealed to us about the sorts of creatures that we are – a great deal has been revealed about the interconnectedness of concepts that inform our understanding of the sorts of creatures that we are. As I have argued above, the *eudaimon* principle is a fundamental structural feature of our attitudinal system and activities, and it is because it plays this prominent role within the system that constitutes our rational existence that the desire for happiness is the ultimate justification for living an ethical life. The desire for happiness, to repeat, plays this justifying role because happiness is something that is achieved when the different aspects that typically constitute our rational existence are ideally unified.

Further, it is because, among other things, *eudaimonia* is an organizational principle – the organizational principle that informs the life of an ideally rational subject – that the method of critical introspection is the means for coming to have an intellectual understanding of it. It is, to repeat, precisely the method that studies the fit between the different aspects that constitute our rational existence (our existence in accordance with *logos*).

Let us now return to Nussbaum's discussion on Cyclopes and Erinyes, and establish how her discussion is linked to the present one. We have seen that one fundamental reason why we would not want to live like these creatures is that these lives do not accord with our *telos*. Nussbaum argues, when discussing the content and social function of Greek tragedy, that we must agree with her conclusions that we would not want to live like these exotic anthropomorphs because the denial of these conclusions would amount to a denial of the form of life of persons. In Nussbaum's words the arguments are, 'self-validating in a deep way; you cannot withdraw your assent from its conclusion, without withdrawing from the entire form of life that, as a procedure, it embodies'.[40] One cannot choose to be a god, a Cyclops or the like, without at the same time (implicitly) denying central defining features of our lives.

The sacrifices involved in choosing lives of the sort just described are far too great. Indeed, seriously entertaining the idea that one wants to become a Cyclops or an Erinye strikes a paradoxical note that also sounds when entertaining the idea of being a god, since in choosing to live lives of these sorts it appears that one would have to be committed both to preserving central defining features of one's identity and to sacrificing these features at the same time. The paradox arises because the reasons for wanting to choose to live a certain kind of life rather than another one are based on the identity (and one's grasp of it) one already has before choosing to change. I might desire to be a god, for instance, because, given my self-understanding, I believe that being a god is a good thing.[41] The problem with the possibility of choosing to be a god is that choosing this entails undermining the very foundations upon which that choice was made in the first place – one threatens the identity of the deliberating person who has chosen to live like a god.

But why would a threat of this sort be a problem? It would be a problem because one, after all, wants to be aware that one is undergoing change but, in ceasing to be who one is, one also loses the possibility of appreciating the change. There is a sense in which desiring to become a god (or such like) is to contemplate suicide, since in becoming a god (supposing such a transformation were possible) one would have to forego one's identity. Accepting then that one wants to change involves, on final analysis, denying certain types of change that threaten to undermine one's identity as a person.

Now that we have studied several cases that show the constraining role of the constitutive relationships between rationality, pleasure, attitudes generally, time, mortality, and so on, I will attempt to make a more general claim about the nature of our lives. But we have said enough already to establish that there is such a thing as the being of persons, and also that there is a procedure for determining our being – a procedure that operates by mirroring the structure that constitutes us *qua* persons.

Generally, one judges whether or not a given mode of life is acceptable by considering one's life as a whole, by considering the fundamental relationships between different aspects of a life. In considering these basic interrelationships one observes that one cannot coherently want to live a purely hedonistic life, or a life of immortality, since such life options are incompatible with the central defining features of our identity as persons. Nussbaum argues that, 'Aristotle explicitly announces that his method in ethics is just the method he uses in all other areas: to preserve the greatest number and most basic of the 'appearances' [*phainomena*] – human perceptions and beliefs – on the subject'.[42] The criterion for deciding whether a given life option is worth living, Aristotle believes (and I agree), involves comparing it with the beliefs one holds as fundamental about ourselves – with a basic largely implicit conception we already have about ourselves.

For example, as argued above, on final analysis we judged that a life that was lived exclusively for the sake of pleasure would be undesirable given that, in such a life, there would be no room for other fundamental aspects of the lives of persons we value and consider to be essential to whom we are. As we have seen, a life that was exclusively lived for the sake of pleasure would be a life in which one could not *plan* for pleasure, or know about the pleasure one would be having (if, indeed, it were possible that someone could have pleasure without ever knowing so). Additionally, in order to be able to plan for anything one would have to be possessed of reason. Moreover, reason is a basic requirement for having knowledge. So, if one were able to plan for, and have knowledge of, pleasure, one would also have to be rational. Further, planning for pleasure involves having the capacity to *choose* to do what one considers pleasurable. And, more generally, the capacity to choose seems to be an essential component in our lives. Choosing, I might add, requires reason, since, quite trivially, choosing involves choosing on the basis of reasons (explicitly or implicitly known). To choose is not merely to select one possible option over others but, rather, to select one option for some reason. One chooses, in other words, implicitly or explicitly on the basis of a certain justification which is itself a constitutive element of the choice. If I chose, for instance, to live a full life rather than to live as a professional automaton it is only because I have reasons – even though the reasons might not be good ones, and even though I might not be fully aware of the reasons – for choosing this particular life option rather the other. Choosing, in addition, involves having a conception of self, given that one chooses by considering one's overall pattern of interests and desires. A big component of the justification for choosing involves justifying one's actions by recourse to the manner in which we perceive ourselves. So choosing involves, at the very least, rationality, desire and self-awareness. It can be observed, then, that we cannot reasonably desire to live radically different lives from those we live already, since I have shown, through numerous examples, that basic aspects of our lives hang together in constitutive relations such that choosing one life option cannot be properly done without taking into consideration a whole range of mutually constitutive aspects that define us.

We also know that our lives are fundamentally lived for happiness, and this knowledge serves to give a fundamental direction to our lives. Insofar as we are persons, even though we might not explicitly know exactly what the good life is, we ideally *desire* the good life (this is just another way of formulating the *eudaimon* principle), and this basic desire ideally informs our pattern of interests and choices. Moreover, since persons are essentially rational, capable of choice and mortal, then a *eudaimon* life must include all these features of our lives simply because they are defining features of our lives.

I have been concerned here with spelling out the constitutive links between different the components that compose a life, and in this way I hope to have shown that there are certain basic rational constraints on what it is to be a person. Since our lives are constrained in at least the ways specified above we may observe that we cannot consistently desire for ourselves a life that is radically different from the basic conception of a life set out here.

We have seen that basic aspects of our lives hang together in mutually constitutive relationships. So, we have good reasons for thinking that we cannot reasonably choose to change an aspect of our lives without taking into account their basic fabric. Protarchus became aware of the importance of rationality in his life when Socrates showed him that the life he initially desired for himself – a life of pleasure and devoid of reason – would not, in fact, be a life he would actually desire to live. Reason is a prerequisite for the sort of life Protarchus thought was best. Socrates does not, Nussbaum argues, attempt '... to correct his [Protarchus'] beliefs by appeal to some point on the outside; the aim is simply to adjust the totality of his beliefs'.[43] Nussbaum's comment suggests that, when asking ourselves about the ideal life, we already have in place a concept of self which is constituted by a totality of concepts intertwined in constitutive relations. Moreover, the only possibility of determining whether a given life option is acceptable is to compare it with this totality. Indeed, as we have seen, the structure of our lives is itself revealed by the application of the method of critical introspection: it is one that gives life its unity, and it is a condition for its intelligibility. In Nussbaum's words:

> ... Protarchus defines himself as a human being, and thinks of the shellfish life as a life "not choiceworthy *for us*". He seems to accept the (tacit) premise that the humanness of a form of life is a necessary and central condition for its being a life for him, a life in which he could see a being identified as him.[44]

Nussbaum is arguing that the method for determining a life worth living is what I have already characterized as the method of critical introspection. I have characterized it in this manner because one can only determine whether a given life option is acceptable by comparing it to the already existing totality of beliefs we have about ourselves. This introspective method presupposes a conception of personhood with which a given specific life option is compared, and it is by systematically applying this method that we are able to establish the ideal ethical unity – the unity that pertains to the manner in which a person ideally ought to act – that is constitutive of *eudaimonia*. We know this because we know that the *eudaimon* ideal is just the ideal of coherence that defines the lives of persons – the ideal of balance between the distinct aspects that define what it is to live the life of a person. The virtues, of course, have a central role to play in this unity, given that they are the enduring dispositions that inform our ideal rational manner of operating in the world.

So, we may conclude that, by studying how the different aspects that constitute our rational existence are related to one another, we are able to establish the ideal ethical unity that constitutes a *eudaimon* life. Moreover, it is by studying this unity that we are able to establish the proper role of the different aspects of our rational existence. We are able to determine, for example, the proper role of the emotions and of our intellectual faculty. We are also, and crucially, able to establish the role others play in our own happiness (as we shall see).

## Appendix: Holism and Indeterminacy

I want to avoid tempting the reader into entertaining the possibility of a total theory of the psychological. It is not hard to see why one might be tempted to think that a total theory is possible. The idea is that if one applies the method of critical introspection consistently then one would eventually end up having a total theory. Clearly, constructing a total theory, were this possible, would be a formidable endeavour given the sheer vastness of the psychological domain, but, we already have some idea why such an endeavour would necessarily fail. First, the task of interpretation is ongoing because life has a narrative structure. However, this is not the only reason. Another related, but more general, reason for the indeterminacy is that one never has a complete grasp of one's life at a given moment. This, of course, follows from the fact that life has a narrative structure, but not only because of this. The indeterminacy also cuts through the system of the psychological simply because there is no sense in which one can have a god's-eye-view of the entire fabric of one's life or, indeed, of the lives of others (I take it that this claim is straightforwardly true). One is always, so to speak, trapped in a hermeneutic circle; that is, any attempt to grasp something will presuppose a background of belief which is not present to the mind's eye. Indeed, there is something rather peculiar about thinking of one's life as a structure that can be unveiled once and for all, either by oneself or by others. It cannot because of certain basic structural features of our minds. I can only, say, delve into the depths of my current situation (sitting in a café writing this book) insofar as I am not thinking about the problems that will besiege me once I am thrown into the situation of having to carve a future in a foreign land – as a stranger. More simply, I can think of one thing at a time, and thinking about a specific thing at one time blinds me to other thoughts. To use a familiar example, I can only think of the drawing presented to me by Wittgenstein as a duck or as a rabbit, but not as both simultaneously. Another way of making much the same point is that one's consciousness can only hone into aspects of the self, and these aspects always form part of a figure/background structure of the sort discussed by the hermeneutic tradition. Light, so to speak, shines forth in relation to a backdrop of darkness. However, the darkness is playing an active role here – it is, one could say, pregnant.

Indeed, it becomes clear that the problem of indeterminacy does not merely occur at the first-person level, and this is simply because the problem of indeterminacy is structural; the mind has an indeterminate structure. When interpreting others there is no hope of establishing exactly which beliefs a given subject is holding, simply because there is no complete set of beliefs. In fact, it is a mistake to view the mind as being structured in a way that can be fully described by a complete theory.

Dreyfus is critical of the holism of both Davidson and Quine while at the same time defending the sort of holism he attributes to the hermeneutic tradition – Heidegger's holism in particular. I do not think Dreyfus is being fair on Davidson, or Quine for that matter, but I do think that his critique, though ultimately flawed, is very informative, and for this reason it is worth giving the critique some time. In 'Holism and Hermeneutics' Dreyfus provides a defence of holism of the sort developed by the hermeneutic tradition – Heidegger particularly – and of Wittgenstein,[45] and he is critical of the holism developed by Quine and Davidson because they, Dreyfus thinks, treat all understanding as theoretical. It is not too hard to see why Quine and Davidson could be construed as holding a theoretical view of understanding. They think that beliefs are primary given that all other attitudes, and indeed the behaviour expressive of these attitudes, are ultimately expressive of beliefs. However, what Dreyfus does not consider in sufficient depth and precision are the repercussions of the indeterminacy thesis, which both Quine and Davidson advocate. And, to be fair to Dreyfus, one cannot blame him too much here given that neither Davidson nor Quine seem to go far enough in their study of the implications of the indeterminacy thesis for understanding the structure of the psychological (implications that would align them much closer to Heidegger than they would perhaps feel comfortable with).[46]

Dreyfus refers to the Quinean/Davidsonian stance as theoretical holism, and he contrasts this variety of holism with what he refers to as practical holism. Unlike a holistic system which is constituted by a network of logically related beliefs, attitudes and behaviour expressive of these beliefs, practical holism is a holism that involves having a system of skills. It is not a variety of belief holism insofar as, according to Dreyfus, beliefs do not underlie skills. Dreyfus's view that beliefs do not underlie skills is a peculiar one, since it is difficult to see how one could come to individuate a certain skill without eliciting beliefs that are expressed by the activities that flow from the skill. Let me quote Dreyfus in order to better understand what he is trying to get at:

> The practical holist's answer to such a theoretical account of the background is...[w]*hat makes up the background is not beliefs*, either explicit or implicit, but habits and customs, embodied in the sort of subtle skills which we exhibit in our everyday interaction with things and people.... Wittgenstein notes that '...it is our *acting*, which lies at the bottom of the language game.'... We just do what we have been trained to do. Moreover, as practices, they have a flexibility which is lost when they are converted into propositional knowledge.[47]

Leaving aside the apparent contradiction between the last two sentences of this passage, the remaining problem with Dreyfus's critique is that neither Quine nor Davidson hold the view that beliefs somehow form a background of discrete beliefs, and such a view seems to be at the heart of Dreyfus's critique even though he does discuss the indeterminacy thesis later on in the piece. Indeed, the very idea that the psychological is formed by discrete beliefs contradicts central aspects of the Davidsonian holistic project. The background is an indeterminate realm of beliefs and, although it is true that skills can be described as being expressive of beliefs – in propositional terms – it is not true that this amounts to creating a rigid account of mind that is unable to explain the plasticity of behaviour amongst other things. Skills are described in propositional terms, but the description itself is never exhaustive. There is always the looming prospect of reinterpretation – of reassessing one's original interpretation. And this prospect is due to the fact of indeterminacy. For any given interpretation of an individual's behaviour (my own or the behaviour of others) there will always be alternative and equally compelling interpretations. If one properly incorporates indeterminacy into one's account of what Dreyfus refers to as theoretical holism, then the motivation for establishing the dichotomy between theoretical and practical holism apparently collapses. One can claim both that the exercise of a skill is expressive of propositions and that there is no rigid structure of beliefs underlying behaviour. Instead, indeterminacy entails that the background of beliefs is more like thick – pregnant – fog.

Revealingly, Dreyfus deals with the Wittgensteinian theme that skills, and not rules move us to behave. What is relevant here is that Dreyfus seems to confound the issue of rule-following with Davidson's concern with the holism of propositional attitudes and rational behaviour. Dreyfus thinks that beliefs function as rules for Davidson, and this is not true. It must be noted that Davidson explicitly and famously argues that there are no psychological laws,[48] and in this regard he aligns himself with Wittgenstein (or at the very least with the Wittgenstein Dreyfus is bent on defending). Eliciting beliefs does help explain why we behave, and in this regard they do seem to have a causal role to play in the production of behaviour (when they operate in conjunction with pro-attitudes – intentions, desires and so forth), but the explanations in question are not lawlike ones.

Indeed, recall what I argued above regarding the virtues. Remember that a virtue is a skill for acting in accordance with the good, which means that Dreyfus would have to be committed to claiming that these skills, like any other skills, would not be explainable in terms of underlying beliefs. Now, what would a skill be if it were not a propositional attitude – an attitude that can be described in propositional terms? It seems that Dreyfus would be forced to claim that, with regard to ethics, there is nothing to be said and there are only things to be done. But, how can one make sense of one's actions, unless, of course, one can do this in plain English, Spanish, and so on?

One thing that is peculiar about Dreyfus's critique is that one is left to wonder about what one is doing when one elicits beliefs in order to explain skill-based action. If beliefs do not underlie, then what role is belief-talk playing in our explanations of behaviour? To repeat, it appears that Dreyfus would have to argue along the lines that behaviour cannot be explained, and that belief-talk, when it comes to explaining behaviour, is ultimately spurious.

As I have claimed above, the background of beliefs which is expressed by the manner in which we behave is more aptly described as a fog than as a rigid structure. And, indeed, the figure/background dynamic – the fluid structure of mind – is also aptly described as a horizonal structure, and is described in this way by the hermeneutic tradition. It is, for instance, the existence of the horizonal structure in question that allows for the open-ended nature of artistic interpretation.[49] One should not think that the open-ended nature of artistic interpretation is a problem that is exclusive to such practices – not at all. The open-ended nature relates to a basic feature of all interpretative processes, and that is that such processes have as their goal to fix meaning in face of the inherent instability of all meaning systems. The instability in question flows from the holistic nature of systems of meaning. The emergent nature of that which is picked out in the task of interpretation points to the fact that what emerges does so clearly out of a background of indeterminacy (like the point of focus in a field of vision).

Meaning emerges, but the question remains as to why it emerges in one way and not in another. To express this in slightly differently, why is it that we choose one interpretation over a plethora of other interpretations when we interpret someone or something (such as a work of art or an event)? We do not, after all, simply interpret; we approach the task of interpretation from some sort of perspective. If I were ignorant about art, and I accidentally walked into a gallery and observed that peculiar colourful rectangular objects were displayed throughout the premises I would not know for sure what to make of my casual encounter with the art world. I might view the spectators whose gazes are transfixed on to these colourful rectangles as very strange. Indeed, to appreciate art as art I must come from somewhere – that is, I must approach the artistic piece with certain (aesthetic) intentions in mind. It is only in this way that the artistic event will shine forth as artistic event. Another way of making this point – one that would more clearly relate what is being said here with what has been discussed above – is that one interprets in one way rather than another by subsuming a given object within a specific interpretative project.

Davidson's indeterminacy thesis, inherited from Quine, points to similar phenomena, except that this issue is not properly integrated with discussions regarding the issue of intentionality (or, indeed, with the related issue of project formation). Indeterminacy follows from holism, according to Quine and Davidson, because there is no point outside a given system of meaning from which to start assigning value to its component parts (or aspects, to be more precise); hence all one can expect to achieve when engaged in the task of interpretation is to maximize consistency, but if there is one maximally consistent set of interpretations, then there will be others also. So, there is no fact of the matter regarding which set of beliefs a given subject of interpretation holds. Total theories, one could say, are the best we could possibly hope for. However, hoping for total theories is already to hope for too much, since the task of interpretation always takes place in a piecemeal fashion, and always presupposes a background.

Instability, then, is an inherent aspect of an interpretative project. But the issue of instability is perhaps less interesting than the issues that emerge by answering the question 'What gets a particular interpretative *project* going?'. The answer is already contained in the question. An interpretation gets started by *projecting* ourselves forward into the fog of the indeterminate.

It follows that the task of self-interpretation is always and necessarily partial and permanently open to revision. Self-interpretation is a labour that never ceases, and it is a labour that epitomizes the sorts of lives we typically live – lives that are always en route to self-discovery. And this labour is an ongoing labour, as opposed to a path towards a complete resolution, precisely because of the horizonal structure – the figure/background structure – that typifies our mental lives. It follows that we can never expect that there will be a moment in which one's life will, to a greater or lesser degree, cease to be a mystery to us. Self-understanding can never amount to a complete unveiling of the self for no such condition is possible given the indeterminacy that pervades the psychological.

Finally, it follows that applications of the method of critical introspection will never reveal a fully determinate structure, for such a structure does not exist. Instead, what an application of the method does achieve is an understanding of aspects of our lives, or of the lives of persons generally, in accordance with specific interests and concerns. But, of course, in order to have any interests and concerns about one's life one must have a grasp of its overall structure insofar as one must have a grasp of the subject matter of one's ongoing concerns.

## Notes

1 Martha Nussbaum, 'Aristotle on Human Nature and the Foundation of Ethics', in J. E. Altham and R. Harrison (eds), *World, Mind, and Ethics: Essays on the Ethical Philosophy of Bernard Williams*, New York: Cambridge University Press, 1995, pp. 86–131. Nussbaum points out that Charles Taylor discusses related matters in, 'Interpretation and the Science of Man', *Philosophy and the Human Sciences: Philosophical Papers II*, Cambridge: Cambridge University Press, 1985, pp. 13–57; and idem, 'Explanation and Practical Reason', in M. C. Nussbaum and A. Sen (eds), *The Quality of Life*, Oxford: Clarendon Press, 1993, pp. 208–31.

2 Part of the refinement, of course, involves fitting the particularities of one's own existence into the general conception of personhood one possesses. Remember that to be a person is to be an individual, not just in the sense that one is a token of a given type, but also in the sense that one is unique with regard to one's qualities – with regard to one's character and the actions that flow from it.

3 Taylor characterizes this method as hermeneutic in his 'Interpretation and the Sciences of Man', *op.cit.*, n. 1. His discussion is based on works on the subject by Gadamer, Ricoeur and Habermas.

4 Issues relating to having a sense of world and the concepts of objectivity and truth will be discussed in the next chapter.

5 Indeed, these hermeneutic considerations apply as much to the natural sciences as they do to the human ones (I disagree with Taylor that one can make a hard and fast distinction between sciences which are hermeneutic and those which are not – the nature of all knowledge is hermeneutic). Einstein, like Newton, Galileo, and Copernicus were creatures of their times – creatures who broke the bounds of the conceptual horizons they were born into, and that is the source of their greatness. They moved us all from the vantage points of their unique historical situations.

6 Nussbaum, 'Aristotle on Human Nature', *op.cit.*, n. 1, p. 90.

7 *EN* 1966a 19–22.

8 In order to avoid confusion let me remind the reader that the kind that I am presently considering is the moral kind person rather than the natural kind human being. On the other hand, the kind membership Nussbaum is considering, following Aristotle, is species membership. This difference in no way affects what is central to the present discussion, so I will simply assume that Nussbaum is referring to persons generally, rather than simply human beings.

9 Nussbaum, 'Aristotle on Human Nature', *op.cit.*, n. 1, p. 91.

10 Ibid., p. 91. Nussbaum cites *EN* 1178a 2–3 in support of her claims.

11 I thank Paul Patton for pressing me to clarify how the method of critical introspection can also be applied at the level of the unique individualities that separate us out from all other members of our problematic species.

12 Nussbaum, 'Aristotle on Human Nature', *op.cit.*, n. 1, p. 99.

13 I thank Justin Tauber for pressing me to clarify these issues.

14 *EN* 1172b 28–32.

15 *EN* 1172b 9–26.

16 *Ph* 1252b 20–24 & *EN* 1180a 28–9.

17 Cyclopes being creatures 'who live in isolation from community ... "... and they have no

concern for one another" (*Od.* 9.112–15) ... they have no awareness that if you have received a man as a guest-friend you ought not to eat him' and Erinyes being '... strange hybrids of the human and the bestial (or bestial/divine), both in appearance and in action. Although in form they resemble human women, they also resemble dogs, sniffing after their prey with dripping eyes, thrilled by the scent of blood. Their deeper beastliness shows in their speech, rational yet solipsistic, impervious to community, obsessed with revenge': Nussbaum, 'Aristotle on Human Nature', *op.cit.*, n. 1, p. 97.

18    I might also add that these gods, unlike persons, have fixed predetermined characters and, as such, there is nothing they can do to change their characters. I think that it is clear that this aspect of divinity is not desirable by creatures like us, and the reasons why having a fixed character is not desirable will be explored below.

19    Nussbaum, 'Aristotle on Human Nature', *op.cit.*, n. 1, p. 96.

20    Nussbaum, 'Aristotle on Human Nature', *op.cit.*, n. 1, pp. 95–6.

21    *EN*, 1178a 3–8.

22    These claims might seem problematic on the grounds that perfection is kind-relative such that if a god is more perfect than a person, then it appears that a god is a person of sorts. But this claim is only partly true, since there is a case for interspecies comparison. Arguably, a cheetah is a more perfect runner than a person ever will be. A god, similarly, is more perfect in many respects than we are, but it is nevertheless a radically different creature.

23    *EN* 1178b 9-17.

24    Nussbaum, 'Aristotle on Human Nature', *op.cit.*, n. 1, p. 120. Whether or not Nussbaum's characterization of what gods are like is adequate or not is of little relevance to the present discussion (although, I might add, if I came across a creature of the sort Nussbaum describes here, I would most certainly be happy to refer to it as a god). What I am interested in showing here is that persons cannot live the lives of the sorts of creatures Nussbaum refers to as gods. I am most certainly not interested in engaging in a theological discussion at this point.

25    Sophocles describes his outcast character, Philoctetes, as he approaches his cave where Neoptolemus and a group of sailors are waiting for him:

> New counsels! For the man is not far from home, but he is in this place; he is not playing the music pipe, like a shepherd living in the wild, but because he stumbles, I think, under constraint he utters a far-sounding shout, or because he descries the ship in her inhospitable anchorage. His cry is fearsome! (*Sophocles: Antigone, The Women of Trachis, Philoctetes, Oedipus at Colonus*, ed. H. Lloyd-Jones, Cambridge, Massachusetts: Harvard University Press, 1994, p. 279)

It is important to note here that, despite the fact that Philoctetes was found in a state close to that of a brute, he is still described as fundamentally human.

26    I am not claiming that creatures of this sort would not be persons. Instead, I am claiming that they could not be living in accordance with the *eudaimon* ideal. They would have the *potentia* that define us as persons insofar as they have ensouled bodies that are relevantly similar to ours.

27    The view that we are essentially political creatures will be defended shortly. I shall argue that the *eudaimon* ideal – the fundamental defining ideal of the lives of persons – is only achievable by social creatures. So, given that gods, as conceived here, need not be social creatures, and if we assume that a *eudaimon* individual is necessarily a social creature, it follows that a *eudaimon* individual cannot be a god.

28    J. L. Borges, 'The Immortal', in D. Yates and J. Irby (eds), *Labyrinths: Selected Stories and Other Writings*, London: Penguin Books, 2000, pp. 135–49.

29    Ibid., p. 145.

30    If an immortal creature thought he or she was mortal he or she would carry on like the rest of us. Sooner or later, though, he or she would come to the realization that his or her

life was endless (or at least he or she would come to the realization that he or she might as well count his or her life as being endless) and he or she would end up living his or her life in accordance with this understanding.

31  Malpas argues along these lines. In his words:

> ... for a life without end there need be no limit on the orderings [the organization of the aspects that constitute a life] that are possible within that life and no sense in which that life need depend on any finite number of choices. Given an endless span of time, the possibilities that a particular life might encompass are themselves endless.... It is precisely because we cannot play through an endless series of choices, an infinite series of possibilities, that the choices we do make become so important to us: those choices establish the character and identity of our lives; they allow certain things to show up as valuable; they establish a certain *ordering of and orientation within the world* [my italics]. It is perhaps for this reason that the idea of immortality can seem to entail a loss of meaningfulness, even a form of boredom. (J. Malpas, 'Death and the Unity of a Life', in J. Malpas and R. Solomon (eds), *Death and Philosophy*, London: Routledge, 1998, p. 131).

32  Even talk of identity as being detached from the subject that has that identity has a paradoxical ring, since one's identity is what one is, as opposed to something one could choose to let go of (and continue to be whom one is). For this reason, I think it is more precise to speak of a purported identity rather than an identity proper in the case under scrutiny.

33  Bernard Williams, in his 'The Makropulos Case: Reflections on the Tedium of Immortality', *Problems of Self*, London: Cambridge University Press, 1973, pp. 82–100, shows us just how bleak and tedious an immortal life would be.

34  An immortal living in a static environment cannot afford to engage in transformative projects because projects of this sort would sooner or later cause him or her to lose his or her sense of identity and purpose given that he or she has all the time in the world. But then, of course, it is hard to see how an immortal subject living in a static environment could have anything like something we would liken to a purposive life. Merely having the purpose of wanting to artificially preserve his or her 'theatrical' identity does not seem to be good enough for an immortal to count as having a purposive life. A desperate need is not necessarily a need that bestows purpose.

35  J. Malpas, *Donald Davidson and the Mirror of Meaning: Holism, Truth, Interpretation*, Cambridge: Cambridge University Press, 1992, pp. 115–44.

36  Ibid., p. 135.

37  J. Malpas and G. Wickham, 'Governance and the World: From Joe Dimaggio to Michael Foucault', *The VTS Review: Cultural Studies and New Writing*, 3 (2), November 1997, pp. 91–108; and idem, 'Governance and Failure: On the Limits of Sociology', *Journal of Sociology*, 31 (3), November 1995, pp. 37–50.

38  There is a sense in which all projects are projects of governance insofar as projects have as their purpose to create a certain order – a certain organization of objects and subjects in relation to a given purpose. Malpas and Wickham argue along these lines.

39  I thank Justin Oakley for pointing this counterargument out to me.

40  Nussbaum, 'Aristotle on Human Nature', *op.cit.*, n. 1, p. 98.

41  For example, I look at myself and see that, in many ways, I am deficient, and I do not like these deficiencies. I compare my finite life with the way I conceive of divine lives and reach the conclusion that I would like to be a god.

42  Nussbaum, 'Aristotle on Human Nature', *op.cit.*, n. 1, p. 102. See also *EN* 1145b 1–8, and Martha Nussbaum, *Fragility of Goodness: Luck and Ethics in Greek Tragedy and Philosophy*, Cambridge: Cambridge University Press, 1994, pp. 240–63.

43  Nussbaum, 'Aristotle on Human Nature', *op.cit.*, n. 1, p. 100.

44  Ibid., p. 101.
45  H. Dreyfus, 'Holism and Hermeneutics', *Review of Metaphysics*, **34**, September 1980, pp. 3–23.
46  Indeed, this is the sort of move that Malpas makes in his *Donald Davidson and the Mirror of Meaning*, Cambridge: Cambridge University Press, 1992.
47  Dreyfus, 'Holism and Hermeneutics', *op.cit.*, n. 45, p. 8.
48  Davidson, 'Psychology as Philosophy', *Essays on Actions and Events*, Oxford: Clarendon Press, 1980, pp. 229–44.
49  See Hans-George Gadamer's, 'Composition and Interpretation', *The Relevance of the Beautiful and Other Essays*, Cambridge: Cambridge University Press, 1986, pp. 66–73.

# Chapter 6

# Personhood and Community

Philosophy begins in the only place it can, here, in the midst of things, with thinkers who are already accomplished at thinking and whose thinking takes time and the world for granted. Without our abilities to move around objects and to see, both of us, the same physical object from different perspectives, to move our tongues and mouths and to make sounds, to remember the past in such simple acts as recognizing this as the same object we saw a moment ago, to enter into countless forms of communal life, there could be no beginning to those acts of communication that ... are basic both to interpretation and to thought. Knowledge ... is held in place by the very contingencies it takes for granted, as are one's mind and one's existence as a self. Neglect these contingencies and we lose a grip on the very idea of meaning.[1]

## Preliminary Remarks

Although the present discussion starts out with an exposition of Donald Davidson's argument for the sociality of thought, its aims are somewhat different from Davidson's in that they are ethical in nature. Davidson's argument establishes that if we did not communicate with others, our lives would not be the lives of rational or thinking creatures. In establishing this, Davidson establishes the bare minimum conditions for rationality, providing a minimalist – Spartan – theory of rationality. I will argue that there are further conditions for rationality, not supplied by Davidson's minimal set-up, necessary for the instantiation of Davidson's minimal conditions. The sort of conditions I have in mind are those that foster expression of difference – that is, conditions that foster an understanding that coming to terms with the world, including coming to terms with those who share the world with us, is ideally a matter of creating the conditions for others to strive to come to terms with the world in ways that are not under our control. The space within which rational creatures can thrive, one could say, must be radically non-hegemonic.

Davidson's argument shows us that the basic set-up required for being rational involves being able to communicate with other thinking creatures about a world that each and every rational creature knowingly shares with all other such creatures. Central to his argument is the idea that we must have a sense that subjects in communication grasp the world from unique vantage points. But, understandably, Davidson's argument goes only so far as to give good reasons for believing that at least two communicators are required for there to be any rational creatures at all, since all he sets out to establish are the bare minimal conditions for rationality. By contrast, I further establish the plausibility of the thesis that a substantially larger community of communicators is required for developing most fully as rational creatures, and that this community must be one that acknowledges difference and fosters its expression. It is only within such a pluralistic community that the minimal set-up established by Davidson can most fully be implemented.

A community such as the one described in Orwell's *Nineteen Eighty-Four* – a community in which all subjective perspectives can at best only be grasped in relation to one dominant master perspective – would not be one in which the basic conditions for rationality, determined by Davidson, could be most fully implemented. One of the conditions that would be found wanting is a proper understanding of the concept of objectivity. Put briefly, the reason why I think a community that could broadly be characterized as pluralistic is required is that understanding the concept of a common world that forms the stage upon which we communicate with others – a world that exists quite independently of interpreting subjects – is to grasp the world as a realm that can never in principle be fully understood. I will argue that living in a community that fosters the expression of difference is a condition for fully understanding this idea, since it is only within such communities that one can fully come to terms with the idea that there is no limit to the possible vantage points from which the world could be grasped. Orwell's dystopia is, by contrast, a place in which the world is grasped vaporously – as if it were a bad dream. Winston Smith's sense of world is subject to the whims of Big Brother and he is only half-capable of making a distinction between what the party wants him to believe and what is actually the case. One could think of his life as one that is being played out within the mind of another, as opposed to being played out in the world. What this means in effect, we shall see, is that Orwell's dystopia is one in which individuals are unable to develop fully as rational creatures – that is, as creatures who are able to communicate about a world known to each to be largely known by the other.

## The Triangle

The argument I will now put forward provides us with good reasons for believing that only social creatures are rational. The minimal set-up required for rational agency has a triangular structure – that is, it consists of two agents communicating about a common world known by each to be largely known by the other.[2] Once this minimal set-up is established, we will be able to determine further conditions that are required for the minimal triangular set-up to be most properly instantiated.

Let me re-emphasize at the outset that what Davidson establishes are the bare minimum conditions for rationality, such that if these conditions were not met by a given creature, then such a creature would not count as being rational. It is because the conditions set out by Davidson are the bare minimal ones, only that the issue of whether or not rationality comes in degrees does not arise for him. I argue, by contrast, that rationality does indeed come in degrees once one progresses beyond the bare minimum. The triangular structure set out by Davidson must be understood as being immersed in an ocean of further conditions for rationality, that, though not minimal, impinge on the fundamental triangular structure. And, indeed, these further conditions are conditions for rationality precisely insofar as they impinge on the minimal conditions.

In 'Rational Animals'[3] Davidson sets out to determine some of the central conditions for rationality and, in doing so, he determines basic conditions that would have to obtain for non-human animals to count as rational. However, his focus on non-human animals is incidental.[4] His primary interest is in establishing the most basic conditions for rationality and, in establishing this, he shows that one can only be a thinking creature if one is able to communicate successfully with others. Moreover, in order to perform the interpretative feat of understanding someone else, the overall subject matter of our meaningful exchanges must be shared. The reason why the subject matter must be shared is that, in order to understand each other, we must know what we are talking about (if, of course, the meaningful exchange in question is verbal); we must also know that those we are engaged with are talking about much the same, and we must know that they know this. Not knowingly sharing a grasp of the subject matters of our engagements amounts to a failure in communication. By contrast, knowing the subject matters amounts to having a grasp of the objects and events that preoccupy us. The sum total of the objects and events we deal with on a day-to-day basis constitutes the world, or, more precisely, the world of phenomena. These last qualifications are important, since what is shared is not the world as described by theoretical physics or some other high-powered science, given that very few of us are scientists. What we share is day-to-day reality; in other words, what we share is the reality that forms the stage upon which all other meaningful exchanges are performed – exchanges such as those performed by scientists and storytellers.

Being rational and having beliefs are closely related insofar as determining the conditions for belief will yield a theory of rationality. This claim is relatively uncontroversial, since rational creatures are thinking ones and thinking creatures are ones who have beliefs. So, what are the conditions for belief? First, Davidson argues, to have a single belief presupposes having further beliefs such that being warranted in attributing one single belief to a given creature would also necessarily involve attributing a whole range of beliefs to that creature. Specific beliefs, Davidson argues, are constituted by the particular logical niche they occupy within an attitudinal system (a system of propositional attitudes and rational behaviour) such that one could not have a specific belief without at the same time having a whole range of beliefs – beliefs which constitute each other. For this reason, it is precise to claim that, in order to have one single belief one must also have an entire world of beliefs; or more generally, having a single belief presupposes having an entire world of beliefs, and attitudes and behaviour expressive of beliefs. Malpas illustrates this basic thesis:

> If I decide to drive from Perth to Geraldton tomorrow, one might expect that this decision will be reflected not only in my behaviour tomorrow, but that it will also presuppose certain beliefs and desires which I have now – maybe I wish to go to Geraldton to visit friends. This, of course, presupposes my desire to see those friends, and also presupposes that I have some expectations of actually being able to see them in Geraldton. That I have decided to drive there presupposes that I have access to a vehicle of some sort – a vehicle, moreover, I believe will get me there. Many other attitudes may also be implicated – not just beliefs, but desires and all the rest. That attitudes do exhibit this sort of interconnectedness is a simple fact about our mental lives.[5]

Davidson's account of belief stems from Quine's famous refutation of (reductive) verificationism. However, it must be pointed out that Quine and Davidson's concerns differ in key respects. Quine's focus is on translation and on developing a naturalized epistemology for the natural sciences and Davidson's focus is on interpretation, and on a theory of mind, meaning and belief. Quine and Davidson also seem to differ on the role played by stimulus in epistemology. That said, establishing the differences that exist between Quine and Davidson is not directly relevant to our present concerns and dealing with them would take us off-track.[6] The basic idea behind the refutation advocated by both Quine and Davidson is that events allow for innumerable descriptions, and, because of this, establishing a correlation between an utterance (or segment of non-verbal behaviour) and an event will by itself never yield sufficient evidence for assigning content to a given speaker's utterances or non-verbal behaviour. There are, to make use of a well-rehearsed Quinean example, innumerable ways of describing events that fit descriptions such as 'a rabbit is scurrying by'. We will, however, have sufficient evidence for making an informed guess of what a speaker means if we correlate a given utterance with an event *under a certain description*. But then we must be in a position to attribute a system of logically related beliefs to a given subject in order to be warranted in assigning one single belief to that subject, since descriptions are expressive of a system of beliefs. Moreover, the pattern of logically related beliefs attributed to the subject of interpretation must, for the most part, be the pattern held by the interpreter, since interpretation involves correlating one's beliefs with those of others.

We might wonder what a theory of interpretation has to do with a theory about belief content. But this question dissipates once we realize that a theory of interpretation involves a theory about the constraints on belief – a theory about what must be held about belief in order to make sense of others. Note carefully what is being done here. Davidson, primarily, is showing us what must be held about other minds in order to be able to make sense of rational behaviour. This is the fundamental reason why a theory of interpretation implies a theory of mind. One creates a model of the mind in the process of working out what is involved in the process of interpretation.

Indeed, because the relationship between theory of interpretation and theory of mind is an intimate one, I find it difficult to understand how anyone could suggest that issues of interpretation and mind should be kept apart. Fodor and LePore make such a suggestion when they establish the distinction between confirmation holism and semantic holism.[7] They believe that holists – Quine and Davidson in particular – make the illicit move of inferring that because holism applies at the level of interpretation or translation, then it must apply also at the semantic level. Fodor and LePore are not quite grasping what we do when we engage in the task of making sense of others. Indeed, what would a theory of interpretation be if it did not imply a model of the mind? If one were not somehow determining the structure of mind when engaged in the process of interpreting others, one would be left without criteria for distinguishing adequate from inadequate interpretations, since to interpret is to interpret what someone *means* – what he or she has in mind, so to speak.

Given that beliefs form clusters of logically related beliefs, we know that if we can make sense of someone, then we must share most mundane beliefs. This should not be taken to entail that, if we are thinking creatures, then we must be able to understand each other. It is quite possible for someone to have a system of beliefs in which not one belief of theirs is a belief that we could have. It is reasonable to suppose that there are incommensurable conceptual conglomerates. We shall see that, on final analysis, such incommensurability could not obtain: if someone has beliefs, then we can understand them. However, we have not as yet established whether or not a thinking creature must be able to communicate successfully with others. Once it has been shown that communication is indeed necessary, we will have established that, in order to have beliefs, one must be aware that others also have them and one must know that those beliefs are typically about a shared world largely known by both of us in advance of any specific communicative engagement.

Without communication, Davidson thinks, thought would be impossible, and by this he means that, if a given creature is a thinking one, we must, with patience and effort, be able to understand it. We will start this part of Davidson's argument by establishing the holistic interrelationship that exists between the truth/falsity pair and belief, and then we will move on to the final stage of the argument where he establishes that communicating successfully is necessary for grasping the truth/falsity pair and hence for having beliefs in the first place.

Davidson argues that in order to have beliefs – in order to hold that something is the case – one must be able to grasp the distinction between truth and falsity, and this is simply because, by definition, to have a belief is to hold true. To grasp the distinction between truth and falsity amounts to having a grasp of the concept of belief; it amounts to knowing that we have beliefs. There is, after all, a fundamental distinction to be drawn between a proposition and a belief. A proposition is either true or false, but it does not involve being committed to its truth. On the other hand, to have a belief is to be committed to its truth. This amounts to saying that to have a belief is to have an attitude towards truth, and such an attitude can only be had if we know what a belief is. Furthermore, knowing that our beliefs may be either true or false just is to know the truth-conditions for belief – knowing what would make a belief true or false. Let me clarify this last claim with Davidson's favoured Tarskian example: to know what the sentence 'snow is white' means is to know what would have to obtain for this sentence to be true – namely, the whiteness of snow. And to know the truth-conditions, moreover, involves possessing the concept of objective truth – of what must obtain, independently of what we happen to believe, in order for a given belief to hold to be true. What Davidson is in fact doing here is establishing a correlation between truth and meaning. This is a fairly basic point, and I find it difficult to understand why it has been such a controversial one, given the straightforward fact that the concept of belief entails the concept of truth, and of truth, I might add, in the sense of what must obtain independently of what we happen to believe. To recapitulate, one can only count as having beliefs if we knows what our beliefs are about and we only know this if we know what must obtain in order for our beliefs to be either true or false. The concept of truth, we could say, implies the concept of objectivity. Hence, the concept of belief entails the concept of objectivity.

After showing that one must be aware that one has beliefs, Davidson moves on to the final stage of his argument where he shows that communication is a necessary requirement for possessing the concept of belief, and hence for having beliefs in the first place. Would one, for instance, be capable of having the belief that the moon is rising if one was unable to communicate with others? Suppose, for the sake of argument, that one could possess such a belief without forming part of a community of communicators (a community of at least two). Obviously, I can quite easily have the belief that the moon is rising even if no one else is around at the moment of the lunar event. Moreover, it seems that the obvious fact that individuals do not need others to have beliefs about particular objects or events counts as evidence against the view that we must form part of a community of communicators in order to be able to determine the content of our beliefs. After all, it seems that if we are sometimes able to have beliefs about objects and events without the assistance of others, then, by extrapolation, we could argue that it is perfectly possible for an individual who has never had contact with anyone else – a radical loner – to, in fact, have beliefs.[8]

Comments of this last sort miss the mark. The point is that we can have beliefs about this lunar event only if we also recognize that other thinking creatures could also grasp the same objects. If we were unable to recognize the intersubjective grasp of a common world, we would be unable to know, as we shall soon find out, whether the beliefs we have are about events in the world, or indeed, if our beliefs have no such referent. And indeed, to admit that we are not able to find out what our beliefs are about is just to admit that our beliefs have no content, since for a belief to have content it must be about something *specific*. We must know the relevant truth-conditions, and knowing this involves knowing the objects of belief. On final analysis, admitting that one does not know what our beliefs are about amounts to admitting that we have no beliefs, which is absurd.

So why would a radical loner not be able to determine the content of his or her beliefs? The reason is that he or she would be unable to determine whether his or her beliefs are about mental representations, sensory promptings, objects in external reality or, indeed, about any point between the subject and an external object. In Davidson's words:

> ... as psychologists have noticed, there is a problem about stimulus. In the case of the dog, why say that the stimulus is the ringing of the bell? Why couldn't it be the vibration of the air close to the ears of the dog – or even the stimulation of the nerve endings? ... Why not say the same about the child: that its responses are not to tables but to patterns of stimulation at its surfaces ...[9]

Davidson's point is that there would be no fact of the matter regarding what the objects (or causes) of a given creatures impressions of external reality would be if one were merely to consider a creature on its own. What we need to consider is (at least) two creatures in communication about a common object in order to locate a common cause. These considerations also apply at the first-person level. What my impressions correspond to could not be determined on my own.

Without a sense that there is a common world to which our beliefs largely relate – a world that forms a stage upon which our communicative engagement take place – we would be unable to tell what the subject matters of our most basic grasp of reality are. Being unable to tell amounts to not knowing what our beliefs are about. But if we did not know this, on final analysis, we could not have beliefs in the first place, since to have beliefs we must know their truth-conditions. It is only if we know that others could entertain beliefs about the same subject matters as we do that we can determine the subject matters of our beliefs. Note here that knowing that others have beliefs like us involves being able to communicate with others. That is the only way of telling.

Basically, we cannot grasp the concept of objective truth unless we also grasp the concept of intersubjective, shared, truth. And, we can only grasp the idea of intersubjective truth if we are able to communicate with others about a world that is common. If I was alone in a radical sense – that is, if I had no sense that there are other subjects sharing a common world –

then all I could do when attempting to understand something is to maximize the consistency of my current impressions (perceptions and beliefs). I would have no sense, for instance, that someone could actually disagree with me about something known to both of us in advance of our engagements. It is this fundamental moment of communication that allows us to establish a separation between the world as perceived, or the world as grasped, and the world as such. Without a sense that others could grasp the world from alternative vantage points we could not develop a sense of what our beliefs are about, for we would have no grounds for determining whether or not what we grasp corresponds to a realm that exists beyond the confines of our minds. We would be unable to tell whether our impressions of reality correspond to a realm beyond mind or whether perhaps there was an evil demon working behind the veils of consciousness deceiving us about the nature of the world. And, unlike the claims of methodological solipsists, knowing that there is a world out there that forms the stage for all our meaningful exchanges matters a great deal given that, as previously discussed, there is an intimate relationship between belief and truth.

Note that we often disagree with ourselves, and this could be construed as evidence against the view that we need others in order to have a proper sense of world. I could, for instance, initially think that a twig dipped in water is bent only then to realize that it merely looked bent or, alternatively, I could confuse a branch with a snake and then correct my beliefs without anyone else having to point out that I am confused. By correcting myself, it could be argued, I am establishing a distinction between what appears to be the case and what actually is the case, thus grasping the distinction between what is believed and what is the case. The problem with this possible objection has already been addressed, albeit implicitly. All we can do on our own is organize our impressions (perceptions and beliefs), and such efforts do not yield the sort of evidence required for having an unambiguous sense of world. We need unambiguously to possess the idea that the world is a stage upon which we can interact, and we can only possess this idea if there actually are interacting others (at least two of us).

To be sure, streams of different impressions of determinate objects and their surroundings pass through our fields of consciousness, and without effort we construct four-dimensional representations of the objects and the spaces they inhabit. Our perceptual capacities, so to speak, do the work for us. However, the task of organizing impressions is carried out between our different capacities. If we were radical loners, if we had no sense that there were others, the question would be left open with regard to what these organized impressions correspond to. However, the question cannot be left open. Or, to be more precise, it can in specific instances, but not on the whole.

This does not mean that I have to be in communication with someone about a shared subject matter every time I entertain beliefs about that subject matter; rather, the idea is that I can only grasp the concept of objective truth in conjunction with the concept of intersubjective – shared – truth. And, I might add that the concept of intersubjective truth just is one of the central concepts that are implicated in my drive to speak and listen to others. Insofar as I even bother to speak to you, I presume that we share a common world. Moreover, to repeat, I can only have a sense of a shared world if I have a sense that I can and do communicate with others. 'The solipsist's world', Davidson elegantly claims, 'can be any size; which is to say, from the solipsist's point of view it has no size, it is not a world.'[10] Davidson explains this as follows:

> It takes two points of view to give a location to the cause of thought, and thus to define its content. We may think of it as a form of triangulation: each of two people is reacting differently to sensory stimuli streaming in from a certain direction. If we project the incoming lines outward, their intersection is the common cause. If the two people now note each other's reactions (in the case of language, verbal reactions), each can correlate these observed reactions with his or her stimuli from the world. The common cause can now determine the contents of an utterance and a thought. The triangle which gives content to thought and speech is complete. But it takes two to triangulate. Two, or, of course, more.[11]

The common cause is the object of belief. The 'triangle' is complete, and we now have good reasons for thinking that it is only because we are able to communicate with others that we are able to determine what our beliefs are about. In other words, it is only because we are able to communicate with others that we can locate the common cause of our thoughts – the subject matter. We may conclude that it is only insofar as we share the world with others that we are thinking creatures.

Davidson shows us that knowledge of self, of others and of world are dependent on one another. Note his strategy: he has developed an account of the constitutive relationships between basic concepts. If we have belief, then we have the concept of belief. If we have the concept of belief, then, on the whole and in the most basic cases, we must know the subject matters of our beliefs. And, if we know the subject matters, then we must know that, on the whole and in the most basic cases, we share the subject matters with others. We must have a sense that the world is the stage upon which and about which we communicate with others. In order to know this we must have a sense that we actually are able to communicate with others, and we can only have this sense by actually communicating. We do have beliefs, hence we also know all things that are implicated in the very possibility of having them.

Knowledge of self – that is, knowledge that one has beliefs – knowledge of others, and knowledge of world are intertwined. One of these basic modes of knowing cannot be had without the other two. A corollary to these claims is that an imperfect manifestation of any of these three modes of knowledge implies an imperfect manifestation of the other two. This is an important implication for it will help us understand why there is a strong case for extending Davidson's argument in order to give us a richer picture of the conditions for rationality.

## Some Ethical Implications of the Davidsonian Stance

Davidson's argument does not merely show us that if we were not social creatures our lives would be very different from the ones we currently live. On the contrary, it shows us something more basic – namely, that we can only be rational in the company of at least one other subject – and thus provides us also with a theory of rationality. However, Davidson's argument gives us no clues regarding the nature of the specific sorts of communicative engagement required of us, nor is it intended to do so. One could say, paraphrasing Cherniak, that it offers the minimal conditions for minimal rationality.[12] This said, I think Davidson's argument by itself has important ethical implications in that it gives us excellent reasons for thinking that an ethic that did not honour the basic principle that we are always and necessarily creatures living amongst others must be radically flawed. This argument can fruitfully be complemented with further considerations regarding our communal nature and the ethic implicit in such a condition. As stated earlier, Davidson provides the very basic conditions for rationality, and I will now specify further conditions that are required for Davidson's basic set-up to be most properly instantiated.

*Prima facie*, there seems to be no reason why a world in which there were only two communicators could not exist. But, multiple perspectives held by persons in dialogue clearly enrich the understandings of the individuals in dialogue, including their understanding of the ethical dimensions of the world. This last claim follows quite naturally from the fact that having to relate to a large variety of different persons and groups of persons places moral demands on us that would not exist were we to live in a world that was radically underpopulated by communicators.[13] Generally it is clear that, to a large extent, we learn by establishing contrasts, by having to confront and compare our particular perspectives on things with a variety of alternative perspectives – perspectives, moreover, that are radically different from those we could possibly adopt given the specific (finite) individuals that we are. The truth of this last claim does not depend on Davidson's argument, but rather points to the fact that Davidson's minimal set-up can only properly be instantiated, as opposed to minimally instantiated, in the right sort of social environment.

Let us focus more sharply on the issue of multiple perspectives. Hannah Arendt claims that '[t]he end of the common world has come when it is seen only under one aspect and is permitted to present itself in only one perspective'.[14] Her reasons for making this claim are similar to Davidson's in important respects. Arendt argues that:

... though the common world is the common meeting ground of all, those who are present have different locations in it, and the location of one can no more coincide with the location of another than the location of two objects. Being seen and being heard by others derive their significance from the fact that everybody sees and hears from a different position.... Only where things can be seen by many in a variety of aspects without changing their identity, so that those who are gathered around them know they see sameness in utter diversity, can worldly reality truly and reliably appear.

Under the conditions of a common world, reality is not guaranteed primarily by the 'common nature' of all men who constitute it, but rather by the fact that, differences of position and the resulting variety of perspectives notwithstanding, everybody is always concerned with the same object.[15]

Davidson, if you like, provides the foundations for rationality and Arendt could be understood as having a largely Davidsonian starting point insofar as she acknowledges the importance of properly grasping worldly reality, and that this can be done only if one is able to communicate with others. She extends the Davidsonian stance by arguing that what is required for having a proper grasp of worldly reality is a sense that others grasp the world from radically different vantage points. Arendt thinks that one must view the world as a common meeting ground for an 'utter diversity' of possible perspectives or interpreations. However, it must be noted that the criterion I am applying for determining the importance of a pluralism of the sort Arendt advocates is whether or not it provides the conditions for Davidson's minimal set-up to be most properly instantiated. Pluralism, of the variety presently being discussed, is what we should be aiming at insofar as it is only within such conditions that we can most fully be the sorts of creatures who we are – namely, rational ones. At this point, ethics, ontology and epistemology converge.

Having a well-developed sense of world involves having an unambiguous sense that the perspectives from which the world could be grasped are inexhaustible given that, if we conceived of the world merely as a place that can be grasped from multiple yet finite perspectives, then we would not be able unambiguously to differentiate objective truth from subjective or intersubjective truth. Indeed, the idea itself of a perspective involves the idea that it is one perspective of innumerable alternative ones. To take a relatively straightforward example, grasping an object of perception involves the idea that one could observe that object from innumerable points of view. Grasping the idea that there is no end to the possible points of view from which an object could be observed is a necessary condition for grasping the distinction between objects as such and our perceptions of them. To admit that I could grasp the world from innumerable points of view is to admit that what I perceive can never be perceived in its entirety, for I could not in principle have infinite representations in my mind. One must have as sense that an object can always be grasped from a new vantage point. That said, notwithstanding the fact that a necessary condition for grasping the objective as such involves having a sense that the perspectives one could take on objects are inexhaustible, this is not a sufficient condition for properly grasping the objective as such, since the question is left open as to whether objects are genuinely external, or if indeed they are mere idealizations, or something of this sort. Having a sense that perspectives are inexhaustible is a necessary, though not a sufficient, condition for grasping the idea that what we perceive unambiguously corresponds to a realm beyond mind.

Malpas notes that, in *The View from Nowhere*, Nagel characterizes our development of the idea of the objective as a process of gradual detachment from our perspectival grasp of reality – from our subjective grasp.[16] He argues that Nagel cannot be right inasmuch as the very idea of a perspective on something already presupposes a realm beyond the 'merely' perspectival, which is to say that the idea of objectivity cannot be derived from the idea that our grasp of reality is perspectival. Instead, the idea of a perspective relies on, although it is not derivable from, the idea of a reality beyond perspective – a reality we grasp from where, in the world, we stand. Indeed, one could say that the very idea of being a subject, and hence of having a subjective perspective, involves the idea of being a subject in the world. The ideas of subjectivity and objectivity depend on one another for their existence and neither is derivable from the other.

But, we already know that more is required for grasping the ideas of objectivity and subjectivity. We must also have a sense that others share the world with us. By ourselves we cannot establish the subjective/objective distinction, since the very idea of having a perspective entails the idea that others are able to grasp the same objects that we do from different locations. Subjectivity, we already know, entails intersubjectivity. The fact that you and I occupy different locations, and hence disagree to some extent, is what allows us to have a sense that there is something that is common about which no perfect agreement can be had. Note that similar considerations to those discussed above regarding the individual grasp of the concept of a perspective apply also at the intersubjective level. The concept of grasping worldly reality from a specific vantage point rests on being aware that there is no end to the possible vantage points from which others could grasp worldly reality. One must have a sense that there is no end to the possible perspectives others can take on the world, and such a sense can only properly be had where individuals are in fact interacting with one another in ways that always present the prospect of a challenge to what could be characterized as one's existential *status quo*. One could say that the ongoing possibility of violence exerted on our present outlooks, and violence exerted from a plurality of directions, allows us to have a sense that our grasp of the world is perspectival, as opposed to a sense that blurs the distinction between the world as such and the world as grasped.

The issues being treated here will become especially clear in the next section when I deal with Orwell's conception of a world in which one overarching perspective rules – the perspective of Big Brother. There we will see in what sense talk about having a partial grasp, as opposed to a full grasp, of the subjective/objective distinction, or of the intersubjective/objective distinction, or to put it slightly differently, of the distinction between what is believed and what exists independently of what is believed, creates a dream-like sense of reality. Having a partial grasp of reality undermines the possibility of being most fully rational, since having such a sense of reality would mean that one only half-knows what one's beliefs are about. Truth, one could say, would be perceived as shifting and moving quite randomly.

We most fully come to terms with the world when we properly grasp it as an inexhaustible realm – a realm that exceeds all possible interpretations or perspectives. Furthermore, we can only experience the world as inexhaustible if we are able to recognize our own finiteness – that is, if we are able to grasp the idea that we are quite incapable of grasping all that the world has to offer, and we can only properly grasp this idea in the company of multiple others who are permanently challenging our present outlooks. Our finiteness, so to speak, must be imbued with a sense of the inexhaustible.

## Orwell's Monolithic Hell

Let us conceive of a scenario in which agents, for one reason or another, grasped the world from one overarching perspective – a world in which the irreducible particularities of each individual perspective are rendered negligible insofar as they are encompassed by one overarching governing world-view. Such scenarios have existed and do exist, albeit imperfectly, in the form of totalitarianisms and fundamentalisms of all sorts (including ones that are not always described in these terms). If, rather than allowing for the play of difference, one tries to coerce people into holding one fundamental account of reality, then one is effectively promoting a community of solipsists of sorts – of individuals incapable, to some degree, of differentiating their understanding of what is *believed* to be the case from their understanding of what *is* the case. The world, so to speak, must be set free from our interpretative noose.[17]

Orwell's *Nineteen Eighty-Four* brilliantly describes how an extreme regime of terror, in which only one overarching master discourse ruled, allows for the victims only a vaporous, nightmarish, unreal sense of reality. The reality of Orwell's hero, Winston Smith, is one in which there is no clear demarcation between the concepts of fact and fiction, which is just to say that he has almost lost the concept of objective truth. Even his rebellion against Big Brother has a certain surreality in light of the nebulousness of his past (and hence of his present, which is largely understood in light of his past) and the lack of differentiation between individuals due to the fact that they are all forced to conform in action and belief, and also due to the solitary nature of life in Oceania. The solitude has a paradoxical ring to it, since there is almost no private realm in Orwell's dystopian nightmare. The sense of self is nebulous. One is alone, but one is, paradoxically, hardly oneself, since there is barely a sense of self to be had, and this partly is due to the fact that one's sense of the past, both private and public, never ceases to mutate under the pen of those who work in the Ministry of Truth. What Big Brother wants members of Oceania to believe is what is believed, and hence there is almost no sense that what Big Brother holds can be called into question. Moreover, there is hardly a sense that the beliefs one might hold about oneself are either true or false. Their truth-value seems to shift quite randomly and this means that the concept itself of truth can only be had vaporously. That this is the case is not surprising given that truth, so to speak, emanates from a single authority. One becomes like a fiction to oneself, or more poignantly, one becomes like a fiction of Big Brother. And, if one is unable to establish a clear demarcation between oneself as fact and oneself as fiction, then it is hard to see how one could have a clear sense of world. If one perceives of oneself as quasi-fictional, then one perceives the world as quasi-fictional. Individuals who perceived themselves as quasi-fictional would walk in a haze never knowing for sure whether or not they will dissolve or mutate, or whether the ground under their feet will, quite unexpectedly, give way to the emptiness of space, or some other incongruous impression. Under conditions of the sort being described here our grasp of what our beliefs are about would start to crumble. Reality, in Orwell's hell, is perceived as shifting and moving; as being fundamentally amorphous and incapable of being grasped properly.

But we should not forget that Orwell's dystopia is one for rational creatures like ourselves and hence most of the most basic beliefs held by those who populate Oceania – the beliefs about the most basic features of everyday reality – must be true. Davidson's minimal set-up is still in place, albeit imperfectly. Here is a passage that clearly illustrates the sort of life Winston has:

> It was as though some huge force were pressing down upon you – something that penetrated inside your skull, battering against your brain, frightening you out of your beliefs, persuading you, almost, to deny the evidence of your senses. In the end the Party would announce that two and two made five, and you would have to believe it. It was inevitable that they should make that claim sooner or later: the logic of their position demanded it. Not merely the validity of experience, but the very existence of external reality was tacitly denied by their philosophy. The heresy of heresies was common sense. And what was terrifying was not that they would kill you for thinking otherwise, but that they might be right. For, after all, how do we know that two and two make four? Or that the force of gravity works? Or that the past is unchangeable? If both the past and the external world only exist in the mind, and if the mind itself is controllable – what then?[18]

Winston's sense of reality, and all that hangs on it (including his capacity to think), is bursting at the seams. Indeed, it seems as if Winston has no clear notion of his own reality, or of reality as such. He only has what is minimally required for being able to differentiate the concept that something is believed to be the case from the concept that something actually is the case. His struggle can be seen as a desperate effort to preserve this distinction against all odds. In the end he fails and the reader is left in no doubt that all members of Oceania will end up grasping the world through the eyes of Big Brother, which is almost not to grasp the world at all.

While it is true that Big Brother is a pathological liar, this is not the only reason why Winston has only a faint grasp of reality. It is primarily faint because he can only vaguely differentiate Big Brother's claims to truth from reality itself, including his own reality, in a way that would allow him unambiguously to grasp the idea that Big Brother could get things wrong at times. This lack of clarity is largely due to the fact that, in Oceania, only one perspective prevails; all other sub-perspectives – namely, those of the individuals who populate that hellish land – are parasitical upon Big Brother's hegemonic outlook. Core problems would still remain even if Big brother were fundamentally honest. Even in an alternative and somewhat less hellish scenario, as the one presently being suggested, Winston would nevertheless still be incapable of grasping the idea that Big Brother's claims could be called into question. The core problem that is of interest to us here is that, in conditions such as the ones being described, reality would be grasped through the eyes of Big Brother, and such a mediated outlook undermines the possibility of a full expression of rationality precisely because a hegemonic perspective does not allow for the proper grasp of a sense of world. We need unambiguously to possess the idea that the world is a radical other in order for rationality to fully prosper. In order to possess this idea we need to possess the idea that multiple others grasp the world in ways that are to some degree foreign to our personal outlooks. The hell offered in Orwell's land is one where the play of difference, which is central for being most fully rational, simply does not obtain – a play, I might add, that is a necessary requirement for the full implementation of Davidson's minimal set-up.

Obviously, Orwell's hell is not a place where we would want to live, but my additional point is that the hell offered by Orwell is not merely unpleasant, but also unpalatable insofar as it is a place where our capacity to be rational, our capacity for thought, is radically hindered. Of course, while we do not require Davidson's sophisticated conceptual machinery to tell us that thinking clearly would be difficult in Orwell's land, what it does allow us to do is clearly to determine why Orwell's land is no place for us. It is no place for us because, as I have said, the conditions in Orwell's hell allow only for the absolute minimal conditions for Davidson's basic set-up to be minimally implemented. With the understanding brought to us by Davidson's minimal account of rationality we are justified in claiming that we are by nature social creatures, and we have basic criteria for judging, in broad outline, what sort of social environment is well suited for us insofar as we are rational creatures. The ideal social environment is, in broad outline, one where the basic triangular set-up required for being rational can be nested properly.

Orwell portrays his dystopia as one that is populated by quasi-solipsists – people without a clear sense of a world that exists quite independently of what the party wants you to believe. On the other hand, characterizing members of Oceania as quasi-solipsists may be rather misleading given the fact that a solipsist is, if anything, a creature with an unduly strong sense of self – creatures who place the entirety of creation under the umbrella of their own being. Members of Oceania are perhaps best understood as thoughts of Big Brother. Their status is uncomfortably close to the status of dreams. Indeed, both the incapacity to think, given that agreement is so radical, and the incapacity to have a clear sense of reality are intimately intertwined. Winston almost completely lacks a private life – a sense of having a private space where he can entertain thoughts that belong to him. His mind belongs to Big Brother. What Big Brother claims is confused with what is the case. The concepts of subjectivity, intersubjectivity and objectivity cannot be properly differentiated in Winston's mind, although they can be minimally differentiated.

The triangle constituted by our grasp of the subjective/intersubjective/ objective modes of knowing is only minimally instantiated in Orwell's hell because conditions for rationality, other than those provided by Davidson, are not present. Certainly, the people inhabiting this hell are minimally rational insofar as they are minimally able to grasp the relevant concepts determined by Davidson, but it seems equally clear that much more is required for us to count as being fully rational.[19] We observe how ethico-political conditions impinge upon the implementation of Davidson's basic triangular set-up.

We know about the world, and we are constituted as the subjects that we are, by sharing a world with others but, importantly, ideally by sharing the world in a way that recognizes differences in perspective. This is, quite literally, what it means to share a world with others. To recognize that others genuinely grasp the world from different vantage points involves more than merely grasping the fact that other individuals occupy different locations – locations that we could fully grasp. Having the idea of objectivity involves recognizing the ongoing possibility that others may challenge our beliefs, and, I might add, challenge them in unexpected ways – that is, in ways that transcend our own spheres of understanding. One could say that a condition for holding the beliefs that I do is that you can, and do, disagree with me to some extent, and disagree in ways that I can never fully envisage. It is only under such pluralistic conditions that the idea of a location, which is clearly necessary for Davidson's minimal set-up to be properly instantiated, can most properly be grasped.

The ethical consequences of the conclusions reached are quite clear, at least in broad outline. Our existence as fully thinking creatures is a function of living with others in a community that fosters the conditions for the expression of unique modes of grasping the world. We ought to understand our lives as ideally embedded within what could be characterized as a regime of difference – a matrix of contrasting relationships aimed at a domain within which we all dwell. The regime at issue is one of differing perspectives on the same world. And there is no paradox here, since the very possibility of talking meaningfully about differing perspectives is that they are perspectives on one single domain – the world. And indeed, the very possibility of having a sense of world involves having a sense that the world is being grasped from a unique location, from a unique vantage point – namely, the vantage point occupied by an individual, properly speaking. One could say that the basic ethical stance I am presently defending is one of sharing difference in light of sameness. More specifically, I have shown that central to our own capacities to grasp the world from unique vantage points, the ones that define individuals as such, is the acceptance of the other as genuinely another.

Davidson establishes the minimal conditions for rationality. I have shown that these basic conditions must be supplemented with further conditions in order to be most properly instantiated. The triangle required is not just one in which two subjects communicate about a common world known by each to be largely known by the other. What is also required, among other things, is that the subjects in dialogue be substantially different from one another. Moreover, the idea itself of a triangle is perhaps not entirely adequate if we consider more than merely the most basic conditions for rationality. What we need to consider instead is a network of subjects. Each individual is a node in the network, and it is within such a network that we can hope to flourish as rational creatures.

Let me finish by adding that the conclusions of the present chapter have repercussions on the account of the virtues (and of the good life that flows from them) that has been developed in this investigation. Given that pluralism is a condition for *eudaimonia*, it also follows that an account of virtue must be pluralistic. This is exactly what I have thus far been arguing. It is not as if there could be a rigid set of virtues that apply to all persons. Virtues are typically developed and called for in the context of our unique engagements with life. Of course, insofar as we are persons, there must be a substantial overlap between the different modes in which complete virtue is expressed, but making this claim is very different from claiming that there is such a thing as a list of virtues. What there is, instead, is a rational system of dispositions that constitutes our practical understanding of life, and this rational system is one that is adaptive – sensitive to the particularities of the unique circumstances within which our individual lives are played out. Indeed, a world in which there was one set of virtues only, which was applied according to a fixed set of criteria, would be a world very much like the one portrayed by Orwell inasmuch as there would be no scope for the differences that define each of us as unique human beings. Further, it is hard to imagine what would be left of virtue in such a homogeneous scenario. In what sense would we be agents at all under such a mechanistic paradigm, and if we were not agents, in what sense would we be rational? It seems that the basic system that defines our rational existence would start to collapse in such an Orwellian scenario, and this is not surprising, given the above discussion.

Let me stress that, as argued above, the virtues are a mode of understanding. Moreover, the understanding at issue must be fluid insofar as our lives are fluid. Indeed, understanding human life rigidly amounts to nothing but a form of ignorance that leads to what could be characterized as a mode of practical dogmatism that is very clearly embodied in, say, colonialisms of all sorts. A typical colonialist is characterized by his or her incapacity or unwillingness to understand those he or she has colonized because of the rigid ethic that informs his or her practical understanding of what is to count as an acceptable mode of being. A paradigm case of colonialism is the one that took place in Australia where the indigenous peoples who populated the land were relegated to the status of natural slaves because their lifestyle did not fit in with the white colonizers' rigid conceptions of acceptability.

Given that we now know that we are persons insofar as we are social creatures, and that we are only able to flourish if we live in a pluralistic social realm, then it follows that virtue itself can only be properly constituted within a regime of difference. So, one could say, the virtues can only properly exist in a realm of ongoing negotiation. This is not surprising, since this is exactly the sort of scenario that we are left with once it has been shown that radical homogeneity undermines our possibilities of flourishing. Negotiation, of course, can only get started if there is a common ground for negotiation – if a subject matter is shared – which is to say that the realm of difference is one that is delimited by our essence (the highest expression of our rational constitution).

### Notes

1    Marcia Cavell, *The Psychoanalytic Mind: From Freud to Philosophy*, Cambridge, Massachusetts: Harvard University Press, 1993, p. 41.

2    I am aware that the views I am about to discuss are controversial, but I do think that, once properly understood, they are compelling. The discussion will touch upon key issues regarding epistemology and the philosophy of mind, and I am aware that much has been written against the sorts of views I discuss here. Nevertheless, this is not the place to engage in a detailed discussion of, for example, the internalism/externalism debate, the realism/anti-realism debate, or the debate about non-human animal intelligence. For an excellent general defence of Davidson's views against some important contenders, and for an exposition of the tradition within which Davidson's views on mind and meaning are imbedded, see Marcia Cavell's, *The Psychoanalytic Mind*, *op.cit.*, n. 1, pp. 9–41.

3    In E. LePore and B. McLaughlin (eds), *Actions and Events: Perspectives on the Philosophy of Donald Davidson*, Oxford: Basil Blackwell, 1985, pp. 473–80. See also Donald Davidson's 'Three Varieties of Knowledge', in A. Phillips Griffiths (ed.), *A.J. Ayer: Memorial Essays*, Cambridge: Cambridge University Press, 1991, pp. 153–66. Other relevant papers by Davidson are 'The Second Person', *Midwest Studies in Philosophy*, **17**, 1992, pp. 255–67, and 'Thought and Talk', *Inquiries into Truth and Interpretation*, Oxford: Clarendon Press, 1984, pp. 155–70.

4    Although his focus on non-human animals is incidental, Davidson provides us with good reasons for suspecting that, on this planet, only humans are thinking creatures. This seems a crazy claim to make given that there seems to be no better way of explaining the behaviour of dogs and cats than to do so in terms of beliefs and desires. However, if Davidson is right, then the difference between explaining non-human animal behaviour and human animal behaviour in terms of beliefs and desires is that, in the case of non-human animals the explanations in question are most probably pragmatic ones – rather like explanations about the 'behaviour' of heat-seeking missiles given by someone who has no idea that missiles are artefacts that 'behave' as they do because they were designed to do so (see Donald Davidson, 'Rational Animals', in LePore and McLaughlin, *Actions and Events, op.cit.*, n. 3, p. 477). Clearly, unlike heat-seeking missiles, dogs and cats are not created, but this is beside the point. What is important is that, if Davidson is right, then our folk psychological explanations about non-human animal behaviour are only warranted because we lack the appropriate conceptual resources to explain animal behaviour properly, and thus we rely on explanations that project our own highly sophisticated attitudes on to furry creatures. By contrast, in the case of human animals, explanations of behaviour in terms of beliefs and desires describe genuine facts about our psychological lives (genuine facts are described insofar as all, as opposed to merely some, of the basic conditions for rationality are met).

In contrast with what has just been claimed one could be tempted to argue that it is crazy to think that our explanations of animal behaviour are pragmatic ones and, further, that, in some sense, the beliefs and desires we attribute to animals are proto-rational. One, after all, wants to keep the distinction between purely causal reactions (such as tripping), and what appears to be an instance of genuine action (such as running away from a hungry carnivore because one, as potential prey, recognizes the looming danger). We would have no grounds for making such a distinction unless we argued along the lines that the efficient cause of an animal is in the animal itself. Now, there certainly are organisms that do have an immanent principle of change and yet are clearly not rational in the sense that is presently relevant. Trees, for instance, grow according to their own impetus, yet we do want to hold that there is an important distinction between mere growth and fleeing from danger (for instance). How can we hold such a distinction unless we were warranted in attributing propositional attitudes to non-human animals that display relatively complex behavioural patterns? The problem is that, in attributing a rational life to an animal, we are in fact eliminating the possibility of making what appears to be the important distinction between the manner we engage with the world and the manner in which other fellow creatures do. It seems that we do not have the conceptual resources required for holding this last distinction and it is perhaps why it is reasonable to suppose that attributing beliefs and the likes to animals is something we do for want of better conceptual resources. What I certainly think we can attribute to non-human animals are representations, and I think it is safe to say that animals react to these. A zebra, arguably, does not see a lion *qua* lion. Instead a zebra forms a representation that triggers a response in it. The response in question is not mediated by beliefs or the likes. Instead, it is purely causal. One, of course, must account for the relative plasticity of non-human animal behaviour but, equally, one must be able to account for the massively higher levels of plasticity human animals display in relation to other fellow creatures. I confess that, although I am pretty certain that the last distinction must be preserved, I am not really certain what sorts of conceptual resource would allow us to explain the distinction. We need not, however, delve into this problem any deeper for, as I have mentioned already, our central concern here is with rationality, and not with the problem of animal intelligence.

5    J. Malpas, *Donald Davidson and the Mirror of Meaning: Holism, Truth, Interpretation*, Oxford: Oxford University Press, 1992, pp. 57–8.

6    A more comprehensive analysis of the similarities and differences between Quine and Davidson can be found in Quine's 'Where Do We Disagree?', in L.E. Hahn's *The Philosophy of Donald Davidson*, Chicago and La Salle: Open Court, 1999, pp. 73–9, and in Davidson's 'Reply to W.V. Quine', in L.E. Hahn's *The Philosophy of Donald Davidson*, Chicago and La Salle: Open Court, 1999, pp. 80–86. See also Malpas, *Donald Davidson and the Mirror of Meaning, op.cit.*, n. 5, pp. 11–50.

7    J. Fodor and E. LePore, *Holism: A Shoppers Guide*, Oxford: Blackwell, 1996, pp. 37–58.

8    Heil is critical of Davidson's views on very similar grounds. See his *The Nature of True Minds*, Cambridge: Cambridge University Press, 1992, p. 218.

9    Davidson, 'The Second Person', *op.cit.*, n. 3, p. 262.

10   Ibid., p. 263.

11   Davidson, 'Three Varieties of Knowledge', *op.cit.*, n. 3, pp. 159–60. The idea of triangulation is not exclusive to Davidson. D. Føllesdal points out that Quine entertains a similar idea in his 'Ontological Relativity', *Ontological Relativity and Other Essays*, New York: Columbia University Press, 1969, p. 28, and *Word and Object*, Cambridge, Massachusetts: MIT Press, 1960, p. 1. See D. Føllesdal's 'Triangulation', in L.E. Hahn (ed.), *The Philosophy of Donald Davidson*, Chicago: Open Court, 1999, pp. 723–24. Føllesdal takes issue with Davidson's causal theory of reference, and his comments are worth considering. In a nutshell, he believes Davidson holds that '... causality can individuate objects' ('Triangulation', p. 724). This is not something Davidson holds. What Davidson does hold instead is that causation plays a central, albeit not exclusive, role in individuating objects. We also need the holistic structure that constitutes the psychological. Indeed, Davidson believes that we need '... the apparatus of propositional thoughts ...' ('Reply to Dagfinn Føllesdal', in L.E. Hahn (ed.), *The Philosophy of Donald Davidson*, Chicago: Open Court, 1999, p. 731). Central to Davidson's philosophy is the idea that 'Perception is propositional: when we look or feel or hear we believe' (ibid., p. 732).

12   C. Cherniak, *Minimal Rationality*, Cambridge, Massachusetts: MIT Press, 1986.

13   Indeed, this claim points to the crucial fact that, given that by nature we are social creatures and, given that engaging with others necessarily involves the ethical, one cannot separate our rational nature from our ethical nature. Acting as a rational agent necessarily involves bringing an ethic to bear.

14   H. Arendt, *The Human Condition*, Chicago: University of Chicago Press, 1974, p. 58.

15   Ibid., pp. 57–8.

16   J. Malpas, *Place and Experience: A Philosophical Topography*, Cambridge: Cambridge University Press, 1999, pp. 61–71; T. Nagel, *The View from Nowhere*, Oxford: Oxford University Press, 1986.

17   A call for the world to be set free is made also by Heidegger in, for instance, 'The Origin of the Work of Art' and 'The Question Concerning Technology', in D. F. Krell (ed.), *Basic Writings: From Being and Time (1927) to The Task of Thinking (1964)*, London: Routledge, 1993, pp. 139–203, and pp. 307–41, and it is also one of the central themes of Nietzsche's post-nihilistic philosophical project.

18   G. Orwell, *Nineteen Eighty-Four*, New York: Harcourt, Brace & World, Inc., 1949, p. 80.

19   I have not dealt with another important issue that is dealt with in Orwell's story – namely, that of torture and other forms of oppression. It seems that there is overwhelming evidence that one's faculties are radically impaired in cases of radical oppression, such as the conditions that prevailed in Auschwitz, and in which one could

say that rationality was temporarily suspended. Imre Kertesz's autobiographical novel *Fateless*, Evanston, Illinois: Northwestern University Press, 1992, brilliantly illustrates the surreal atmosphere predominant in such extreme conditions of torture and depravation. So, there is much scope for extending the present inquiry further in a way that makes it even plainer to what extent our ethical engagements are constitutive of our rational nature.

# Chapter 7

# Our Political Nature

## The Embeddedness of Individual Narratives in Greater Historical Meta-Narratives

This section has the sole purpose of establishing some central *formal* aspects of the lives of persons and their relationships with their communities. More details will be supplied in the subsequent sections of this final chapter. However, given the breadth and scope of this investigation I will be unable to set out more than some very general, albeit central, guidelines for understanding the political within a *eudaimonistic* framework.[1] What I *will* provide here is a direction for further, ongoing, investigation.

By now we know that the *telos* of the lives of persons is *eudaimonia*. In other words, the lives of persons are ideally organized by the unitary purpose of having a good life. What this means, in turn, is that the particular (chosen and non-chosen) goals one might pursue, and which contribute to shape a particular life, should ideally be embraced because they play a fundamental role in the formation of a *eudaimon* life – because they are constitutive of the rational pattern that makes up an ideal life. To express this slightly differently, being a unitary creature is a necessary condition for *eudaimonia* not just because life has a unifying *telos*, but, more specifically, also because the *telos* itself – the *eudaimon* life – is life lived in accordance with a certain ideal rational unity which is constitutive of *eudaimonia*. Our *telos*, I have already argued, does not stand over and above life itself as a kind of epiphenomenon; it is just the refinement of the practice of living – it is the overall dynamic composition that defines the lives of person as just that.

The choices we make typically have a unifying function to play insofar as these choices are ideally made taking into account the totality of one's life. And, indeed, our choices are constrained by our evolving history since this is what determines our possible moves in life in ways that render the choices we make intelligible. This basic feature of choice-making, combined with the *eudaimon telos*, form two basic principles involved in the formation of a *eudaimon* life. One ideally chooses for the sake of *eudaimonia*, and *eudaimonia* comes about by informing one's activities – activities which, to a large extent, draw their meaning from the evolving history within which they are framed – with the appropriate complex of qualities of character; that is, with the possession of complete virtue.

Another fundamental component of the unity of individual lives, which I have only touched on so far, is, to use words that echo MacIntyre's treatment of the matter (and are reminiscent of Hegel's), their embeddedness in historical meta-narratives – in cultural narratives.[2] I shall now proceed to argue that an account of *eudaimonia*, which only considers the lives of persons independently of considerations pertaining to the 'specific settings' (to use MacIntyre's terminology) which place constraints on the form lives are able to take, and within which particular lives are played out, is a hopelessly incomplete account. Given what I have said thus far regarding the circumstances for action, it may already be fairly clear why this should be the case.

In arguing that life has a narrative form, MacIntyre claims that individual narratives cannot be understood in isolation from particular historical narratives.[3] Individual narratives are embedded in, and constituted by, the histories of those who are closest to us, such as friends and relatives; and these histories, in turn, are embedded in, and constituted by, the history of a community. Furthermore, this net of relationships covers the whole of humanity (past and present) simply because, at present, the whole of humanity forms one complex network of diversely defined relationships that are constituted by the cultural heritage of the entire human race. Indeed, given the intimate relationship that exists between individual lives and history as a whole, individual lives are best understood as forming part of a net that covers an entire field of dialogically entwined lives and, in our time, is constituted by the entirety of humanity.

The plausibility of MacIntyre's claims becomes apparent once one recognizes, say, the basic structure of biographical narratives. Biographers know (as evidenced by the contents of biographies) that, if one is to have a relatively good understanding of a life, it cannot be separated from the specific setting of intertwined lives in which that life is played out simply because the playing out of a life depends on where and when that life is being played out. Specific settings constrain us in specific ways and offer us with certain specific possibilities for action. The constraints to which our specific settings subject us are constitutive of the manner in which our lives are formed. This inseparability of an individual life from its setting is not confined only to well-known lives. All lives *qua* lives of persons must be understood in this manner, since lives are dependent on circumstances. We are all forced by circumstances to act in certain ways that define individual lives as just those lives. Taking a biography as a paradigmatic way of understanding a life, think of how crucial an accurate account of the specific setting (and the specific interactions of the biographical subject with that setting) within which the life described is played out is for understanding that very life.

It might be worth noting here that innumerably different narrative descriptions may adequately describe the life of any given subject. But I also think that if these narratives are narratives of one and the same subject, there must be a way in which different accounts can be integrated in order to help shed light on the life of the subject being described. However, such an integration is not incompatible with a degree of inconsistency and conflict, nor is it incompatible with a certain degree of indeterminacy. Rather, the integration, if successful, should shed light on the inconsistencies and make them intelligible in relation to the general and complex pattern of a given individual's life.[4] The unity that is made intelligible in the form of a narrative is complex and multifaceted. A narrative that did not bring this complexity into light, like the narratives Hollywood is so systematically bent on producing – narratives that provide 'black and white' psychological profiles – are clearly unsuccessful descriptions.[5]

Let me clarify my concerns regarding the multifaceted nature of the lives of persons by means of an analogy. Objects, even the simplest of them, are multifaceted – they have innumerable faces. This is not to say that the object in question does not have an identity – not at all. An object *qua* object has an identity insofar as it can be referred to as an object – one thing. It may have many colours and different textures; it may even be used in countless different ways, and hence be understood under countless distinct descriptions, and nevertheless still count as a single object. Indeed, the very fact that I am able to claim that a given object can be understood under varying, and even at times antithetical descriptions, presupposes that there is an object – one object – that I am describing. Analogous considerations apply to the 'object' person.

The fundamental type of setting a life requires is a social one;[6] a setting that is understood by historical narratives – that is, a setting which is described and understood as an organized temporally-extended network of collective narratives. If this is so, and it seems clear that it is, then individual narratives can only be properly understood as embedded in collective narratives, thus making the existence of collective narratives essential for the possibility of there being individual narratives. I take it as given that collective narratives are a function of individual narratives since, clearly, there would be no history without the individuals who make history. So, the relationship at issue between collective narratives and individual narratives is one of mutual constitution. These claims should come as no surprise given that I have already determined that we are by nature social creatures – that it is only by communing with others that we can be the types of creatures that we in fact are (that is, rational creatures, creatures with propositional attitudes, that behave in ways that are expressive of these attitudes).

A person, we know already, is defined as a creature whose *telos* is *eudaimonia*. Moreover, since persons are necessarily social, it follows that only social creatures can achieve *eudaimonia*. The fact that we are, by nature, social creatures helps us visualize the importance social settings have to play in the formation of our lives. Indeed, we have already seen how the particular settings, within which specific lives are played out, have a necessary role to play in the formation of those lives. In addition, because the formation of our lives is so closely tied up with specific settings, then it must be the case that flourishing is only possible if the settings are appropriate. For this reason, it is not hard to see how the possibility of achieving *eudaimonia* is intimately tied in with *particular* types of settings (which we have yet to determine) that provide the conditions for the possibility of achieving *eudaimonia*. The good life, we may conclude, can only flourish in what could be characterized as a good society.

Roughly, I define a good society as one that offers the appropriate conditions for flourishing. I leave this characterization of good societies conveniently vague for the time being. I will soon argue that an ideal society offers the necessary external conditions for the flourishing of *each* member of that society, although I am not claiming that every member of an ideal society will, in fact, flourish. There will, after all, always be the possibility of genuinely inevitable bad luck creeping its way into some unfortunate lives, such that individuals who lived these lives would be genuinely incapable of achieving the *eudaimon* ideal, even in optimal social conditions. I am thinking of individuals who, for one reason or another, would simply be incapable of acting in ways that are constitutive of *eudaimonia* – individuals with severe and irreversibly brain-damage, or individuals who suffer immense personal losses. It must be emphasized that I am not thinking of individuals who are victims of injustice or neglect.

All I have intended to do in this section is to show not only that we are social creatures, but also that our well-being depends on the specific sort of intersubjective environment within which we dwell. I have shown that considerations regarding the quality of an individual life cannot be separated from considerations regarding the social setting within which that individual life is played out. So far, I have said nothing of substance about the specific sort of intersubjective or social environment required. I will now attempt to establish some more specific features of a *eudaimon* life, which, I hope, will provide grounds for discriminating between flourishing individuals and societies from those that are not so good.

## The *Eudaimon Telos* of the Social

To be a person, we already know, is not merely to be in a certain state but, rather, it is to have a life and, ideally, to have a good life. We also know that to live as a person is to live primarily for the sake of *eudaimonia* since our *telos* – the ethical ideal that defines us as the creatures that we are – is *eudaimonia*. Being a *eudaimon* individual involves having the active capacity to form our lives by working on perfecting the already existing fit between the different aspects of our lives that define us as rational creatures (behaviour, dispositions, desires, emotions, circumstances, beliefs, goals, and so on). In this manner a *eudaimon* individual is able to form an ideal unity, which is implicated in, and dependent on not only the intermeshing of lives with those closest to our hearts, but also on the great narrative of history within which the individual lives of those closest to us are embedded.

I shall now turn to what Aristotle considers to be a basic type of intersubjective relation, namely *philia* (loosely translated as friendship), to show that, in fact, a substantial ethic informs our lives – an ethic of shared lives.[7] Moreover, I will uncover a crucial link between the ethical and the social. We will see in more detail why individual good lives cannot be separated from their embeddedness in a social setting that promotes general well-being. We shall also see that it is only by engaging with others as *philoi* that we are able to acquire the relevant practical knowledge required for engaging with others who are not our *philoi* in ways that are expressive and constitutive of the *eudaimon* ideal. I shall argue that having, as a defining feature, the ethical ideal of *philia* – what we could characterize as the ethic of reciprocal love – constitutes both the condition for the possibility of having a good life and the condition for the possibility of a good society.[8]

I am deliberately establishing a distance from Aristotle at this point, since I believe that his relative lack of emphasis regarding the ethic that ideally informs our active concerns for those individuals that make up the social at large – those individuals one will never know – makes for an extremely parochial ethic. Indeed, I shall argue that Aristotle's relative lack of interest in others beyond his immediate circle of acquaintances is inconsistent with the central tenets of his work, particularly with the *eudaimon* principle. But let us not get too far ahead of ourselves.

The question forced upon us by the discovery of our social nature is 'What constitutes a good society?' or, in other words, 'What is the *telos* – the ethical ideal – of the political realm (the social setting for a life)?' By 'political realm' and 'society' I mean a complex, multifaceted and dynamic fabric of spatio-temporally extended human engagements (at present, the political realm spreads out to cover the entire globe). Given this particular characterization of the social, and if we presume that the *telos* of the social, like the *telos* of persons and unlike the *teloi* of shoemaking and medicine, is not an end product over and above the engagements themselves, it follows that the *telos* at issue is just a refinement of the complex fabric of intertwined activities that constitute a given political realm.[9] Given this particular understanding of the political, another manner of formulating the question at issue – a formulation which is suggestive of the relationship between *philia* and the political – is 'What are the basic modes of engagement that are constitutive of the ethical ideal of political existence?'. But, it must be stressed, this is only a reformulation of the question at issue if we presume that the *telos* of the political is a refinement of the activities that constitute the political realm. I think there are good reasons for holding this view, as we shall now see.

Since the *telos* of individual lives is to achieve *eudaimonia*, then the *telos* of the associations of individuals must be an aspect – and a fundamental aspect as we have seen – of the *eudaimon* ideal. So, ideally, *each* person is engaged in associations with other individuals because these forms of engagement are constitutive of his or her *eudaimonia*. It follows that each and every member of a given association is ideally in that association because that association is constitutive of his or her *eudaimonia*. Further, since the social realm cannot be said to have a *telos* over and above the ideals pursued by the members of that association, because the political realm is nothing but the multifaceted fabric of human associations that constitute it, then the *telos* of each and every form of political engagement is the achievement of *eudaimonia* by each of the members of that association.[10] It is also important to note here that I am not claiming that the relevant social conditions are sufficient conditions for human flourishing; rather, I am simply claiming that the social conditions are necessary external conditions for human flourishing.

I have argued that the *telos* of the social is to create the conditions for the flourishing of each of its members.[11] It is also important to stress at this point that the claims being made here, though based on certain key features of Aristotle's ethics, are not claims that Aristotle himself would make. Aristotle is explicitly an aristocrat. He holds that few individuals can actualize the potentials that define persons as such. This last claim is not merely a matter-of-fact sort of claim – the claim that most persons are in actuality incapable of embodying the ethical ideal that defines them. On the contrary, Aristotle explicitly holds that the many (including all women) ought to provide the few with external goods that purportedly cannot be provided otherwise, and which are necessary for the flourishing of an aristocrat – the only sort of individual who is actually able to live a *eudaimon* life. The ethical ideal of a human life is, for Aristotle (but not for me) primarily an ideal achievable only by the small elite of male citizens of the Athenian state. Nussbaum clearly describes Aristotle's stance with regard to slaves (and much the same applies to females generally).[12] She claims that 'the slave is like "something of" the master, an extension of the master's own good'.[13]

There are good reasons for believing that Aristotle's conception of slavery is inconsistent with his overall account – his teleological account – of what it is to be a person. The slavery Aristotle is mainly concerned with, I must stress, is what he understands as natural slavery – that is, the type of slavery in which the slaves are defined as such by the ethical ideal, the *telos* – of being useful to their masters. The problem with this account of slavery is that it entails that slaves of this sort are not persons, since persons as such are defined by the ethical ideal of living the life of a *eudaimon* individual. It is important to note, however, that Aristotle explicitly claims that natural slaves are human beings, and also that they are a kind of instrument.[14] Aristotle explicitly claims that 'he [a slave] may be said to be another's man who, *being a human being* [my emphasis], is also a possession'.[15] There is clearly a contradiction here, since to be a possession contradicts the *eudaimon* ideal of self-sufficiency discussed above. So, it appears that Aristotle must either abandon his conception of natural slavery, because it is not consistent with the central tenets of his *Ethics*, or he must abandon the central principle that informs his ethics – the *eudaimon* principle. Aristotle cannot consistently argue along the lines that there are 'half persons'. More specifically, he cannot consistently hold, as he seems to, that women (slaves or otherwise) and natural slaves are half-persons because he defines persons as such in relation to the ethical ideal of personhood. It seems that the only reason he could possibly provide for claiming that someone is a half-person is to claim that he or she is defined by the *telos* of half-persons. But this would be a different *telos* altogether. So, either one is a full person or no person at all. Certainly, as I have discussed above, there are individuals who might be closer to actualizing the ethical ideal that defines us than others, but we are defined as the types of creatures that we are not because we have reached the *telos* that defines us but, rather, because we possess the *telos*. So a person cannot, in any sense that is consistent with the central tenets of Aristotle's ethical system, have the ethical ideal of being an instrument or an extension of a master's body.

It is also true, however, that Aristotle is, to a large extent, a thinker who believes that there are hierarchies of existence, as we have seen when studying Aristotle's theory of *psyche*. And, of course, the very idea of a *telos* – a good – is a hierarchical notion. In this light, his doctrine of slavery could be seen, and quite rightly so, as an expression of Aristotle's hierarchical mode of thought. Nevertheless, even though Aristotle's doctrine of slavery is a reflection of his hierarchical mode of thought, it is inconsistent with his teleological account of human nature. Inasmuch as a slave or a woman is a person, he or she must have the same *telos* as the male citizens of Athens.

It seems clear that it is the doctrine of natural slavery that must be discarded since in this way we preserve what is central to Aristotle's thought and at the same time we get rid of the unpalatable doctrine of natural slavery. No person can be properly understood, *qua* person, as a living instrument of others by virtue of the fact that persons are defined as such by the *eudaimon* ideal of self-sufficiency.

It is perhaps worth mentioning at this point, again against Aristotle, that a community cannot be understood in a manner that is analogous with the way in which one understands the hierarchical organic unity that composes a given agent. The organic unity at issue here is hierarchical in the sense that some of the component parts of the unity in question are conceived as existing for the sake of other parts;[16] a unity in which most members of Athens, namely slaves and females, were conceived by Aristotle as having a relative existence – that is, an existence that was for the sake of the noble caste (we have seen that Aristotle explicitly characterizes slaves as living instruments).[17] I mention this to avoid the temptation of understanding the social as ideally (in the sense of an ethical ideal) hierarchically stratified in this manner. Persons, we already know, are defined by the ideal of self-sufficiency – they are defined by an ideal of autonomy that an organ does not have. So, when talking about a community at large – our global contemporary community in our case – we must not forget that we are talking about a group of *individuals*. By understanding this we avoid the temptation – a temptation Aristotle succumbed to – of holding that some individuals ought solely to play an instrumental role in the lives of other, more fortunate, individuals.

When claiming that individuals ought not to be instruments of others, I do not mean more generally that individuals should not be useful to others. We all have different things to offer each other and there is clearly great merit in sharing these resources (we need friends, providers of all sorts of products and services and so on). The types of associations I am opposing are, paradigmatically, exploitative ones or, more generally, relationships that undermine the paradigm of self-sufficiency.

Let me immediately proceed to defuse a possible counter claim regarding my claims about the *telos* of the social – namely, that having a single *telos* would imply a homogeneity of sorts. Obviously, there are many distinct types of human associations and this suggests that the *teloi* of these associations vary accordingly. I think this claim largely true – to the extent to which we are *not* talking about the *ultimate* justification for human associations, which, we already know, is the achievement of *eudaimonia* by each and every one of the associating individuals. We know also that *eudaimonia* is a complex, dynamic, and temporally extended unity. More to our current point, *eudaimonia* is constituted by distinct, variously interrelated sub-*teloi*. And, indeed, as we have seen above, given the manner in which the formation of human lives is dependent on circumstances (both internal and external), it follows, quite obviously, that each human life will be unique. Also, given the diversity of dispositions, interests, talents, histories and so on, that differentiate us from one another, it is clear that there will be innumerably distinct manners of instantiating the *eudaimon* ideal or, more specifically, of instantiating the fabric of sub-projects that are constitutive of the *eudaimon* ideal. It is clear, then, given that the *telos* of the social is to create the necessary conditions for the development of the *eudaimon* ideal by each of the members of a given social group – of a given association – that the *telos* of the social is to create the necessary conditions for the realization of the diverse systems of goals that constitute *each* individual *eudaimon* life.[18] We may conclude, then, that the apparent problem at issue here only arises if one forgets that the issues discussed here regarding what is common to us all and what makes each of us unique are cast at different levels of generality – at the level of particular differences between individuals and at the general formal level which defines us as tokens of a given type.

It is for reasons of this sort that I think this investigation is immune to possible 'attacks' on the grounds that it places unduly strict restrictions on what are to count as morally praiseworthy lives. Certainly I have principally focused on that which is common to us all (our ethical ideal) rather than on the irreducible particularities that differentiate individuals (and the specific cultures they inhabit) from each other. And indeed, this generalist focus could be seen as limiting in some important respects. However, while I concede that my inquiry is limited, I do not think that it is limiting. The main aim of this investigation is to show that we have a common purpose and that this purpose not only shows that the quality of each of our lives is intertwined with the lives of those who share this world with us, but also shows that we should willingly embrace our interconnectedness, as our well-being depends on it. No doubt there is much detail to be filled in with regard to how exactly ethical lives express themselves, as well as much work to be done with regard to how inevitable conflict is dealt with within a *eudaimon* society. But, and I have made this point more than once throughout this investigation (in slightly different terms), I think that it only makes sense to talk about differences amongst us if we are working within a common overarching framework that is binding – that unites us as persons. Moreover, I cannot make sense of the moral demands of other persons unless I can first make sense of them as being one of us (moral agents). I must be able to make sense of difference, and I can only do this if there already is much in common, *qua* moral agents, between us. You and I must already, so to speak, co-inhabit the same moral space.[19]

It is also clear that, built into the above claims regarding the intersubjective intermeshing of projects, there must be considerations pertaining to the inevitability of conflict of interests among individuals constituting a community (nowadays the global community). And, indeed, since a constitutive aspect of the *eudaimon* ideal is how our lives are implicated in the lives of others, then the very process by which our goals are determined already ideally implicates concerns about others or, more relevant to the present point, already ideally implicates the general fabric of goals and interests that constitute the social at large. This said, just as I doubt whether conflict within a given individual could be eradicated, I also have serious doubts that it would ever be possible to eradicate social conflict – nor do I think that the eradication of conflict at these two levels is always and necessarily desirable. There are many differences among us, and many conflicts within us, and these conflicts often help to enhance the richness of our lives even if pain is sometimes involved, such as the pain involved in the sorts of conflicts that typically arise in face of the loss of loved ones. I might add that an understanding of the sorts of creatures that we are, which includes an understanding of how the lives of others are implicated in the fabric of our own lives, puts us in a much better position to understand human conflict, and deal with it in ways that reflect an understanding of our common overarching goal. If conflicting parties understood that their conflicts are ideally related to the manner in which we think our common goal ought to be achieved, then it seems to me that we would be much better placed to deal with the conflicts in good faith.

I am not thinking here of conflicts of the sorts that arise, say, between the selfish interests of those managing some large corporations and the enslaved workers that work for these evil Cyclops-like institutions. At the moment I am considering possible conflict within a *eudaimon* society in which blatant injustice would have no place.

I am very aware of the charge of naivety that may arise from the above comments (and from the general tone of this investigation). The world clearly has been, and is, in many ways and for many people a very nasty place indeed (examples abound). I think the charges of naivety would indeed be justified if I thought that somehow we could simply change things from one day to another. But I do not think this is the case. The central purpose of the present investigation is to provide a direction – a target – so that we are able to see that we are, and why we are, way off-track, and to provide a *general* direction for positive change in a way that brings our common humanity – our common purpose – into prominence.

Referring back to the above discussions regarding the nature of projects, and the constitutive role conflicts play, remember that individual projects are framed within dynamic, fluid and open-ended networks of projects and that, because of the dynamic nature of these networks, perfect harmony can never be guaranteed. This means that the matrix within which our lives are played out is necessarily unstable. Indeed, it is within this unstable matrix that our individual endeavours derive their meaning and purpose. An immortal living in a static environment, remember, will not be living in conditions in which he or she can have a meaningful life. So, creating a better society cannot be understood as creating a conflict-free society. The issue of social improvement, then, is bound up not with the eradication of conflict, but rather with the eradication of certain varieties of conflict – namely, as we shall see, conflicts such as those involving exploitation. Generally, the sorts of conflict that should not exist are those that do not acknowledge the humanity of conflicting others – that is, dehumanizing conflicts.

## Communion of *Philoi*

### A Basic Taxonomy

What are the social conditions for human flourishing? There is a sense in which a society can be seen as a project and, as such, it is defined by its *telos* – by an ethical ideal. That a society can be seen as a project follows from the fact that it can properly be understood as a network of variously interrelated purposive activities that are unified by one central *telos* (which is the achievement of *eudaimonia* by each of its members). The ethical ideal at issue here, we already know, is the ideal of providing the right conditions for human flourishing. Studying the conditions for the social, then, will help us understand the nature of *eudaimonia*, since it is only in the appropriate social environments that one is able to stay active in ways that are constitutive of the *eudaimon* ideal. The particular ways in which we engage with others – the specific projects in which we become involved – and not merely the fact that we are by nature social creatures, are an aspect, and a fundamental aspect, of what it is to live as a *eudaimon* individual.

Aristotle argues that the fundamental conditions for the social are relationships of *philia*. *Philia*, he argues, 'hold states together'.[20] Societies (or the *polis* at any rate), Aristotle seems to believe, are best understood as spatio-temporal networks of *philia* (ideally, not any type of *philia* as we shall soon find out).[21] *Philia*, we know, is standardly translated as 'friendship' and, with a few qualifications, this translation is adequate, although not perfect, because *philia* encompasses not only what we normally refer to as friendship, but also all sorts of relationships involving reciprocal care and concern for persons.[22] Other possible translations of *philia*, which help bring out different aspects of Aristotle's notion, are 'bonds of care and concern' or 'reciprocal bonds of love'.[23]

Aristotle divides *philia* into two different types; primary and secondary. Primary *philia* is the sort that is played out between *eudaimon* subjects (or at least by practically wise individuals) and are for the sake of *eudaimonia*. Secondary *philia*, on the other hand, are the sorts of bonds of *philia* that are paradigmatically represented by what could broadly be characterized as instrumental or advantage bonds.[24] I am thinking here of everyday examples such as the relationship one might have with one's physician. One might actually care for one's physician, and want to spend time with him or her (in his or her practice), but more often than not, the caring and the desire to spend time with him or her is conditional upon the specific service being provided. This example is of the type referred to by Aristotle as instrumental *philia* for the sake of utility. He contrasts this variety of instrumental *philia* with *philia* for the sake of pleasure. The latter sort of instrumental relationship is exemplified by sexual relationships where the pleasure gained by the relationship is what holds those involved together, such that were one to cease to take pleasure (or take pleasure to the same degree) or to cease to be interested in taking pleasure in this manner, the relationship would terminate simply because there would be nothing left to sustain it.[25]

In addition, instrumental *philia*, as Nussbaum notes,[26] must be distinguished from purely exploitative relationships which do not involve care and concern at all. This last sort of relationship is the sort in which one party regards the other party as nothing but a piece of living equipment, and treats him or her accordingly. It is exemplified by the relationship of master towards slave. In addition, instrumental *philia*, as John Cooper notes,[27] must also be distinguished from other less radical forms of association that do not involve genuine care and concern, such as purely commercial associations. These are relationships, which, falling short of being exploitative, nevertheless do not involve care and concern for the other members of the association. In purely commercial relationships, as in purely exploitative ones, one does not regard the person one is engaging with as a genuine person.

Engaging with someone in ways that are expressive of the primary sorts of friendship, on the other hand, fundamentally involves caring for someone for his or her own sake as opposed to caring for someone chiefly in relation to something specific that is of interest to me and which someone else can provide.[28] I care for my primary sort of friend mainly because I value his or her character; I value him or her *qua* the specific person that he or she is. In relation to this, Aristotle claims that, '... the friend [the primary sort of *philoi*] is loved by the friend *qua* friend, and not *qua* musician or doctor ...'.[29] Love amongst *philoi* of the primary sort can also be characterized as disinterested precisely because one cares for one's *philos qua* person as opposed to *qua* specific attribute that one finds useful or pleasurable. By contrast, for example, if one purportedly loved one's *philos* primarily because of his or her external appearance, one would not in actual fact love one's *philos*. Rather, one would be in love with one's friend's appearance (if, indeed, one could properly love in this way).

I emphatically do not want to suggest here that one should not love one's *philos* because of some aspect he or she has that one values but, rather, that the love one ought to have for one's *philos* must have a disinterested component. One must love one's *philos* independently of any of the specific features that one values. In a primary sort of friendship, one chiefly values one's friend because of his or her character and the pattern of activities that flow from it.

Instrumental relationships, by contrast, involve engaging with someone in a way that is similar, but not identical with, the way in which one engages with artefacts that one considers useful.[30] We care for artefacts mainly because artefacts perform certain functions that are useful to us, or to put the matter in slightly different terms, because we somehow perceive some artefacts as being beneficial to our lives. If a given artefact ceased to interest us because the service it provided no longer interested us, or because we no longer needed what it provided or indeed, more generally, because we no longer perceived it as beneficial to our lives, we would dispose of it quite easily. Aristotle characterizes instrumental *philia* thus:

> Now those who love each other for their utility do not love each other for themselves but in virtue of some good which they get from each other. So too with those who love for the sake of pleasure; it is not for their character that men love ready-witted people, but because they find them pleasant. Therefore those who love for the sake of utility love for the sake of what is good for *themselves*, and those who love for the sake of pleasure do so for the sake of what is pleasant to *themselves*, and not in so far as the other is the person loved but in so far as he is useful or pleasant.[31]

In this passage, and as we have seen above, Aristotle differentiates two distinct, but closely related, categories of instrumental *philia*: relationships for the sake of pleasure (pleasure is not, in these types of relationship, bound up with the relationship itself, but rather is for the sake of which the relationship is carried out) and relationships for the sake of utility.[32] It is also important to note here that Aristotle does not want to suggest that *philia*, of the primary variety, cannot have an instrumental component. All I am claiming, and all

Aristotle claims, is that it is not the instrumental component of genuine *philia* that defines the engagement as such. Of course a genuine friend typically engages with his *philoi* because this engagement is, at least on the whole, enjoyable. But the enjoyment one gets out of the engagement *completes* the activity rather than being that for the sake of which the engagement is constituted.[33] I engage with my *philos* (in the case of friendships of the primary sort) because my *philos* is an inherently valuable person (and I perceive his or her value and get enjoyment out of this 'perception') and not simply or fundamentally because he or she is of value to me.

Now that we have a rough idea of what *philia* is, we can start to fill in some gaps by establishing why primary and secondary varieties of *philia* are just that. We already know what, according to Aristotle (and I agree), the primary and secondary varieties of *philia* are. What we do not as yet know in sufficient detail is what makes one of them primary and the other secondary. Following Aristotle, I shall argue that primary *philia* are those sorts of relationship in which one is best able to express one's goodness, and in which one is best able to learn how to act in accordance with complete virtue. Indeed, since the *telos* of life is *eudaimonia*, then the primary type of *philia* must be the type that is best able to play a role in the formation of a *eudaimon* life (since anything we do in life is ideally done for the sake of *eudaimonia*).

To my account of the distinction between the two basic varieties of *philia*, we can add that, in Sherman's words:

> Within the threefold classification of friendship, into friendship based on pleasure, utility, and good character, the former two are ... accidental, and inferior primarily because they are more transient and less enduring sorts of friendships than those based on the mutual pursuit of virtue....[34]

I agree with Sherman's account of Aristotle's 'threefold classification of friendship' and, indeed, I find Aristotle's classification to be of great importance.[35] Sherman then claims that secondary forms of friendship are just that primarily because they are 'more transient and less enduring'. She is not suggesting that primary friendships are just that simply because they are more enduring. Rather, she contrasts the less enduring relationships with those 'based on the mutual pursuit of virtue'. And, indeed, Aristotle thinks that it is much more difficult for a primary sort of *philia* to end given that they are founded on an appreciation of not just this or that aspect of the character of one's *philoi* (or on some particular shared interest) but, are based instead on a mutual appreciation of each other's noble character – a character that instantiates the ideal of complete virtue.[36] Endurance comes as a consequence of these latter defining aspects of primary *philia* rather than being its principle defining feature. For instance, Aristotle claims that '[n]ow those who wish well to their friends for their sake are most truly friends; for they do this by reason of their own nature and not incidentally; therefore their friendship lasts as long as they are good – and goodness is an enduring thing'.[37] He contrasts this characterization of virtue friendship with the following characterization of friendships based on utility:

> Now the useful is not permanent but is always changing. Thus when the motive of the friendship is done away, the friendship is dissolved, inasmuch as it existed only for the ends in question.[38]

To repeat, Aristotle is not primarily interested here in establishing a distinction between friendships that last a long time and friendships that do not. Rather, he is primarily interested in the conditions for stable relationships. A stable relationship, if the conditions are bad enough, could end. Also, a stable relationship could come to an end if one of the friends, say, moved to a foreign land permanently. By contrast, an unstable relationship could last a lifetime if the conditions are adequate. I might, for example, have a lifelong unstable relationship with, say, an accountant (and I am in the relationship primarily, though not exclusively, because he or she is my accountant) if the need for his or her services happens to be ongoing. In the above-quoted passage Aristotle claims that useful relationships – that is, instrumental relationships – are not as stable because our interests are always changing.[39] Moreover, in this passage Aristotle is suggesting that all friendships that are not stable are instrumental in nature, as opposed to relationships that are based on character.

Relationships are instrumental because they are not based on who one's friend is (that is, on his or her character and the activities that flow from it), but, instead, on a specific aspect of a friend that one appreciates. If one appreciated only a specific aspect of a given individual it would be because one is primarily interested in that aspect, and not so much interested in whom has the given aspect.[40] Moreover, one is interested in this aspect, rather than that one, because one primarily perceives it as important, not so much to the owner of the aspect, but to oneself – the concern for the owner of the aspect is secondary (incidental). Relationships of this sort are not stable precisely because they are based on some specific aspect of a person – such as an aspect of his or her character, wealth, social status, specific abilities, beauty, and so on) rather than on the complex fabric of aspects that constitute his or her character and the actions that flow from it.

Conversely, virtue friendships (friendships based on the ideal of complete virtue) are desirable to virtuous subjects because virtuous subjects have a practical understanding of the role played by these friendships in a *eudaimon* life. Virtuous subjects have an appreciation of the character of their companions, and because of this appreciation, they find sharing time with their companions enjoyable or, at any rate, desirable.[41] A further necessary component of virtue friendships is that they take time to develop, but crucially, these sorts of friendship do not develop once and for all. The task of cultivating these sorts of relationship is ongoing.

## *Why are* Philoi *Necessary for* Eudaimonia*?*

It might be doubted that *philia* is necessary for *eudaimonia*, but I see no good reason for sustaining this doubt. It should become clear as the discussion proceeds that we must form intimate reciprocal bonds of care and concern – reciprocal bonds of love of the primary sort – if we have any hope of living a good life. One of the main reasons Aristotle provides for holding this thesis is that to have a good life one must not only be continuously active, but continuously active in the right manner. Moreover, to be continuously active in the right manner, Aristotle believes, involves having friends towards whom to express one's goodness. And more relevant to our present interests, Aristotle holds that one can only learn and express one's goodness fully in the company of *eudaimon* friends – friends who live their lives in accordance with complete virtue.

Let us explore this last claim in more depth. It is clear that *philia* is desirable and useful (in the sense that it is able to play a positive role in the achievement and perpetuation of *eudaimonia*), but why is it a *necessary* component of a *eudaimon* life? Sherman agrees with Aristotle that perfect friendships are necessary for living a *eudaimon* life. She quotes Aristotle in support of this claim:[42]

> The friendship of good persons is good, being augmented by their friendship. For the individuals seem to become better by their activities and by improving each other. For they mould themselves from one another with respect to those characteristics they approve.[43]

Implicit in this passage are two of Aristotle's reasons for holding that friendships are necessary for *eudaimonia*. The first reason is that, with good friends, one is able to be active in ways that are expressive of complete virtue (if the friendship at issue is a virtue friendship). The second reason is that virtue friends are able to improve each other – engaging with others for the sake of virtue plays a pedagogical role in relation to the ongoing development of complete virtue. It must further be noted here that the idea is not merely that what virtue friendships contribute to good living can also be attained to the same degree in other ways. The idea here is that what virtue friends contribute to good living is not merely a means towards a greater end that may be achieved in other ways. On the contrary, as Sherman notes,[44] virtue friendships are an intrinsic part of good living. I shall deal with both of these reasons in turn.

It is perhaps worth noting at this point that the two reasons why virtue friendships are necessary for *eudaimonia* are closely linked because learning how to act in accordance with virtue, like any other skill, is learned in the act of exercising the skill – exercising the virtues in this case (with a greater or lesser degree of competence). Further, as previously argued, there is no end point to the task of learning how to act in conformity with virtue. Each

opportunity to exercise virtue is also a possible opportunity to perfect one's character and the manner in which one's character is expressed in action.
Sherman argues that:

> Aristotle calls friends the 'greatest' and 'most necessary' of external goods ... without whom we would not choose to live 'even if we had all other goods'.... As suggested, friendship creates a context or arena for the expression of virtue, and ultimately for happiness. More strongly, it extends and re-defines the boundaries of the good life in such a way that my happiness or complete good comes to include the happiness of significant others. Happiness or good living is thus ascribable to me, not as an isolated individual, but as a self extended, so to speak, by friends.[45]

The sort of friendship Sherman is mainly alluding to here is virtue friendship. Friendships of this sort are 'the "greatest" and "most necessary" of external goods' because they provide the 'context or arena for the expression of virtue', which is a necessary aspect of a *eudaimon* life. Additionally, it is because the expression of complete virtue plays this central role, and it is because the expression of virtue, in the case of friendships of this sort, has as its *telos* to improve one's friend's living, that my individual *eudaimonia* comes to incorporate the *eudaimonia* of my friend. It must be emphasized here that the principal reason that Sherman provides here for supporting Aristotle's view that *philia* is necessary for *eudaimonia* is that the network of love constituted by perfect friendships provides the necessary scenario for the complete expression of complete virtue – for the expression of the goodness of a *eudaimon* individual's character. If this claim is true, and I think it is, one cannot separate individual *eudaimonia* from a network of *philial* relationships of *eudaimon* subjects within which an individual *eudaimon* life is played out.

Annas identifies a further reason Aristotle provides in order to show why *philia* is necessary for *eudaimonia*.[46] Following Aristotle, Annas argues that *philoi* are necessary for self-discovery. By using others as reflections of ourselves, and by communing with others intimately we are able to develop an understanding of ourselves. Annas follows Cooper in holding that this claim is best supported by *Magna Moralia* 1213a 10–26 and *Ethica Nichomachea* 1169b 28–1170a 4.[47] Given the clarity of the *Magna Moralia* passage just mentioned, I will quote it extensively here:[48]

> If, then, when one looked upon a friend one could see the nature and attributes of the friend ... such as to be a second self, at least if you make a very great friend, as the saying has it, 'Here is another Heracles, a dear other self.' Since then it is both a most difficult thing, as some of the sages have said, to attain a knowledge of oneself, and also a most pleasant (for to know oneself is pleasant) – now we are not able to see what we are from ourselves (and that we cannot do so is plain from the way in which we blame others without being aware that we do the same things ourselves; and this is the effect of favour or passion, and there are many of

us who are blind by these things so that we judge not aright); as when we wish to see our own face, we do so by looking into the mirror, in the same way when we wish to know ourselves we can obtain knowledge by looking at our friend. For the friend is, as we assert, a second self. If, then, it is pleasant to know oneself, and it is not possible to know this without having some one else for a friend, the *self-sufficing* [my italics] man will require friendship in order to know himself.[49]

We already know that the idea of self-sufficiency is central in Aristotle's *Ethics*. A self-sufficient life, we already know, is a life that is complete (and not a life that is radically autonomous). More specifically, a life of this sort is one that is lived out in accordance with the *eudaimon* ideal of completeness – the ideal of living in accordance with one's *telos*. In addition, we already know that, given that we are by nature social creatures – given that an aspect of our *telos* is the manner in which we relate to others – the ideal of self-sufficiency cannot be understood independently of an understanding of the manner in which we ideally relate to each other.[50] In the above-quoted passage Aristotle gives us reasons for holding that virtue friendships are one fundamental sort of interaction that is constitutive of a complete life. He argues that, without friends, one would necessarily be limited with regard to how much one could learn about oneself. Friends, Aristotle argues, allow us learn about ourselves in that we can compare our actions and emotional dispositions with those of our friends. In this sense, friends act as a kind of mirror, although Aristotle is not claiming that friends must be identical with, or a mirror image of, one another. One also learns about oneself by contrast – by comparing the differences between one's friends and oneself. I shall have more to say about the issue of self-discovery and the central role *philia* has to play in this process below.[51]

Remember that Aristotle argues that the good life is an active one. Remember also that, to have an active life, one must be in the right circumstances for being active in the relevant ways. The ways that are relevant, we have also seen, involve being active among and towards one's *philoi*. It is for reasons such as these that establishing bonds of *philia* are constitutive of the possibility of being a *eudaimon* individual. Indeed, Aristotle argues that:

Further, men think that the happy man ought to live pleasantly. Now if he were a solitary, life would be hard for him; for by oneself it is not easy to be continuously active; but with others and toward others it is easier. With others therefore his activity will be more continuous, and it is in itself pleasant, as it ought to be for the man that is supremely happy; for a good man *qua* good delights in virtuous actions and is vexed at vicious ones, as a musical man enjoys beautiful tunes but is pained at bad ones.[52]

A radical Philoctetes (or Cacus) could not have a good life because the range of good activities he or she can perform is greatly reduced by their solitude. But it is not necessary to consider such extreme cases to see how we need to be with others in specific ways to have a good life. Aristotle argues that we are at our best with respect to the possibility of performing good actions when our good actions are directed toward our *philoi*. This might sound counterintuitive if we consider the Gandhis of the world who have greatly helped those they never knew. One could even conceive of a *eudaimon* individual (although it still remains to be seen if this individual could actually exist) who had no *philoi* – an individual who lived amongst others and acted appropriately only towards those he or she did not know. Could such an individual exist? If Aristotle is right, and I think he is, then having intimate *philial* relationships is a necessary condition for learning the virtues, such that an altruistic hermit of the sort described could not in reality develop the relevant dispositions for acting in ways that promote the good of persons in general.[53]

This last claim might be contested on the grounds that, at times, intimate friendships have the opposite result, that is, they separate the circle of friends from the community at large, leading to the exclusion of the wider community from our sphere of concerns. Obviously friendships of this exclusive sort exist, but I consider them to be corrupt because they reflect a misunderstanding about how the very possibility of establishing intimate relationships, and the character of those relationships, depends on the embeddedness of the network of those intimate friends within the wider fabric of relationships that constitute the social at large. I think it is clear that caring for oneself in a way that reflects a proper practical understanding of human flourishing entails care for those conditions that make one's flourishing possible, and these conditions are, among other things, constituted by the community at large.

Here I do not want to suggest that one ought to care for the wider community for instrumental reasons – that is, simply because the wider community provides the conditions for the possibility of the existence of my immediate circle of friends (although my circle of friends is certainly just that circle only insofar as the circle is embedded in a wider network of relationships). Rather, I believe our concerns for the community at large ought to be based on a genuine *appreciation* of how our lives depend on the overall pattern of relationships which constitutes the social at large. Ideally, I love my community because I appreciate my life and I appreciate how others have contributed, and are contributing, to the possibility of living my ideally fine life.[54] I see, for example, how a provider of a given service (say, a doctor or a builder) is contributing to the edification of the society that has gifted me with the possibility of being who I am. Since, ideally, I genuinely appreciate my life and I genuinely appreciate the role my community plays in the possibility I have of living this specific life, I direct myself towards my community in ways that reflect and constitute my appreciation. And indeed, to understand the constituting role my community has on my good living involves perceiving my community as part of myself (because there is no sense in which I can appropriately conceive of myself independently of my embeddedness in a particular community). My community is part of me in the sense that my identity hangs on the unique identity of my community.

Note that the case is different from, say, the purported appreciation I could have for my organs insofar as I depend on them for living. The case is different because my relationship to my organs is contingent – incidental – and not necessary. Identity is not defined in relation to the identity of my organs, but my identity is most certainly defined in relation to my communal belonging.

In sharing with intimates we also ideally learn about human joy and suffering, and we learn to understand how circumstances (internal and external) impinge upon the quality of our lives. Moreover, in sharing with virtue friends, one most perfectly learns about virtue, and hence one is in the best possible position to act towards others as demanded by our ever-changing circumstances. In learning these things, to use words that echo the wonderfully expressive title of Nussbaum's influential book, one also learns about the fragility of one's own goodness, and of the goodness of others. Because one is (ideally) content with who one is and one is able to recognize the fragility of one's own good fortune, one is also able to appreciate how others may not be in the same position, and one is able to act in ways that are expressive of this understanding – one is able, for instance, to feel compassion for others and to act accordingly. Moreover, one can only act compassionately or, more generally, one can only act in an appropriate manner, if one has a practical understanding of the good of persons – an understanding that is most perfectly learned and perfected in the company of those who live in accordance with complete virtue – because only with this sort of understanding will one be able adequately to inform the actions one directs towards those who are not living in accordance with the good. And indeed, the more sophisticated one's practical understanding of the good for persons is, the more clearly one will know how to direct one's actions towards others. With a practical understanding of the good for persons one is better able to put oneself in the position of someone else because one has a general practical understanding of how (internal and external) circumstances mould the lives of individuals. Learning from engaging intimately in friendships that are expressive of goodness teaches one to see the complex intricacies of the human soul, and to act in ways that constitute and express this profound understanding.[55]

It might also be worth mentioning here that this capacity to put oneself in another person's shoes, even if imperfectly, as is, more often than not, the case, is further evidence that we are creatures of the same sort. Of course, these projections are always subject to revision. But we are only able meaningfully to revise our interpretations if we already have a reasonably good idea that, on the whole, our interpretations are adequate.

It could be contested that a person like me, a white, middle-class male, living comfortably in the West, is not able to understand what it is to be, say, a member of some discriminated against minority group (an indigenous Australian for instance). Indeed, it could further be argued, and quite rightly so, that arrogant claims to understanding have had disastrous consequences. Although I think that many injustices have undoubtedly been committed, at least in part, in the name of purported universal ideals (think of the crusades and the destruction of so many pre-Colombian civilizations), it is equally true that the recognition of our common humanity is what leads many aid workers to help people in need across the globe. Indeed, I think the world would be a very sad place if we could not come to understand other people as fundamentally similar to us. Fortunately, we can make sense of others, and we can do this quite well. Many have recognized the suffering of others that, for instance, forms of imperialism have produced, and we have been able to recognize this suffering insofar as we have been able to recognize the common humanity we share with those who have suffered from injustices. I can recognize the plight of the slum dwellers in South Africa, indigenous Australians, Tibetans and the Palestinians because, even though I do not belong to these social groups, I am able to recognize them as similar to me in many relevant ways – I can empathize with their suffering. In general, it seems to me that our common humanity underlies the very possibility of making sense of difference. Differences among us can only be made intelligible in light of what is common to us all. Generally, recognizing evils inflicted upon others presupposes our capacity to empathize with those who are suffering. We must be able to tell that they are suffering, and we can only do this because there are bridges that connect our 'worlds'.

A person who has a practical understanding of the good possesses the measure of the good. Like the measure of health a doctor possesses, which allows him or her to identify particular ailments that affect us, a *phronimos* possesses a measure that allows him or her to identify states of privation with regard to our practical rational fabric. However, there is a fundamental difference between the sort of understanding a doctor possesses and the understanding of a *phronimos*. The understanding of a *phronimos*, we know, necessarily reflects itself in the manner in which he or she conducts his or her life, whilst this is not necessarily the case with a doctor's understanding of medicine (a doctor does not have to live in a manner that promotes his or her health, or anyone else's health for that matter, in order to count as possessing knowledge of medicine).

Indeed, a *phronimos* is the sort of individual who lives his or her life in accordance with the *telos* – the good – of persons. He or she understands that every person is fundamentally good in the sense that we are defined by a given ethical ideal. It follows that any act of evil can only be a consequence of ignorance – of ignorance of our defining *telos*.[56] And second, it follows that a *phronimos* will have a practical understanding that all evil comes as a consequence of practical ignorance.[57] Although this claim could be contested on the grounds that many evil actions are premeditated, I nevertheless do not think it counts as evidence against the view I am currently defending. One could, after all, deliberately plan to harm for certain reasons and be mistaken in one's reasoning. A high-flying entrepreneur, to take a paradigmatic example, could, for certain bad reasons, systematically and deliberately exploit Third World labour for the sake of amassing capital. He or she could reason along the lines that power is all that matters in this world, that this world has always been a nasty place and, indeed, that if one did not play to the tune of this nastiness, one would simply be another worthless loser (like the people he or she exploits as he or she would exploit any other 'natural resource'). There might be several ways of showing why a purported argument of this sort is flawed, but there is one reason that is of particular interest to us here. The argument is 'blind' to the *eudaimon* ideal. So, even though the entrepreneur in question is, in some sense, fully aware of what he or she is doing, and why he or she is doing it, he or she is nonetheless still acting out of (practical) ignorance.[58]

In sharing intimately one ideally learns to understand, and thereby appreciate human joy and suffering, and also the intimate nature of being a person – one learns about the rational fabric that constitutes a given individual as a person. In sharing with others in this manner one learns that others are like oneself, and in this way one learns to empathize with others. Of course, understanding how others are like me does not involve seeing others as identical to me. Rather, it involves, among other things, having a grasp of how my character would have developed in different circumstances (both internal and external) and having the capacity to identify these counterfactual possibilities in others. In this manner I am able to empathize with others, not because they are identical, but because I have an understanding of how they have developed as individuals with unique characters. If I was in these circumstances, and I had these capabilities, I would have lived much the same life he or she is currently living. I appreciate, say, my partner not because he or she is identical to me (although I might appreciate some aspects of him or her because they are similar, in some respects, to the way I am), but because I am able to understand how he or she has become the unique individual that he or she is. Additionally, I can only perform this marvellous interpretative feat because there is a great degree of similarity between us – because I am able to identify him or her as a person.[59]

Nussbaum quotes a passage from Aristotle, which clearly presents Aristotle's view on the pedagogical role *philia* plays in the formation of a good life:[60]

The love of base people is harmful: for, being unstable, they share in base activities, and they become base through assimilation to one another. But the love of good people is good and increases with their association. And they seem to become better by their activity and their correction of one another. For they model their tastes and values on one another's – from which we get the proverbial expression 'excellence from excellence'.[61]

In thinking how to act in morally demanding circumstances – circumstances that test the strength of one's character – one often thinks of how others, or possible others (invented by basing ourselves on the concrete experiences we have of others), would act, and one compares these projections with one's own views regarding how to proceed. And, indeed, it seems that being able to have a good idea of how others would act in a given situation depends on having observed how those closest to us have acted in comparable circumstances.[62] Crucially though, knowing how others would act in any given situation or, indeed, knowing how one would act in any given situation is not something that can typically be established once and for all precisely because ethical action, as already discussed, is not typically rule-governed.[63] Rather, it is, amongst other things, by assessing the ongoing moves in life by those closest to us, and comparing these moves with moves we have made or with moves we would make or could have made, that we come to develop and perfect the appropriate qualities of character. The proximity to the other participants of a given relationship is crucial given that one can only learn to grasp the relationships – the rational pattern – that exist between the different beliefs, intentions, desires, goals, etc. of a given individual, and the relationship of these attitudes with the behaviour of the same individual, in the intimacy of our ongoing close relationships. That this is the case shows how crucial virtue friendships are for developing a good character.

One could imagine a situation in which one went about substituting virtuous friends with other virtuous friends in such a way that none of one's friendships were continuous, but in which one would permanently be engaged with some virtuous individual(s). The possibility of there being cases of this sort would seem to provide good evidence against Aristotle's view that virtue friendships must be continuous. Since, arguably, one could, in such situations, have all that is significant in continuous virtue friendships. But, on final analysis, I do not think this is the case, given that fleeting relationships of the sort just described do not provide the level of intimacy required for developing a deep understanding of the fabric of a given individual's character (to come to understand the particular manner in which a given individual instantiates the ideal of complete virtue – the rational ideal). The duration of a relationship is an important factor in its quality.[64] An individual who spent his or her life moving from short-term friendship to short-term friendship would only develop a correspondingly superficial understanding of how people are. For this reason, he or she would not have any significant point of comparison between the ongoing journey of his or her character and the character of others. Additionally, it is only in the ongoing company of specific virtue friends that one is able to weave one's life together with the lives of one's friends by the mutual choices of activities, and in a way that is constitutive of the *eudaimon* ideal. It is in the continuous and ongoing engagement in shared activities with someone of good character that one can learn and further develop the habit of acting in conformity with the good.

Clearly, to be able to learn from a friend, one must be similar in many ways to one's friend. Indeed, more radically, Aristotle argues that the nature of *philia* is very much like the nature of self-love. I am able to commune with someone if I am able to recognize someone, so to speak, as another me. Aristotle strikingly puts it thus: 'Further, we say about friendship such things as that friendship is equality, and true friends a single soul.'[65] He is not claiming here that there must exist a relationship of qualitative identity between my friend and me.[66] Rather, he is claiming, to use a passage quoted by Sherman,[67] that 'friendship is not consensus concerning everything, but a consensus concerning practical matters for the parties involved and concerning those things that contribute to living together'.[68] So, my friend, according to Aristotle, is like me with regard to those fundamental aspects involved in sharing a life together. We could say then, that the agreement at issue here is a practical one – an agreement with regard to a common ethic and a common set of general interests and aspirations. In other words, it is a kind of consensus regarding that which one considers to be good and desirable – a consensus which allows friends to weave their lives together in a fabric which contributes to the good of each *philoi*.[69]

A crucial factor that differentiates close friendships from other sorts of ethical engagement is that, ideally, when one engages with a close friend, one engages with an individual not just for this or that reason, but in ways that summon the mutual expression of our characters. One engages with someone's whole life. It is by engaging in these sorts of dialogical engagement that one is able to recognize one's humanity in the fullest sense – one is able to recognize that one is relevantly like those one is sharing with. And in this manner, one is best able to inform one's actions towards others (not just friends, but to persons in general) in a way that reflects a sensitivity to the subtleties of the human spirit.

I must stress at this point that one does not learn the virtues once and for all such that, once they are learned, there is nothing more left to do but to act virtuously. I have already described how the circumstances for action are innumerable, making it, in principle, impossible to provide an exhaustive list of universally applicable principles for action. Like painting, acting in accordance with complete virtue is a kind of know-how which allows an individual to act virtuously in innumerably distinct circumstances and in ways that are not constrained by a rigid set of context-neutral totalizing maxims. At best, all we can provide is a series of rules of thumb. Like doing exercise, perfecting the technique of living well is an ongoing practice. Like a sport or the act of painting, good living is a practice that is perfected in the ongoing company, in this case, of virtuous individuals. Given this thesis, it is clear that there is great scope for differences with regard to the manner in which different individuals act in accordance with complete virtue – ways that might not always be fully compatible with one another.

Indeed, moral demands placed on us by life are many, and they often compete for our attention with each other. For example, the demands one's children place on oneself might conflict with the demands of caring for one's ageing parents. And these sorts of demands might in turn compete for one's attention against demands such as those of the environment or world poverty. It seems clear to me that there is no single ideal way of catering for all the conflicting demands placed on our lives, nor can one always successfully satisfy all these demands. If one decides to give large proportions of one's time and energy to one's children, then one might be unable to pay due respect to other equally important and urgent demands. Working through all these conflicting demands is perhaps one of the central tasks of our complex and multifaceted lives, and it is clear that many conflicts with others can and do arise from the choices we make with regard to how we prioritize, even with the best of intentions and the clearest understanding.

Sherman argues, correctly I think, that to have a character is not just to have qualities that inform this or that particular course of action but, rather, a character is expressed by an overall network of specific modes of operation that define a specific individual as such.[70] But if specific individuals are defined as such in this manner, then one simply cannot hold that to act in accordance with complete virtue is to act in ways that make for the homogenization of persons. Persons typically have different histories, interests and dispositions and any complete ethic must take these variations, which have an effect on action, into account. Indeed, by taking into account the variations of character one must also take into account the inevitable problem of conflicts of interest amongst even the best of us (in even the best possible community). I do not think that the genuine possibility of conflict in even the best social organization presents a problem for the thesis, which I shall defend more fully in the next section, that there is a *telos* of social organizations (the ideal social organization being that which provides the ideal conditions for the flourishing of its members). Remember that a *eudaimon* subject, among other things, is an individual who takes other concerns into consideration when making a given practical choice. But concern for others does not entail that one will always be able to resolve particular conflicts of interest. For example, at times we encounter situations in which there are fewer resources than required for realizing a whole range of projects, and choices must be made regarding how to channel the resources. If all these projects are perceived to be of equal or similar importance, then obviously conflicts might arise, even with the best of intentions. A *eudaimon* subject is able to work around these conflicts and make appropriate concessions when necessary. More generally, a *eudaimon* subject is the sort of individual who is best able to work around these irreconcilable differences (where possible) because he or she understands that the overall pattern of his or her good life is embedded in a greater social fabric without which he or she could not have become that very individual. Because a *eudaimon* individual understands this, he or she will be in a position to make concessions with an understanding that the concessions are for the overall good of his or her life (a good which implicates the lives of others).

In the next section I shall argue that the very possibility of establishing the best sorts of ethical relationship with others we do not know depends on having learnt to act in accordance with complete virtue towards, and with, one's *philoi*. In this way I will establish a bridge between what could be characterized as an ethic of social engagements and the ethic that defines *philia*. Peta Bowden lucidly argues along similar lines. She claims that:

> Thus, though the virtues of citizen relations may appear to be quite independent of those that structure more personal caring relations, success in understanding and practice of citizenship depends on recognition of the crucial ways in which it is strengthened and supported by caring values. Once the social conditions for public contracts of trust, promises, rights and responsibilities are in place, it is easy to take this impersonal morality in its own terms and to ignore its all-important conditions. As a result, the ethics of citizen practices are seen as quite self-sufficient and independent of the ethics of informal interpersonal practices.[71]

In establishing this connection I will also have established in broad outline the fundamental relationship between specific sorts of social organization and individual flourishing.

## *Philia* and Justice

> ... *in one sense we call those acts just that tend to produce and preserve happiness and its components for the political society.*[72]

I shall refer to the ethical ideal that informs our interactions, including our emotional responses, with our community as communal justice.[73] By so doing I am consciously basing myself on the notion of justice expressed in the following passage by Aristotle:

> We see that all men mean by justice that kind of state of character which makes people disposed to do what is just; and similarly by injustice that state which makes them act unjustly and wish for what is unjust.[74]

This characterization of justice as a state of character (and of the actions that flow from it should come as no surprise given that Aristotle lists justice as one of the virtues.[75] Justice, in the sense expressed above, is a state of character which a just individual possesses, and which makes him or her act justly. Indeed, Aristotle further claims that:

> This form of justice, then, is complete virtue, but not absolutely, but in relation to our neighbour. And therefore justice is often thought to be the greatest of

virtues, and 'neither evening nor morning star' is so wonderful; and proverbially 'in justice is every virtue comprehended'.[76]

So, not only is justice a virtue according to Aristotle, but it is complete virtue, 'but not absolutely'. It is not complete virtue absolutely because it is complete virtue only in relation to others rather than being virtue both in relation to others and to oneself. A given action counts as just if it is the sort of action a person of good character would direct towards others and which reflects his or her goodness. Of course, this Aristotelian conception of justice is not as wide-ranging as the conception of justice I am most interested in discussing here. Aristotle's conception of justice extends no further than the bounds of an aristocratic city-state. Nonetheless, I do think communal justice, as characterized above, flows from Aristotle's conception of justice as complete virtue in relations to others.

In the previous section I argued that one could only fully develop the best possible character if one's intimate relationships are healthy and, more particularly, only if one has virtue friends. It follows that having healthy relationships, and particularly having virtue friends, is a prerequisite for being ideally just (in Aristotle's sense of justice), and this is simply because complete virtue is cultivated amongst these ideal sorts of relationship.

I will now proceed to argue that communal justice flows from Aristotle's basic notion of justice. Indeed, given that the *teloi* of individual lives is *eudaimonia*, it follows that the *telos* of justice, however construed, must also be, in some sense, *eudaimonia*. And, I might add, it is in relationship to our *telos* that justice, however construed, is ultimately rendered intelligible, such that a conception of justice that did not consider what it is to live as flourishing persons would be a radically incomplete conception – it would be a conception that did not address the question 'Why does justice matter?'. Justice, however construed, must ultimately be for the sake of *eudaimonia*, and it is in this relationship that it is ultimately rendered intelligible. This follows simply because, as we know by now, the very purpose of human associations generally (and justice, however construed, is a fundamental regulator of human associations) is the achievement of *eudaimonia* and, crucially, it is the achievement of *eudaimonia* by each and every one of the members of a given community (currently the global community).

Before continuing, I must confess that I am not sure whether it is possible to even come close to instantiating the ideal of justice in our global community. Such an ideal might perhaps only be reached in smaller, more localized communities (a city-state, for instance) for the good reason that there is very probably a psychological limit which restricts the scope of our possible moral concerns, and that this limit may not extend as far as our global community. It is clear that we can only have a relatively small number of close friends, and there seems to be equally good reasons for suspecting that our sphere of moral concerns, which is typically much wider than our circle of love, cannot stretch out to cover the entire globe. If it were the case that there is no chance of achieving the ideal of justice in our global community, then I think we would have to conclude that a global community is a corrupt (de-formed) form of community.

It might be protested here that maybe the problem is not so much that our global community is just too big, but that it lies in the concept of 'global community' itself. Perhaps the concept of community should be defined in relation to the purported psychological limits of our moral concerns (or something of this sort). The problem with a counterargument of this sort is that it does not consider what we are doing when arguing that a community is best defined in terms that, in some sense, exclude the possibility of there being global communities. What we are doing when defining community in a way that takes into consideration our psychological limits (or something of this sort) is, in fact, defining an ethical ideal of community. And indeed, it is in relation to this ideal that one is able to judge that a global community might not really, in a sense, be a community at all. A global community might be defined as 'not really' a community at all in a way that is quite different from the way in which we would define, say, a tree or a silent morning as not really being communities. If our global community was, in some sense, not a community at all, it would not be because of a category confusion (as in holding that trees and silent mornings are communities), but because a community of that purportedly monstrous size would be a grossly deformed community. A global community, we may conclude, is indeed a community, even though it might be a corrupt one by virtue of its size. It might just be that the ideal of justice could not, in principle, be established in a community of this size.[77]

Furthermore, I think it will not do simply to argue that we should attempt to instantiate the ideal of justice in sub-communities of our global community, given that this would ignore the fact that the ideal of justice is an ideal that can only be achieved when the conditions for individual flourishing for every member of a given community have been achieved. And every member of our community is every member that is linked to a web of dialogical relations, which in our case covers the entire globe.

Yet perhaps instantiating the ideal of justice is not important for achieving individual *eudaimonia*. Maybe all that is required is that a given subsection of the global community, within which a given individual lives, is a flourishing quarter of the global community for that individual to flourish. I certainly think that living in a relatively morally rich subsection of a community would be greatly beneficial for individual flourishing. But, I also think that the *best* life, as I hope to show below, can only be lived if an entire community, and not merely a subsection of a wider community, within which a given life is couched, is a flourishing one.

I must also add, by way of clarification, that it is important not to confuse the second sense of justice – the communal sense – with a third, and in my view, less philosophically interesting sense – namely, the one that refers to that which is stipulated in the law. I think this third, stipulative sense of justice, is less interesting from a philosophical point of view because stipulations have no persuasive force, if ungrounded.[78] Laws should not, after all, command respect and obedience exclusively because they are created by the judiciary, or because they are widely accepted (or some other reason of this sort). Rather, what ultimately gives the law its *raison d'être* are certain standards of goodness, and these emanate from the core of our rational existence. Indeed, we have already seen how goodness is explicitly determined by an analysis of the sort of creatures that we are – creatures who ideally live *eudaimon* lives.

Let us now return to the issue of *philia* and better integrate it with the issue of justice. A community, and not just an ideal community, can be seen as a network of *philia* precisely because individual friendships are embedded in a network of friendships that constitute a community at large – including our contemporary global community. One could say that, in this respect, friendships (and not just virtue friendships) are the glue of the social. Moreover, it would also be appropriate to claim that in an ideal community – a community which could be characterized minimally as a community which lacked the basic forms of morally unacceptable relationships identified in the previous section, namely exploitative and purely commercial ones – virtue friendships and other acceptable forms of relationships such as the love towards one's children and instrumental friendships would be the basic bonds which constitute the social. But it is also crucial not to lose sight of the fact that even the best community would not be one in which one's concern would only stretch as far as those one loves. There are other important forms of communion that also establish valuable links between persons, such as indirect relationships – for example, that between a leader and those he or she leads or that between a distant provider of services and a consumer. Indeed, communities that totally lacked an appreciation of indirect relationships would be communities in which there would be no practical understanding of the role communities at large play in providing the conditions and determining the character of individuals' direct circles of love.

Given that having a good life involves having a practical understanding of what it is to be a person, and given that being a person ideally involves living amongst others, then a *eudaimon* individual must have a practical understanding not only of how to commune with those closest to him or her, but also of how to commune generally. But even though it is important to stress that a good life cannot be a life that is ignorant of the demands placed on it by the 'life' of its community at large, it is equally true that a *eudaimon* subject learns about human joy and suffering – about what is generally important and not important in human life – in the intimate company of his or her friends. Furthermore, learning about human joy involves knowing how to rejoice in the joy of others when warranted, and learning about human suffering involves being able to share that suffering to some degree, and to act accordingly. The relevant knowledge is primarily learned and exercised in the circles of love within which we dwell.

It is worth mentioning here that, as discussed above, the *telos* of human associations is to create the ideal conditions required of a community for the achievement of *eudaimonia* by *each*, and not merely by most members of that association.[79] So, there is a sense in which my *telos* is implicated in the *telos* of each member of our community. This claim, of course, does not in and of itself imply that we ought to direct our concerns not just towards those closest to us, but also towards our community at large. I am aware that, as it stands, this discussion is inadequate. I only intend it as a first step. But, nevertheless, I think this first step is an important one. It is a big step forward given that it helps us further recognize our deep *interconnectedness*.

Our interconnectedness is also evidenced by the fact, already discussed above, that communities can be appropriately characterized as outwardly expanding webs of love. Understanding the nature of communities in this manner helps us visualize how the right conditions of our direct circles of love are dependent on our community at large, such that we could not reasonably conceive of the health of our immediate circles independently of considering the health of the community within which our lives, and the lives of those closest to us, are played out. But there is more to be said here, and at this point the metaphor of a circle of love could be slightly misleading in that it suggests a clear demarcation between those inside and those outside a circle, when in fact no such clear demarcation exists. The notion of a circle may also be misleading both because what I have been referring to as a circle of love is in fact a dynamic and changing *web* of relationships, to use a more appropriate metaphor, such that the limits of the fabric of relationships that constitutes our 'circle' at a given moment are never clearly demarcated; and also, more importantly, because almost inevitably each individual who forms part of our immediate web of love also belongs to other such webs, such that the love cultivated in one region of the fabric of relationships, which constitutes our entire community, overflows into other webs in this direct and outwardly expanding manner.

This brief sketch allows us to observe how the love cultivated in one zone of our social fabric flows through the delicate fibres that link us all into one community, such that one cannot properly consider the well-being of those closest to oneself without at the same time taking into account the general framework of interlocking dialogical relationships which constitutes a (global) community, and within which one's web of love is embedded. So, if my brief description of the general structure of communities just specified is correct, and such a description is hard to deny, then it is simply not consistently possible to separate self-concern and our concern for our direct web of love, from the concern we ought to have for our community (broadly construed). There is a relationship of mutual constitution between the quality of the webs of love that constitute the social and the quality of the social as a whole. In this manner we can see how the concern for one's own *eudaimonia* and the *eudaimonia* of those we love ideally implicates our concern for the *eudaimonia* of our community at large. Individual *eudaimonia* is not simply constituted by the relationships which constitute one's direct web of love given that one's direct web of love is constituted as such by its embeddedness in a whole network of complexly interlocked webs of love which spread out to constitute, in our contemporary case, and perhaps unfortunately, the entire global community.

It is also important to note here that I do not think that my account of how love spreads out through the webs of love that constitutes our community is just a description of an ethical ideal. Indeed, I think it is uncontroversially true that the great majority of us form part of some localized web of love, although, for the most part, these webs are to a greater or lesser degree imperfect. So, given my account of how localized webs of love are embedded in communities (the global community in our case), and given that the love cultivated in these localized webs is imperfect, then the imperfection must spread outwardly in the manner described above. It must also be noted that the problems in one area of our community do not spread out homogeneously throughout the community. No doubt there are pockets of our population that are better off, morally speaking, than others, but I also think that it is hardly possible that these pockets that are 'better off' can remain immune from the rest of our community. I think it is clear that if, for the most part, or to a large extent, the intimate relationships of the members of our community were unhealthy or corrupt, then corrupt forms of love would spread out through the web that constitutes our (global) community in ways that would significantly influence the general fabric of our community, and hence the quality of our individual lives.

For example, it is common knowledge that the consumption of goods produced by Third World labour by affluent quarters of the population has a direct impact on those producing the goods. I will focus on this example and attempt to draw some crucial conclusions from it. It is not hard to see, given that the evidence is overwhelming that those who have the relevant resources to purchase products produced by Third World labour, on the whole and despite knowing where the products come from and under what conditions they are made, prefer to purchase those products rather than do without them (even if, as is often the case, these products are not of primary necessity and even if it is a well-established and universally known fact that a great deal of human suffering could be avoided by ceasing to buy them). It seems clear that, on the whole, the pull to possess these consumer goods is stronger than the pull to stop investing in human suffering. Why do consumers (and I do not consider myself to be an innocent bystander here), on the whole, prioritize in this incredible way? More interestingly, how is it that an individual, who at an intellectual level recognizes that human lives are more important than possessing relatively cheap products, is nevertheless able to continue this seemingly immoral practice? I think the reason is plain, given what has already been discussed regarding the virtues. One must, we have already seen, possess the right dispositions in order to be able to act in accordance with the good. These dispositions are developed in the company of the right sorts of people. The right sorts of people – namely, virtuous individuals – are rare, particularly in societies where the cultivation of virtue is not valued.

I am not, however, attempting to de-emphasize the role cultural climates play on individual lives. Cultural climates no doubt play a central role. But we learn to value these climates through those to whom we are closest. Those we love, one could say, are our gateways to history. Moreover, and crucially, cultural climates are neither abstract entities, nor a kind of fog that sets in on groups of individuals. On the contrary, they are constituted by the ways in which particular individuals conduct their lives. The responsibility must be placed on individuals and on their bonds of intimacy.

However, it does not follow from this all too brief description that one ought to be concerned in the same manner and to the same degree for every member of one's (global) community. It would be crazy to suggest such a scenario. As I argued in the previous section, it is only possible to have a few good friendships, and psychological limits of this sort apply also to friendships generally. One reason it is not possible to have more than a few good friends is that close bonds require time and effort, and obviously one's energy reserves are not inexhaustible. Also, and relatedly, not only is it clear that there are unavoidable hierarchies in even our closest relationships, but also that most of our relationships with others are indirect. Indirect relationships are precisely that because they involve no level of intimacy whatsoever (one knows only a minute proportion of our global community, and one's intimates are, for the most part, a minute proportion of those whom one knows). So when I say that one must be concerned for one's community, I am not making the radically unreasonable claim that one must love every member of one's community (if someone claimed that they loved everyone then either they would be lying or they would simply have no idea of what they are talking about). Rather, I merely think, following on from what I have thus far discussed, that one must *care* for one's community at large.[80]

Let me also add here that it is not merely the case that, because there happen to be psychological limits regarding how many we can love, we ought not even to attempt to love everyone in the same manner. It is also a good thing that love is hierarchical. Indeed, the exclusivity of our closest bonds of love is a fundamental condition for those relationships to have the level of intimacy that defines them. A mark of my love towards you is that you are special to me, and you are special to me insofar as you are not, for me, one person amongst many. You stand out from the background of human associations within which my life is embedded and defined.

To recapitulate, there is no sense in which one can reasonably separate one's well-being from that of one's community. For this reason, I have said, we ought to *care* for our community. Given the above account of our radical interconnectedness, I think it is safe to claim that the basic motivation for caring for one's community at large is ideally a practical understanding of how one's *eudaimonia* is implicated in the well-being of one's (global) community. The manner in which one ideally engages with one's community is analogous with the manner in which one ideally engages with others intimately in that one ideally engages not solely for one's own benefit, but, rather, with an understanding of how the *eudaimonia* of one's friend, or indeed of one's (global) community, is part of one's own happiness, rather than being merely a means to an end. One ideally does this because there is no sense in which one can consistently separate one's own well-being from the overall well-being of one's community. I ideally see myself as genuinely *forming part* of my community not only because, ideally, my community yields the conditions for my continued *eudaimon* existence, but also because my happiness contributes to, and is constituted by, the overall happiness of my community.

We have seen how individual justice (complete virtue) spreads out through the community thus forming communal justice. There are, of course, other forms of justice, such as retributive, stipulative and distributive justice of which I have said nothing, or almost nothing. My intention in this section has merely been to provide the basis from which justice derives its *raison d'être*, and I think I have done just that by specifying how individual justice entails communal justice. I have, so to speak, established the ethical basis for justice, and this is all I have space to do here.

And, indeed, in establishing how it is that our lives are intertwined, I think I have also established some, though clearly not all, of the fundamental aspects of the ethical ideal of social organizations. In particular, I have shown that, to a large extent, the responsibility for constructing an ideal society rests not so much on our leaders, but on the manner in which we relate to those we love. I have shown that it is from this basis of love that we learn how to relate to our community at large. Finally, and perhaps most importantly, I have shown that the quality of one's own life cannot be separated from concerns about others generally. Of course, much important work remains still to be done with regard to how the practice of love fostered in one's web of intimate relationships ideally involves developing the practice of care towards one's community at large. This is a topic waiting to be developed in another book. But what is important here is that the basic structural features of what could be characterized as our radical interconnectedness have been laid out. The *telos* of a community is to create all the conditions a community can provide for each of its members to flourish. And, indeed, if one considers how one's network of intimate relationships is embedded in the larger network of the social, then one can observe how one's care for those closest to us cannot properly be separated from an ethical outlook directed towards the community that creates the conditions for the very existence of one's specific network of intimates.

## A Politic of Happiness

It must be stressed that the sort of ideal being advocated here cannot be one of perfect harmony. Indeed, the only environment in which perfect harmony could be achieved is a perfectly homogeneous one, and such an environment could hardly foster the development of good character. Recall the discussion in Chapter 6 where I dealt with Orwell's over-homogeneous world portrayed in *Nineteen Eighty-Four*. The uniqueness of our individual histories makes each of us special – it makes us different from each other. And, indeed, the uniqueness of our histories is a function of differing social circumstances – differing circumstances that could not be instantiated in radically homogeneous environments such as the one conceived by Orwell. Moreover, as further discussed in Chapter 6 (following Davidson and Arendt particularly), difference could be characterized as an 'epistemic necessity'. What I mean to say here is that being a person in the fullest sense involves having a full sense of the self/other/world relationship – a sense only to be had in a pluralistic environment. In such a community conflicts will be unavoidable and, in many cases, they are desirable. For instance, dwelling in a system of difference helps one better understand where one is coming from. The fact that you do things differently is an invitation for me to reconsider the way in which I do things. So, a community of friends must also be a community of difference. Another way of making much the same point is to claim that an ideal community is one of individuals – strictly speaking.

Relatedly, and as discussed above, two paradigmatic sorts of relationships with others that should be avoided, because they undermine the autonomy that defines individuals as such, are purely exploitative relationships and purely commercial ones or, more generally, those that are blind to the humanity of those who form part of one's social group (the global community). Blinding oneself to the humanity of others – to their irreducible individuality – amounts to blinding oneself to the *telos* that defines each of us. It is typical, for instance, that, in states of war, adversaries erase the humanity of their enemies, and this is something that seems to be a requirement for killing them. Primo Levi argues along similar lines in describing his own experience, and those of others, in the Nazi camps. He argues that the central reason for the systematic mistreatment and humiliation of prisoners in Nazi camps was to create the conditions for killing. Levi reminds us of the words of Stangl – ex-commandant of Treblinka – who, when asked 'Considering that you were going to kill them all ... what was the point of the humiliations, the cruelties?', replies, 'To condition those who were to be the material executors of the operations. To make it possible for them to do what they were doing.' 'In other words', Levi continues, 'before dying the victim must be degraded, so that the murderers will be less burdened by guilt.'[81] Erasing the humanity of others amounts to erasing the fact that our lives are intertwined by the common ideal of a collective pursuit of happiness. The attitude that is necessary for killing, as one kills when one kills in a battlefield or in a concentration camp, is one that places others – the enemies – beyond humanity, which is in effect to act in ways that do not pay homage to the *eudaimon* ideal. Consequently, it is an attitude that turns against those who erase the humanity of others. So, the sort of community we should aspire to live in is a pluralistic one and one that fosters relationships that do not involve blinding ourselves to the humanity of others.

Indeed, it is not merely in extreme cases such as, to use yet another example, the attitudes of US officials towards Saddam Hussein – portrayed as a monster or a caricature but certainly not as a fallible human being – and towards the Iraqis in general who are portrayed as something like Hussein's shadow, that the humanity of individuals is erased. There are many other types of relationship in which we engage daily that undermine the humanity of our fellow humans. I am thinking of male attitudes towards women (which is exploited to great effect by Hollywood, and the tabloid press), of the attitude of transnational corporations in their relentless pursuit of cheap labour in Asia (in particular), of the way in which we engage with providers of goods and services, and of the manner in which dominant groups typically treat disadvantaged minority groups, such as indigenous peoples, criminals and beggars on the street. Indeed, it is perplexing that contemporary pluralistic Western countries and their populations quite easily engage in dehumanizing relationships with others, given the pluralistic ethos they purport to embody. However, there is a general reason why such exploitative practices are fostered – namely, that the pluralism embodied in contemporary neo-liberal democracies is radically individualistic. The ethos embodied is one that blinds people to one of the fundamental conditions for individuality – our radical interconnectedness.

Let us briefly study the sort of pluralism embodied in the West. Contemporary neo-liberal democracies are ones that archetypically privilege the expression of difference, and they do so, I might further add, to the detriment of a sense of our common essence – our common purpose. And I might also add that the lack of a sense that we have a common essence is, not surprisingly, linked to the fact that the contemporary subject is archetypically one that tends towards moral emptiness. MacIntyre's critique of the modern democratized self parallels my critique of the contemporary self – the self who dwells in what could be characterized as the age of consumption. In MacIntyre's words:

> This democratised self which has no necessary social content and no necessary social identity can then be anything, can assume any role or take any point of view, because it *is* in and for itself nothing.[82]

MacIntyre's critique of the 'democratised self' – the sort of self fostered by contemporary consumption-driven neo-liberal democracies – is based on a critique of what he refers to as 'emotivism'.[83] MacIntyre defines emotivism as the thesis that states that 'all moral judgments are *nothing but* expressions of preference, expressions of attitudes or feelings ...'.[84] It is not hard to see why this characterization of emotivism ties in very neatly with the moral bankruptcy of the contemporary subject. If, indeed, one embodies emotivism – the sort of ethic embodied in neo-liberal communities – then there is ultimately no reason, except the whimsical reason that this is simply what one desires, to behave in one way rather than in another, for there is little sense that life has a direction.

Let me frame the problem in slightly different terms. The problem with the contemporary subject, or one of the problems at any rate, is that a particular kind of contradiction cuts through his or her identity in that there are very strong social pressures for such individuals to develop fully as individuals, strictly speaking, but with the added condition that they do so in a groundless fashion. What this in effect means is that contemporary subjects are left without the relevant motivational resources that are required for choosing one life option over a plethora of other such options. But then the question forced upon us by reason is 'In what sense is one choosing if one is doing so arbitrarily, or almost so?'. Certainly, one might sometimes have to choose in an arbitrary fashion (when weightings are equally distributed over a field of alternatives), but the problem here is more extreme. The problem here is that when there is no fact of the matter regarding what is best, then there is no fact of the matter regarding how to form our lives through the choices we make. Any old life will do, or almost so. The arbitrariness might not be as extreme as I am portraying it here, but that is only because the ideals being fostered have not been taken to their extreme consequences. Not surprisingly, such a feeble condition as that fostered by contemporary nihilism makes us more manipulable – more gullible – and this mouldability seems to be the mark of individuals who inhabit our market-driven neo-liberal societies. If no goal in particular guides our lives, and no goal in particular is perceived as being more worthwhile than a plethora of alternative goals, then one will quite naturally be moved by the forces that sustain and define the *status quo* – namely, the forces of the market, the forces of a consumer-driven world. Paradoxically, it turns out that the pluralistic vision embodied by neo-liberal democracies are, on final analysis, anti-pluralistic in so far as they foster the perpetuation of the homogenizing forces of one overarching paradigm. In an important sense, the social pathology I am describing is akin to the pathology that would infect an immortal's life. As discussed in Chapter 5 the central problem of an immortal life is that it is a life that will inevitably be, or become, meaningless because the motivational resources required for meaningful choice-making cannot properly be embodied, and the reason why the orderings fail is that the sorts of constraint that define us as persons cannot properly be embodied by an immortal creature.[85] Similarly, the constraints that define us as persons cannot be properly embodied in a regime that fosters a nihilistic ethic, since one is unable properly to build one's life unless one has a sense of the good.

To recapitulate, as I have claimed, it is the arbitrariness of the contemporary subject's life that makes him or her gullible to the whims of the market. He or she follows what his or her fancy dictates (and he or she at the very least half-knows that the fancy in question is indeed just that), and fancies are easily manipulable. Indeed, a fancy-driven ethic is what informs our neo-liberal lives, and such an ethic is appropriately characterized as emotivist.

MacIntyre argues that one of the clearest manifestations of contemporary individuality is the one fostered by Sartre's extreme individualistic existential project. Following MacIntyre, I will focus on Sartre's *Being and Nothingness*. The problem with Sartre's existential project, or one of its problems at any rate, is that his project is one that purports to offer an account of how a free life ought to be lived, but it is an account that speaks of freedom in a groundless fashion. One could say that Sartre wants to ground a moral outlook – an existential moral outlook – on thin air, and of course, air is too ethereal to serve as a ground for anything. Sartre argues that:

> Indeed by the sole fact that I am conscious of the causes which inspire my action, these causes are already transcendent objects from my consciousness; they are outside. In vain shall I seek to catch hold of them; I escape them by my very existence. I am condemned to exist forever beyond my essence, beyond the causes and motives of my act. I am condemned to be free. This means that no limits to my freedom can be found except freedom itself or, if you prefer, that we are not free to cease being free.[86]

What is freedom if it is limitless? How can I act 'beyond the causes and motives of my act'? And, moreover, if one is free in such an extreme way – a way which I find almost impossible to comprehend – then it is a wonder that our lives do not simply fall apart and become totally amorphous; it is a wonder that our lives are not like those of jellyfish. Furthermore, if our freedom is so extreme, if it lies beyond causes and motives, if it lies beyond the narrative structure that seems to define our lives and from which our projects acquire their significance, then being free apparently amounts to little more than living like an actor who is able to change the roles he or she plays precisely because he or she is only contingently attached to such roles (if roles – all roles – are founded on whims, then roles are as whimsical as the whims that motivate them).[87] And, indeed, if Sartre's account of freedom is correct, then we might very well be condemned to be free. But fortunately we are not so condemned. Indeed, this investigation can be seen as an attempt to show why in fact we are not condemned at all. Instead, there is an invitation within us – an invitation to direct our lives in ways that are maximally fulfilling. If anything, we are condemned to keep on searching for happiness – for its embodiment. Our lives, if you like, are ideally condemned to be lived in a certain manner by the mere fact that we are persons. But, quite clearly, the language of condemnation is not appropriate in this context. Life offers itself to us as a gift and it comes with an invitation to refine it – with others.

Sartrean existentialism is only one version of the post-nihilistic project propelled by Nietzsche whose brilliance and perception are unquestionable, particularly when it comes to describing the modern condition. Nietzsche famously pronounces the death of God and, with God's death, the death of all ethical foundations. This fundamental pronouncement could be seen as one of the central inaugural acts of the nihilism that typifies our times. Indeed, Nietzsche was correct in seeing that no external authority could possibly ground morality and that is why he turned his gaze inwardly. Unfortunately, he never managed to overcome nihilism by this shift in gaze, and his lack of success was due, among other things, to inadequacies in what could be characterized as his existential psychology. In this regard I agree with MacIntyre's critique of Nietzsche, although his critique is somewhat different to mine. MacIntyre argues that although Nietzsche holds that his agenda goes against modern conceptions of the subject, in actual fact his emphasis on radical autonomy and on the purported fact that the source of the ethical is the radically autonomous individual, makes him a major proponent of liberal individualism.[88] Indeed, Nietzsche's failure to overcome nihilism is evidenced by the failure of the Apollo/Dionysus dynamic which is largely implicit throughout his entire corpus, and which is famously made explicit in *The Birth of Tragedy*. I shall not focus on this particular piece, but rather on an often-neglected essay which is, I think, outstanding for its relative clarity in dealing with the issues that presently concern us – namely, 'On the Uses and Disadvantages of History for Life'.[89] In this essay Nietzsche develops his doctrine of *forgetfulness* which is of primary relevance to our current concerns and, moreover, is intimately related to the Apollonian/Dionysian dynamic, which is meant to explain the human condition. I might just mention that nowhere in the above-mentioned essay is the Dionysian principle explicitly mentioned, but it is clear that Nietzsche is referring to it when discussing his conception of history. Nietzsche thinks of history – actual history primarily, as opposed to written history – as chaotic, deterministic, nonsensical and endlessly repetitive. And, like Borges's immortal discussed in Chapter 5, Nietzsche's historian is prototypically a grey-bearded one – an individual whose creative vital impulses have been exhausted by a deeply embodied understanding that there is nothing new to build and nothing new to do that is of any importance – vital impulses which would, so to speak, ideally transport us into a kind of divinity that lies ever beyond our grasp (the *suprahistorical*, to use Nietzsche's terminology). Nietzsche thinks that what is required in order to build, in order to live most fully, is a sense that what was built was permanent as opposed to impermanent – that is, divine, as opposed to merely earthly. History teaches us about the impermanent, the fleeting and the nonsensical, and too much of this will destroy us; it will render our lives meaningless. For the creative vital forces of the 'Apollonian oracle' – the oracle through which '[t]he Greeks gradually learned *to organize the chaos*'[90] – to have an effect on us we must be able to forget history to a certain extent. But this is not to say that such forgetfulness ought to be permanent and complete, for history plays a vital role in our lives. Without history, Nietzsche thinks, we would be as happy as grazing animals, but this is a happiness that is ultimately undesirable, since it is not human happiness:

> Consider the cattle, grazing as they pass you: they do not know what is meant by yesterday or today, they leap about, eat, rest, digest, leap about again, and so from morn till night and from day to day fettered to the moment and its pleasure or displeasure .... Then the man says 'I remember' and envies the animal, who at once forgets and for whom every moment really dies, sinks back into night and fog and is extinguished for ever. Thus the animal lives *unhistorically*....[91]

Either too much history or too little history will render our lives meaningless; it will thwart our creative impulses, and render our lives stagnant (like those of the grey-bearded historians or cattle). It is in the middle ground between the remembrance of history and its forgetfulness, Nietzsche thinks, that humans can flourish. The fundamental idea Nietzsche defends is that of a dialectic between the principles of chaos and order – the Dionysian and the Apollonian – and this dialectic can only be had if one is able both to remember and forget the chaos and insignificance of the reality that underlies our lives. In setting out his basic thesis Nietzsche claims that living fully depends:

> ... on one's being just as able to forget at the right time as to remember at the right time; on the possession of a powerful instinct for sensing when it is necessary to feel historically and when unhistorically. This, precisely, is the proposition the reader is invited to meditate upon: *the unhistorical and the historical are necessary in equal measure for the health of an individual, of a people and of a culture.*[92]

One of the problems with Nietzsche's account is that he is acknowledging the metaphysical priority of Dionysian chaos and also claiming that too much truth – too much knowledge and understanding – can only be destructive for us. So, he thinks, what we must do is learn to systematically lie to ourselves: the truth is unbearable without a healthy dosage of untruth – of self-deceit. Quite frankly, Nietzsche is asking for too much. He is quite literally asking us to build our lives like one creates a piece of fiction, and he asks us to do so half-knowing that we are, in fact, building celestial castles. Indeed, Nietzsche's super-subject – the *Übermensch* – is a kind of actor (like an immortal), an idea that we can explore further.

In his 'Nietzsche and the Problem of the Actor'[93] Paul Patton takes issue with contemporary conceptions of self, and does so by basing himself on Nietzsche's understanding of the modern subject as a kind of actor. Following Nietzsche's steps, Patton takes issue with the idea that the social roles taken up by an individual should be understood as akin to the roles of an actor on a stage, which is indeed the manner in which the contemporary neo-liberal subject understands him or herself (or, more precisely, the manner in which neo-liberal subjects tend to understand themselves). The problem is that the involvements of actors on a stage, unlike our ideal involvements with others, are archetypically detached from the roles they play (like Camus's outsider). An actor *qua* actor plays a role whilst a person *qua* person ideally *inhabits* one.[94] If we become role-players as opposed to role-inhabitors, then we fall into the trap Nietzsche thought modern Europe had fallen into (and which Nietzsche himself never really escapes). The roles that the modern subject can play are practically inexhaustible, and we modern subjects typically see ourselves as only weakly attached to these roles. What criteria might one have for choosing one role rather than another if the world is perceived as a kind of space for play-acting? As Patton points out, the issue of the actor cuts through the Nietzschean corpus; I might add that he – Nietzsche – never properly comes to terms with it, and the fact that he does not come to terms with it is a wonderfully clear expression of what is wrong with his post-nihilistic project and the defunct pluralism that flows from it. As Patton points out, Nietzsche's problem with actors is not that they take on roles, but that they are not committed to the roles they take on. The modern European, Nietzsche thinks, is fickle – that is, he or she is committed to nothing and will change his or her roles in accordance with passing fancies. Character under such conditions becomes a kind of accessory – a kind of ornament.

Nietzsche had no way of knowing about the development of the so-called 'entertainment industry' in our times, and of the almost divine nature we assign our most famous entertainers – our superstars. They are prototypically our role models; we dress like them, imitate their gestures and, typically, fantasize about being just like them. Our role models are individuals on stage playing roles and, moreover, the roles they play are chiefly those of actors in a fantasy world which is meant to be real, and which is to some extent perceived as real by us. It is as if the stage has become reality. Indeed, what we find most appealing about our superstars is the image they convey, and we care little about whether the image in question is conveyed on- or off-stage (in the roles they play for Hollywood, or in the roles they play at home in Beverly Hills). Another curious facet about our admiration for superstars is that they are admired as disposable items, and their disposability is evidence that superstars cater primarily for our whims. They are like fashion accessories. Indeed, the impermanence and the fickle nature of our admiration for these individuals we do not know is a very powerful sign that we are still living in a culture like the one Nietzsche so thoroughly despised.

However, Nietzsche is not opposed to the idea of an actor *per se* – not at all. As Patton points out, his super-subject is one who has a creative and dynamic commitment to his or her roles, and these views are consistent with what I have said thus far about the ideal Nietzschean subject. Unlike the Europeans of the Middle Ages, the ideal Nietzschean subject is not straitjacketed into a particular set of roles (the ideal subject knows about the Dionysian as well as the Apollonian) and, unlike the Modern European dandy, he or she is not fickle. However, the problem with Nietzsche's account of the super-subject is that this sort of subject is left with no grounds for commitment to the roles he or she purportedly ought to be committed to. One does not simply commit. Instead, one commits for certain reasons, and these reasons must ideally be good ones. In short, Nietzsche does not provide us with the motivational resources required for committing to a given mode of existence. He tries to overcome nihilism through his doctrine of forgetfulness, but how could one deliberately choose to forget knowing that one must forget in order to be able to commit to a role? Certainly, there is a sense in which we must forget things in order to move on, but Nietzsche wants much more of us, and I think he is asking for too much. He wants us to partially forget what he thinks is our tragic condition (as is evidenced by his description of the grey-bearded historian, who is grey-bearded precisely because he knows and cannot forget). In a way he wants us to ride the cusp of a contradiction. In short, he thinks that we must (selectively) hide from ourselves the meaninglessness of our existence in order for our existence to take on the appearance of meaningfulness. One is left to ask 'Why even bother living or, shall I say, surviving?'. Nietzsche ultimately offers us nothing for which to live, except what appears to be an antidote to suicide; he invites us to construct an Apollonian fantasy in order to conceal the meaninglessness of it all. Moreover, the antidote to suicide that Nietzsche offers is a philosophically sophisticated account of the grounds for modern selfhood – an account of a self who continues to populate our busy streets. Fortunately, we need not be as tragic as Nietzsche is, since there are strong grounds for holding a *eudaimonistic* ethic. We are not condemned – not at all.

Nietzsche offers us a lucid account of Modern subjectivity, and his observations are consistent with my observations relating to neo-liberal sensitivities. The contemporary subject is like Nietzsche's dandy except that he or she is a more extreme embodiment of dandyism. Note also that Nietzsche's Modern dandy is not unlike the immortal discussed in Chapter 5, and this is not surprising given that the Modern dandy, as Nietzsche observes, is permanently aware of the purported relativity and impermanence of it all, and this is purportedly because he or she cannot forget the meaninglessness of the never-ending narrative of history.[95] The contemporary neo-liberal subject is not merely a consumer of goods; he or she is also a consumer of roles, which amounts to saying that, to him or her, roles are like commodities – something to be desired and possessed, like being a superstar or possessing a fashion accessory. Nietzsche, more lucidly than anyone else, captures the spirit of our times, but his remedy for the malady that affects us does not allow us to overcome nihilism; it merely perpetuates it, and makes it more philosophically appealing.

After this perhaps far too brief tour through the post-nihilistic landscape that informs neo-liberal pluralism, we will return to what is central to our present concerns. But first let me restate the reason for the detour we have taken. The reason for engaging with Nietzsche and Sartre was to further illustrate the moral pathology of the contemporary subject. And, although both Nietzsche and Sartre are powerful proponents of pluralism insofar as they are proponents of a radical sort of individuality, as I hope to have shown, they defend the wrong sort of pluralism – the nihilistic and consequently ultimately self-defeating variety. As we know, a much better alternative to nihilistic pluralism exists. Given the sorts of creatures that we are – creatures ideally directed towards the ideal of achieving *eudaimonia* – we are ideally suited to living in a pluralistic yet communitarian community. We are who we are only insofar as we live amongst others, and we are best able to live fully in accordance with the what-it-is of persons in so far as we live in a community that fosters difference.[96]

What this investigation has revealed is that a study of the conditions for individuality implicates a study of our radical interconnectedness. Personhood is primarily an activity: to achieve *eudaimonia* is to be active amongst others – to engage in the sorts of relationship that are constitutive of *eudaimonia*. Further, to engage in these activities is to engage in activities that have as their goal the promotion of collective *eudaimonia*. Individual *eudaimonia*, we know, implicates collective *eudaimonia* such that the activities involved in living happily involve extending oneself towards others in ways that foster the good of the collective within which one's life is played out. However, since our energy reserves and our time are limited, we cannot extend ourselves indefinitely. What is crucial, however, is that overall goodness hangs on individual efforts, since collective happiness flows from the happiness of the individuals who constitute a given community. What transpires is that the task of forming a good social order is a task that flows from the specific organization that constitutes individual lives. This means that a good society is a function of individual initiative: a good social order flows upwards – from the individual to the collective. It therefore follows that one cannot expect to live happily if one delegates social responsibility to leaders. This is not to say that leaders are not required; it would be naive to think that central coordination of some sort is superfluous. Rather, the task of a central body should be to coordinate the different efforts made by individuals bent on the idea of achieving the social task of happiness. And, indeed, leaders do not stand over and above us. They are members of our community and, as such, they are bound by our essence. They, too, should see their task as one of promoting overall well-being. Their well-being, like the well-being of everyone else, hangs on this.

Leaders and public institutions seem to be necessary for coordinating the flow of difference that constitutes a healthy social order. However, given the role individuals should play in a healthy social conglomerate, it is apparent that we must reconsider the importance we typically assign to our leaders. The purpose of leadership and of our social institutions generally should not be seen as replacing individual responsibility. Individuals are not isolated marbles that need to be controlled or coordinated by a central power. Our beings are not delimited by the boundary of skin that physically separates us from the rest of the world; they extend themselves towards others, and implicate a community. The sort of ideal social organization that is constitutive of who we are is one of active participation in the common good – a good which is pluralistic, complex and dynamic. The goodness at issue in no way stands over and above individual interests. Collective goodness is that which is constituted by the goals of the individuals who comprise a community. There is no central unifying purpose above the goals of each of us, and that is simply because my individual goals are ideally a function of the goals of my collective. The unifying ideal of my community, as I have already said, is part of my own *eudaimonia*.

As previously mentioned, there will inevitably be conflicts which cannot be resolved between different interest groups, but understanding these differences within a *eudaimon* framework makes all the difference for it shows that my goodness is tied up with the goodness of those whose interests are incompatible with mine. Belligerent attitudes are attitudes that flow from the mistaken conception that conflicting interests should be understood atomistically rather than holistically. Part of the very essence of living amongst others in a pluralistic community is the ongoing negotiation of conflict. But, because the system of the social is a holistic one, the negotiation at issue is not negotiation between two or more parties who have nothing to do with each other – not at all. My goodness is a function of the manner in which I conceive of my own projects within the system of the social – a system which is constituted by conflicting others.

Think of differences that exist amongst friends and, indeed, differences within oneself. One is not a homogeneous substance; rather, living with oneself involves permanent negotiation. Similarly, we are not always in agreement with our close friends – and, indeed, may sometimes have with them deep differences – but this does not to mean that we will enter into a state of war with them: we typically respect that which is different in our friends. Differences, even radical differences, can exist side-by-side harmoniouly so long as we are able to understand where those we do not agree with are coming from. To understand others in this way is to lovingly embrace them as genuine others whose lives are intertwined with ours.

Let me reiterate that I cannot care for everyone in the same way that I care for those who are closest to me. This is a limit, and it is a limit that is constitutive of the very possibility of caring, since to care intimately is to care in an exclusive manner. Similarly, my sphere of concerns is limited by my psychological limits. I cannot care for everyone in the same way in which I care for those who are closest to me insofar as I cannot even identify the individual identities of each and every individual. I can genuinely care for those who are closest to me, and I can also care for humanity, but only insofar as I identify all members of my kind as having goals and aspirations that define each member as an individual; and I can do this even though I am ignorant of what those specific differentiating goals, or systems of goals, might be. The expansive move from those closest to me is inevitably a move up from particularity to generality – from the specific 'you' to the 'you' of humanity. This move has inevitable moral consequences. I can direct myself towards your specific problems insofar as you are close to me, and I can embrace specific concerns that touch me closely, but I cannot embrace all concerns. In this regard, solving every problem on Earth is well and truly beyond my capabilities. Indeed, there is no limit to the number of problems that might besiege our fallible species. A finite creature cannot extend itself indefinitely.

More generally, our psychological limits set constraints on the power we can exercise over others, and these constraints have inevitable social consequences. One cannot have a grip on everyone. This means that top-down governance, whose force emanates exclusively from the core of one or a few individuals, has no hope of succeeding. This in turn means that abuses of power can always be resisted. One can always choose to cease to listen, and if this resistance ripples through the fabric of the social then the despot might very well be left with no power at all. The case of the Danish resistance to the Nazi occupation during the Second World War is a glaring example of how leaders require a network of others in order to exercise power.

I can, at best, set off minor ripples in the social fabric and hope that this outwardly expanding force joins other such forces so as to produce a tidal wave of care that will upset the calm waters of indifference (for instance). Let me emphasize that I am not implying that individuals cannot produce great social change. There is ample historical evidence that individuals do, indeed, effect such changes, but no one can do this single-handedly. Those who lead us in ways that radically change the fabric of our societies are individuals whose guidance, for good or for bad, has inspirational force. What I am suggesting here is that social transformers only produce the impact that they do insofar as they are able to set off an outwardly expanding wave that embraces an entire people. This means that the effect an inspirational figure might have on the fabric that constitutes his or her community is not merely a function of what he or she has to offer as an individual. Instead, it is also, and perhaps even primarily, a consequence of the specific position he or she occupies in a given social fabric. That this last claim is true is evidenced by that fact that not only inspirational figures have power. Many non-inspiring figures seem to be able to have massive social influence, although the influence of these less inspiring figures is not transformational (the case of John Howard in Australia is archetypal). An individual is able to have great social influence if he or she is located along what could be characterized as a social fault – a fault that allows a given message to be transported in an outwardly expanding manner by the combined forces of many individuals who are receptive. The force of a leader's message is a function of the manner in which it is received – on the willingness of many to listen. The force of a given individual, then, is a function of the location he or she occupies within the fabric of the social.

To be sure, the 'logic' of the rifle and the tank complicates this picture, given that the 'logic' at issue here is not, *prima facie*, merely the 'logic' that unfolds by the actions of those who occupy a given social fault. This logic is the logic of the few invested with the power of rifles and tanks (or other technological means, including the means for producing effective propaganda) over the disempowered many. However, on final analysis, what I am saying here merely qualifies the claims made above. Technology needs operators, and it needs to be developed by individuals. In short, an entire gamut of individuals must be working together even in regimes where the force of technology is used as a means of oppression. The case of Danish resistance mentioned above suffices to exemplify how generalized oppression can only be initiated if there are chains of power which spill out to infect an entire community. Without these human tentacles, aspiring oppressors have no chance of living out their morbid dreams.

So, we can appreciate that the power leaders hold over us is also and inevitably a consequence of many joining forces together. And, indeed, as with any social order, an ideal social order is a function of individual efforts. In this regard, centralized power is only a myth, although it is certainly true that power can be more or less centralized. Power is always mediated by chains of cooperation and the extent to which loci of power are constituted is demonstrated by the manner in which individuals who constitute a social group align themselves in relation to centres of power. The manner in which individuals align themselves constitutes these centres.

Even Big Brother can only exercise his power because there is a system, which is constituted by the members of Oceania, that allows him to have the influence that he does. I am certainly not suggesting that members of Oceania voluntarily surrender to the power of Big Brother – not at all. Indeed, I think the situation in Oceania is so pathetic precisely because people are trapped into a narrowly defined mode of being and they are, on the whole, unable to conceive of any better options that may exist for them. They follow Big Brother blindly. Moreover, it would not be far-fetched to claim that centralized conglomerates of power require governed individuals to be blind to a certain extent – blind to the role they play in the perpetuation of power conglomerates. For instance, it is no exaggeration to say that today, in the West at least, we are blind consumers. We are to a large degree incapable of perceiving to what extent we are cooperating in the formation of new, and as yet unheard of, centres of power by our consumer practices.

Centralized power depends on the (blind or otherwise) cooperation of the community at large.

The story I am telling is not meant to be a pessimistic rendition of our hopeless condition. On the contrary, it is meant to point out to what extent individuals are in fact the loci of power, and to what extent any positive social transformation hangs on individual cooperation. Moreover, given the *eudaimon telos*, it is clear that positive social transformation requires active cooperation for the simple reason that a good society is a flourishing one, and a flourishing society is one in which its individuals flourish – and individuals flourish by actively participating in our common purpose.

Individual *eudaimonia* is the locus – the *arche* – of positive social transformation. Of course, the relationship between the individual and the collective is a holistic one, and to express things in this way is simply to restate the fact of our radical interconnectedness. We cannot achieve *eudaimonia* on our own. We must work together, as individuals – as *philoi* – in order to achieve the *telos* that is determined by the mere fact that we are the sorts of creatures that we are – persons.

## Neil Alcock: White God of the Zulus

Implicit in what has been discussed in the previous section is the idea that what could be characterized as communitarian pluralism is very different from what could be characterized as liberal pluralism. While this, of course, is not a surprising claim, its implications are perhaps somewhat more surprising. A *eudaimon* subject is one who extends him or herself towards others and this amounts to claiming that he or she adequately implicates the lives of others into his or her life. He or she is one who understands that the goals and aspirations of an individual cannot be separated from the goodness of the complex, multifaceted, dynamic, and inherently conflictual, tapestry of the social. Indeed, this means that, when one asks a question such as 'Where do I want to go from here?', one is also implicitly asking questions such as 'What is required of me here?'. Note the explicit introduction of the universal element in the second question. Let me qualify what I mean by 'universal element' here. The move from the first question to the second amounts to a move from individual interests to what could be characterized as universal interests, and also illustrates to what extent the individual interests of a *eudaimon* subject are, indeed, universal. What I am in fact surreptitiously introducing here is something akin to the Kantian imperative, but I am doing so from an angle that is perhaps radically un-Kantian. In acting for the sake of my own happiness I am indeed acting for the sake of my own happiness, but let it be said that my happiness, as argued above, incorporates the happiness of my entire community. In this regard my happiness radically transcends the boundary of skin that isolates me from the world. When I act for the sake of happiness I ideally act for the sake of a happiness that is not only mine, but also for the sake of a happiness that is all-encompassing. When acting for the sake of myself, ideally I am acting for the sake of something that radically transcends me. Indeed, that my good radically transcends me is a powerful sign that perhaps too much emphasis has been placed (by the liberal tradition) on the boundary that is my skin. Of course, many of our decisions do not seem directly to implicate others, but my claims regarding the universal element are claims regarding the general direction a life ought to take. Personal interests, whether they directly implicate others or not, do play a central role here, and these interests are expressive of one's unique character. But this should not be seen in any way to conflict with my previous statements, since the ideal life being advocated here is that of an individual whose unique set of interests are properly understood by him or her as forming part of a complex and dynamic network of such interests – an expansive network which constitutes the social domain.

Certainly, 'I' exist; that is undeniable. What is deniable is the precise ontological status of the 'I'. I am an individual insofar as I have a substantial form, but this is only to say that I have a relative degree of autonomy given that my substantial form – *eudaimonia* – is defined with reference to social *eudaimonia*. My *eudaimonia* is an ethical ideal, and it is defined in relation to the ethical ideal of the social. There is indeed a fact of the matter about what *eudaimonia* is and there is a fact of the matter about how my goodness is parasitical upon a certain universal social ideal of goodness. It is for this reason that such questions as 'How do I want go on from here?' imply such questions 'What is required of me here?'.

Few amongst us could be characterized as living in accordance with our ethical ideal, even in a slightly imperfect form, and this is not surprising given the intimate interrelationship that exists between individual and collective happiness. However, some individuals are certainly far more virtuous than others. And there is one individual – two, in fact – whom I have recently heard about, and who are indeed outstanding.

The first individual is Neil Alcock (the second is Creina, his wife) and his achievements are magnificently described by Rian Malan in his life-transforming *My Traitor's Heart*.[97] Neil died tragically in 1983, caught in middle of one of the many Zulu wars – a war he was bravely, indeed almost foolishly some might think, attempting to appease. He was killed by one of the rival groups from Msinga (a region of KwaZulu-Natal). There were rumours that local white people were also plotting his assassination, but they did not get to him on time. They perceived him as a traitor; in their eyes Neil was a *kafferboetie* – a term used by racist Boers, which in their mouths means 'nigger-lover'. His death was caused by the madness – by the nihilism – that comes about as a consequence of multigenerational desperation. Neil died for what he believed in and he believed that all South Africans should learn to prosper together. His many deeds attest to this.

Neil was a farmer and spent most of his adult life working to improve the conditions for indigenous South Africans. His main efforts concentrated around agricultural developments which aimed to revegetate land occupied by Africans who were on the brink of starvation. He was consumed with a passion for finding the grass under the dead soil of Msinga. His last development site carries the name 'Mdukatshani' – Place of Lost Grass. I will not recount the details of his exceptional life except where they directly assist our present concerns. Neil was a very brave man and one who believed in justice and in what Creina refers to as love. He was by no means condescending, and he seemed to have little time for people who stood on the high moral ground – distant from the problem, so to speak. Indeed, it seems as if he simply did what had to be done – no questions asked. Undoubtedly he was a man with incredible initiative and personal strength, and it is also clear that his actions were guided by a deeply embodied understanding of the universal in all of us. It is as if his actions were guided by a force that transcended the boundaries of his own skin and this is because he saw himself, and his value as a human being, in relationship to the overall community in which he was embedded. That is why he could not be a racist. He did not aim to solve all problems on Earth – indeed the very idea of undertaking such a formidable task did not seem to pass through the landscape of his mind. Instead, he was focused on issues that touched him deeply and personally, and these were the issues that still, to a large extent, besiege his country. Neil could not countenance the idea of living a white life in South Africa in face of the fact that the affluence of that group was a direct consequence of treating most people in the land as, at best, half-human.

As previously mentioned, his wife, Creina, describes Neil's deeds, and hers also, as being propelled by love. The love in question is not exclusively, nor even primarily, the love that one has towards specific individuals, but instead is nebulous and all-encompassing. What motivated their actions was a universal embodied understanding of the good. And what is crucial about their story is that, although they clearly suffered a great deal, they also consider that their lives were blessed, and the reason for believing this about themselves is precisely because they embraced the universal in them (their joy and their suffering, one could say, was expressive of the joy and sorrow of humanity). However, and this is a crucial point, the universal love that informed their actions flowed and was informed by direct engagement with specific individuals and specific problems.

Neil and Creina's lives are exemplary, and their example has transformed many lives (including mine to some degree, although I did not have the honour of meeting them). Indeed, their example has helped some black people lose the distrust they understandably had in whites – a distrust that was bred into them for centuries – and it has given them a sense of what can be achieved with few resources and a lot of solidarity. Equally, their example has had an influence on many white South Africans.

I might also point out that the universal element by which the Alcocks lived was one that was not blind to cultural difference. Indeed, one of the outstanding features of their quest is that the good they wanted to bring about was a good that was mediated by a sensitive and caring engagement with cultural difference. One of the outstanding features of the Alcocks is that part of their effort to bring about the good was an effort to come to terms with difference. They themselves moved with, as much as they were moved by, their encounter with the radical other embodied in the form of a Zulu. Neil and Creina learned Zulu and learned to understand where the Zulus were coming from. And it must be emphasized that their attitudes towards this bereaved people carried no trace of condescension: since the Zulus' problems were also their problems, there was no space for such an attitude to arise. Instead, there was love and a deep understanding of the Zulus' plight – which included a willingness to act. To repeat, Zulu suffering was also Alcock suffering.

I am emphatically not suggesting that everyone should act as the Alcocks did. Indeed, the Alcocks' crusade was, in a manner of speaking, idiosyncratic. Neil was a farmer, and the land was his passion; Creina was a journalist, and her contribution reflected this interest. Their willingness to embrace the problems of their country came from the vantage point of what defined them as unique individuals. A world populated exclusively by Neils and Creinas would be a world where the flow of difference could not obtain, which is, as we saw in the previous chapter, a necessary requirement for being ideally rational. Certainly, the Alcocks' repertoire of interests was severely limited – determined – by a clear understanding of their radical interconnectedness. If their world, indeed if our world, was a place of many riches, and if possessing luxuries in no way adversely affected other individuals, or the environment for that matter, then the Alcocks might well have ended up living in a mansion. But instead they lived, and so far as I know Creina still does, in utter poverty. There are other exceptional individuals who have clearly understood the fact of our radical interconnectedness and who have lived radically different lives from those lived by the Alcocks, but what is characteristic of the lives of these exceptional individuals is that they are informed by an understanding of how their unique individuality is tied up with the lives of others (whether this be in the slums of Calcutta, the Chile of Pinochet, or the Australian outback).

It would clearly be rash to claim that Neil and Creina are *eudaimonists* in any explicit sense, but most of their actions seem to have been expressive of a deep understanding of the sort of life that I have been arguing is the best sort of life. Neil and Creina understood the fact of our radical interconnectedness in an embodied manner. This understanding allowed them to make sacrifices that most of us would never make, and that is simply because they had a lucid lived understanding of what is truly relevant. Their motivational structures are, or in the case of Neil were, informed by a deep understanding of the human situation, such that trivial commodities seem exactly what they are to them – trivial. The same applies to trivial pleasures generally. Neil is now considered to be a white god by Zulus of Msinga. No other white person has ever received such an honour. The desert has been halted, and life is slowly growing back into the region. Neil found the grass he was looking for.

## Finding One's Whereabouts in Ethical Space

In this last section before concluding this investigation I would like to draw on some of the central issues that have been addressed in this piece in a way that presents them in a slightly different light. My hope here is that this new focus will complement the above discussion in a manner that will further help clarify at least some of my central concerns. What I will do here is use a few closely related examples in order to highlight the central epistemic role that our ethical attachments play for making sense of reality.

Imagine that you suddenly materialize in a solitary forest that you do not, as yet, know. You have a map of the place, but there is no way of locating yourself on that map. There are no points of reference from which to determine your present location. It is clear that in these circumstances the map is quite useless, even though it is a map of the region in which you have materialized. You are lost.

Well, in what sense do you not know where you are – in what sense are you lost? After all, you do recognize trees, a flowing stream, the rays of sunlight softly making their way through the thick foliage of this lush forest. So there is a sense in which you do in fact know where you are. You know where you are in the sense that you can recognize that at least some aspects of the scenery are *familiar* to you. Nonetheless, it is still true to say that you are well and truly lost. Although some of the features of the landscape are familiar, this landscape cannot be located within the network of relations represented in the map you were materialized with. The chances are that you will feel bewildered and panic stricken on account of the fact that this alien landscape is *meaningless* to you.[98] Of course, you might initially be fascinated with all that is new, but this fascination will sooner or later dissipate, and negative emotions such as panic and an overwhelming sense of meaninglessness will take over.[99]

Think of another similar scenario: imagine yourself following a track and reaching the same place as the one described in the previous example. In this case, by contrast, you know where you are. You have followed the map and, although you have never been in this part of the forest before, you are nonetheless not lost and, most importantly, you do not *feel* lost. The place is not familiar but you can relate your present location to a place or places that are familiar to you. You can, so to speak, make sense of the landscape in relation to locations that are already familiar.

One could argue here that you know where you are because you can locate your present location on a map, and this is in a sense true. But it is only true in a sense though, rather than simply being true, because you could also locate yourself on a map and nevertheless still be lost. Take the first example again in which you simply materialized in an unknown forest. In this case you are lost because the place is not familiar and because you cannot position your current location in relation to a place that is familiar. Suppose, to use a slightly different example, that you materialized in an unknown forest (with a map). Suppose you were able to find your location on the map in relation to other unfamiliar locations (suppose, say, that you materialized on a high vantage point from which you could observe the most outstanding features of the landscape and locate them on the map in relation to your present location). Even though you could locate yourself in this sense it is clear that, in a fundamental sense, you are nevertheless lost. What you would have to do in order to make sense of your present location is to relate this location to a place that is familiar. You would have to be able to relate your current location, say, to your home town or to several locations you are already familiar with. So there is an added condition that allows us to locate ourselves which a map does not provide. One makes sense of one's present location, to repeat, by relating one's present position to a place, or places, that are familiar.

But, what makes for a familiar place? A place that is familiar is a place one can *relate to* – a place one can, so to speak, call 'home' (one could, of course, have more than one home). Home, as I understand it here, is not necessarily a physical location as one could, after all, arguably be a nomad who had no significant attachments to the landscapes in which one temporarily dwelled without this necessarily making one feel displaced. Rather than being a concrete location in physical space, home is necessarily a place of belonging – a place one can identify with. The sort of 'place' at issue is a place to which one is *affectively* attached. This place could be one's family, or one's circle of friends, one's immediate community or, more illuminatingly, this place is constituted by a hierarchical network of relationships which is in turn constituted by our network of love and the community in which it is embedded. Of course, features of our geographical landscape might play an important role in providing us with a sense of place, but the important point that must be emphasized here is that the possible role played by the landscape is mediated by one's emotional ties – by one's sense of belonging among others one is familiar with.

This sense of *belonging* is primarily constituted by our ethical practices – by the specific ways in which we live and share our lives with others. The use of 'belonging' in this context is an important one because it establishes an important correlation between knowing one's whereabouts in geographical space and knowing one's whereabouts in what could be characterized as ethical space. Belonging, of course, is a concept that pertains to location, but what is interesting about the use of 'belonging' in the present context is that the belonging in question does not primarily pertain to physical location. And I might add that I do not think that the sense of belonging that pertains primarily to physical location, and the sense of belonging that pertains to one's affinities with a particular social group, are two different senses of 'belonging'. That this is not the case is evidenced by the central point I have thus far been discussing – namely, that one cannot fully locate oneself in physical space independently of what I have been referring to as 'home'. One cannot fully separate the issues of knowing one's physical location from the issue of one's ethical attachments to others. It is for this reason that I think it is appropriate to speak in terms of one's ethical location in this context. It is even tempting to claim that one's ethical location is a fifth dimension for this very reason.

To a large extent, I identify myself as belonging somewhere in relation to the individuals with whom I am intimate – in relation to the specific practices that define my web of intimacy, and in relation to the wider community within which I can carry on intimately in ways that specifically define me and those who I care for as who we are. Also, and no less importantly, I identify myself as belonging to a given place because I am able to locate myself in contrast with everyone else. It is only because I can do this that I can have a sense of identity – a sense that I am a unique subject who has a place of belonging.

It must be emphasized here that one does not homogeneously identify with one's community – that is, one does not identify with every member in one's community in the same manner and with the same degree of emotional attachment and commitment. Rather, one can only identify with a given community if one is able to establish an affective hierarchy within that community. Let me explain: suppose there was an individual who related to each member of his or her purported community in a manner that expressed no hierarchy of preferences among those members. Could an individual who engaged with individuals in this manner consider this community to be his or her home – his or her space of familiarity? I do not think so. Such an individual would be like a foreigner in a strange land. One enters into a community in a way that makes that place home, through one's direct web of love and, generally, through establishing hierarchies of commitment within one's community.

Additionally, one can locate oneself not only because there is a place one can identify with, but also because there is a sense in which one can establish that one's home is a unique place. And one can only do this if one has a point of comparison. And, indeed, the nature of the points of comparison will help one appreciate (positively and negatively) certain features of one's place. One can identify one's own place, say, as a warm one, by comparison with other places one has been, or of which one has heard, that are not so warm. Equally, one is in a better position to recognize certain outstanding, or indeed not so outstanding, features of oneself or of one's immediate community by comparing these with other individuals or local communities. In short, it is by the play of difference and sameness that one can locate oneself – that one can find one's bearings in ethical space.

Suppose you decide to spend some time in a foreign and exotic land. You know no one there and you are totally unfamiliar with the country's practices. You are a foreigner – a kind of detached onlooker. You are fascinated by how different this culture is from your own, and, in fact, it is largely by comparison with your home that you are able to appreciate this exotic culture. Indeed, spending time in this exotic place may help you gain an understanding about yourself and your own local community. But also, and fundamentally, you can only fully appreciate this new culture from the vantage point of what is already familiar. And, moreover, you feel comfortable in this new location not only because you feel that there is no danger, but also, and more to the point that is relevant here, because you know (or are confident) that you can get back home with relative ease. You are comfortable in your anonymity, but this is largely because you are someone somewhere. Of course, this new place might eventually become familiar and this is fundamentally because what were originally homogenous relationships might give way to a hierarchy of levels of intimacy. You will start to feel at home in this new place once you have developed a sufficiently deep dynamic network of friends of differing levels of intimacy. But the main emphasis here must be placed on those relationships that are most intimate, for it is those sorts of relationship that contribute the most to making one feel most truly at home. And, indeed, it is mainly because these most intimate relationships take time to develop that it takes time for a given place to become home.[100]

Note the role that difference is playing here. If we were all more or less identical there would be no way of establishing the relevant hierarchies required for establishing our locatedness. We would be adrift in an ocean of sameness, and we would lose a sense of our own specific orientation with respect to the world, and to those who inhabit it. I would be no one, for I would be just like everyone else. I would certainly be the bearer of my own experiences yet, given that my experiences and those of others would be much the same, it seems that there would be no sense in which my unique experiences define me as someone who is more than a specific yet undifferentiated location for the endless repetition of type-identical experiences. But I am not merely a location – not at all. I am a location only insofar as I am a unique and irreproducible ocean of experiences. But then, one could further speculate, what if one were all by oneself? Again, if one is alone, one cannot establish the sorts of relationship required for determining a location for oneself. I am how I am to a large extent because I am not like you. What I value about myself, and about the sorts of dream I pursue, is largely determined in relation to other concrete modes of living. One could certainly imagine counterfactual possibilities, but one's imagination is not limitless and it must be refreshed with the newness that continually emerges in one's ongoing relationships with others who are not like oneself, and who always stand there – away from me but with me – as an ongoing threat to one's existential *status quo*. One's uniqueness, one could say, is determined in relation to the ongoing threat of violence offered by the matrix of differential relations within which personal identity is constituted.

What I am suggesting in this section is that one is only able to make sense of one's life if one is able to find one's ethical location. And, indeed, in one sense, the main purpose of this investigation has been to find and explore the basic 'topographical' features of the lives of persons (which are defined in relation to an ethical ideal). I hope to have shown how we are able to locate ourselves – to make sense of our lives – in relation to the lives of others and, more specifically, to the specific ways in which we relate to the lives of others.

A crucial aspect of finding one's ethical bearings, I might add, is the ideals one entertains. In this investigation I have tried to spell out the basic features of the ideals that ought to inform our engagements with others, and with oneself, in a way that renders our lives maximally intelligible. I have spoken of the rational ideal that constitutes the ideal life for persons, and how the general character of our direct involvement with others is constitutive of this ideal. One could say that this investigation is a map that has the purpose of helping us find our whereabouts in ethical space – a map which will help us find the sense and purpose of life, and how this sense and purpose cannot be dissociated from the manner in which we relate to others. Finding sense and purpose, one could say, amounts to learning how to love – how to relate to other in ways that are constitutive of communal *eudaimonia*.

## The End of our Journey: Concluding Remarks

My aim in this investigation has been to provide an account regarding the nature of happiness and how, on final analysis, our lives are intertwined with the lives of others such that individual happiness cannot be separated from the overall happiness of our intimates and of our community as a whole. I think this is an important conclusion because it links the fundamental concern each individual has for his or her own well-being with the well-being of the community at large. In addition, I have aimed to demonstrate that one cannot separate the issue of well-being from that of being a good person. Indeed, to be a balanced, contented human being is to be a person who has a good character, and who expresses this character in ways that promote the goodness of his or her immediate web of love and, also, of his or her community at large. It is important to note here that I do not want to give the impression that one is able to have a good character and nevertheless not express it in the manner just specified. Rather, an integral part of having a good character involves acting in ways that flow from the dispositions that constitute a good character. In other words, there is no such thing as a character in a vacuum – a character does not exist independently of the manner in which that character expresses itself. The virtues, one could say, are active rather than passive dispositions – that is, dispositions that are exercised in actuality.

In this investigation I have also aimed to establish that the ethical ideal defining a good person also defines persons as such. If this is the case, and I have shown why this is the case, one cannot separate the issue of understanding oneself from the issue of understanding how to live a good life. Indeed, the ethical is so tightly knitted into the fabric of our lives that it is simply not possible to establish a separation between being a person and being an ethical creature. This establishes the immense importance of putting ethical matters back into the centre of our everyday concerns. In fact, ethical skills are not just skills we should exercise sporadically when forced to confront difficult and morally demanding situations. Rather, these skills define us as the creatures that we are, which means that they are skills that inform the general direction of our lives and the specific steps we must take in order to reach and perfect the art of living.

There is indeed a purpose to life which is common to us all and which defines our common humanity, and this purpose is to achieve *eudaimonia* in the act of working together to constitute a community based on establishing meaningful and loving relationships with those closest to us. But, although we are defined by a common goal, this is not to say that the *telos* of life does not make allowances for the obvious differences that exist between us. Indeed, to hold that the ethic I have been developing does not take into consideration these obvious differences is simply to miss the point of the entire exercise. I most certainly do hold the view that there is an ethical ideal that we all share and which defines us as rational creatures and as moral agents. But the ethical ideal at issue here is common to us all at a general level only. And, because of this, it is possible for this ideal to be instantiated in innumerably different ways, but, of course, not in any way. In fact, it is not difficult to see why being unable to exhaustively specify how an ideal moral subject ought to be is a good thing given that, if it were possible to do so, there would be no strong sense in which each of us could be the architects of our own destiny – to conceive of ourselves as being responsible for our own lives. Instead, we would, at best, be blind followers of rules with no strong sense of identity nor of being the caretakers of our own unique lives. Indeed, if the ideal moral subject were like 'this' specific subject, then the ideal world would be a world in which there would be no substantial difference between subjects. We would have lost the particularities that separate us out as individuals and allow us to see the world in ways that permit us to make an original contribution to the lives of others. A world of fundamentally indistinguishable individuals would no doubt be a very daunting place indeed – a world akin to the one portrayed by Orwell.

Let us, for instance, take the case of the ethic of friendship in order to clarify some fundamental aspects regarding the nature of ethical concepts. I think it is uncontroversially true that we are all, for the most part, able to recognize friendships as such, and this is because we have a good idea, even if this idea is mostly implicit, about what it is to be a friend. Nonetheless, even though we know this, it is not possible to specify in exact terms what constitutes a friendship. We can certainly claim that relationships of friendship are relationships that involve care for one's friends. And I think that it is straightforwardly true that relationships of friendship are relationships that involve care. But what, specifically, does caring consist of? Given that no such precision exists in the conceptual landscape of ethics, I think this is the wrong question to ask. Although, for the most part, we do recognize when someone is caring and loving, it is not possible to give an exhaustive rendition of what caring amounts to.

I have established, following Aristotle, that a *eudaimon* individual is the sort of subject who lives an ideally rational existence – that is, he or she is an individual who has maximized the coherence amongst the different aspects that constitute his or her rational existence. Moreover, the coherence at issue here, I have argued, is not incompatible with some degree of conflict; maximization should not be confused with perfection. In order to perform this compositional *tour de force*, a *eudaimon* subject must have, and by definintion has, the right states of character – states of character that inform the manner in which he or she ought to act. Such states of character are the virtues. However, it must be added that the ideal of rationality that constitutes the life of a *eudaimon* subject cannot properly be separated from an ideal of rationality that constitutes an ideal community. Indeed, we could say that the task of shaping an ideal community is continuous with the task of shaping an ideal life. To put matters slightly differently, one could rightly claim that the work of living a good life and the work of forming an ideal community are aspects of one and the same *eudaimon* project. In making this move, I have established that the fields of psychology and the social are inseparable, such that understanding the subject-matter of one of these fields cannot properly be achieved independently of understanding the subject matter of the other.

A basic intuition I have implicitly been attempting to undermine throughout this piece – an intuition which I think has been extremely influential in the formation of contemporary Western culture – is that the happiness of a given individual is something that has little or nothing to do with the happiness of the community within which that individual lives. I think this intuition is an offshoot of the contemporary paradigm of radical autonomy in which each individual is seen as having his or her own goals, expectations, and so on, quite independently of how those goals or expectation are intertwined with the overall *telos* of the community those individuals constitute.[101] An individual holding such a view quite naturally would also hold that the community at large is at best a mere facilitator for individual good – a kind of contingent adjunct. By contrast, on my view (a view strongly informed by Aristotle's) one simply cannot consistently conceive of oneself in isolation from others. Indeed, one's whole psychological life – the life that constitutes us as rational creatures – is unavoidably bound up with the psychological lives of others in such a way that it is not wholly unreasonable to describe a given community as having a mind of its own. It is precisely the intermeshing of the rational lives of the subjects who constitute a given community that constitutes this overarching social 'mind'.

A further issue that crops up when considering the crucial role that our interconnectedness plays in the constitution of individual well-being is how it is that one ideally cannot produce a strict separation between caring for others and caring for oneself. Indeed, as I have argued above, one can only reach one's own *telos* if one engages with others in non-exploitative and non-purely commercial relationships – in relationships in which one considers the needs and wants of others, in the light of an understanding of the basic needs persons generally have, and on the particular needs 'this' particular individual has in 'this' particular situation. In general, *eudaimonia* can only be achieved if one genuinely cares for the network of love that constitutes one's community. Of course, the nature of the caring will vary depending on the nature of the specific relationships – on whether a given relationship is, for example, a virtue friendship, a relationship between a mother and her child, a professional relationship, and so on.

Indeed, in establishing our radical interconnectedness I have also established the *raison d'être* of social affiliations. The overall ethical ideal of a community is to create the conditions for the attainment of *eudaimonia* by each of the members of a given social affiliation. Furthermore, justice, understood as the basic regulative ideal of human engagements generally, I have argued, is primarily developed in the intimacy of our particular webs of love. In following this line of argument I have established a fundamental relationship between private virtue and public justice, such that one cannot consistently and deeply conceive of a just community independently of considering the make-up of the intimate relationships (particularly relationships based on good character) that would constitute an ideal community.

### Notes

1    It is important to note that the use of 'political' here differs from the prevailing contemporary usage. I use 'political' here as a translation of *politicon*. As Nussbaum notes, *politicon*:

> ... is both more concrete and more inclusive than the English word. More concrete, in that it refers above all to our aptness or suitability for life in a city or *polis* – not in other forms or levels of political organization. More inclusive, because it takes in the entire life of the *polis*, including informal social relations, and is not limited to the sphere of laws and institutions. In this respect, 'social' would be more appropriate, but it would, even more than 'political' lack the concreteness of the Greek word. (M. C. Nussbaum, *The Fragility of Goodness: Luck and Ethics in Greek Tragedy and Philosophy*, Cambridge: Cambridge University Press, 1994, n. p. 345).

> I shall use both 'political' and 'social' interchangeably. But, as we shall see, my understanding of the political and social realm will be wider than Aristotle's.

2   A MacIntyre, *After Virtue: A Study in Moral Philosophy*, Notre Dame, Indiana: Notre Dame University Press, 1984, pp. 204–25. Charles Taylor, *Sources of the Self*, Cambridge, Massachusetts: Harvard University Press, 1989, pp. 3–107, holds much the same views as MacIntyre. Taylor argues that:

> I define who I am by defining where I speak from, in the family tree, in social space, in the geography of statuses and functions, in my intimate relationships to the ones I love, and also crucially in the space of moral and spiritual orientation within which my most important defining relations are lived out. (Ibid., p. 35)

3   Ibid., pp. 204-25.

4   A given biographer might decide to focus on a biographical subject's brilliant scientific career or, alternatively, he or she might want to focus on his or her subject's more than dubious relationships with his or her multiple partners, and his or her ruthlessly carried out careerist ambitions. To use yet another example, one might want to describe the life of this subject in a way that brings into prominence his or her unusual generosity towards dispossessed children. Indeed, the amount of ruthlessness displayed in certain aspects of this subject's life might not fit in nicely with the immense, and seemingly disinterested, generosity displayed in other areas of his or her life. One might be unable to provide an account which adequately explains why these inconsistencies have come about, but pointing out these inconsistencies, and framing them within a comprehensive account of the subject's life, will nevertheless help us further understand the life of the subject under investigation. By appropriately framing inconsistencies, we will be in a position to make sense of the inconsistencies under scrutiny – we might, so to speak, come to understand the *rationale* of these inconsistencies.

5   Examples of Hollywood's unidimensional characters abound. Perhaps the most striking cases of unidimensional character-making are those in which the good/bad contrast is most clearly exploited. The movies at issue are those in which the 'forces of good' prevail over the 'forces of evil'. Think of movies such as *Independence Day*, most classical westerns, and many, though by no means all, war movies.

6   A social setting, of course, requires a natural environment within which to be set, but this is a topic that transcends the scope of this investigation (although it seems to me that some interesting consequences for environmental philosophy could be drawn from it).

7   Sherman appropriately characterizes the role that *philia* plays in a good life. She claims that:

> On Aristotle's view, the specific ends in a life are sustained and given their finest expression through friendship. Ends that are valued become more highly prized as a result of being shared; actions that are fine become finer when friends are the beneficiaries. Nowhere is the collaborative nature of good living more pronounced; nowhere is the dependency of the good life upon what is external more pervasive. (N. Sherman, *The Fabric of Character: Aristotle's Theory of Virtue*, Oxford: Clarendon Press, 1989, p. 118)

8   Love, like most concepts pertaining to the domain of the ethical (concepts such as that of complete virtue), is open-ended. But this is not to say that we mean nothing when conversing about love. That 'love' means something is evidenced by the fact that not any form of human interaction counts as a relationship of love. There are many sorts of interaction we would most certainly be unwilling to categorize as relationships of love (although no doubt there are also other cases where such consensus cannot be reached). We know, for example, that one is not expressing one's love towards someone if the relationship in question is fundamentally exploitative. Further, I would like to stress that engagements of love are a paradigmatic sort of ethical engagement, since among other things this sort of relationship clearly illustrates the inherently open-ended nature of the

virtues (that ideally inform action). The case of love illustrates the claim, substantiated above, that it is not possible to provide a comprehensive list of procedures that exhaustively characterize what it would be like to act in accordance with virtue (and in the present case, the virtues constitutive of love).

9    It might seem that my presumption that in fact there is a *telos* of the social is problematic. And, indeed, I think it would be a problematic claim if it were considered in isolation from what I have thus far claimed regarding the *telos* of persons. It seems clear that if persons have a *telos*, then the associations that constitute the political or social realm must also have a *telos*, which is determined in relation to the *eudaimon telos*. I shall have more to say about the *telos* of the political very soon.

10   I do not want to suggest here that persons exist prior to these multifaceted associations, which constitute the political realm. I have already established above that we are by nature social creatures.

11   It is important at this point to clarify that I am not suggesting that, because the *telos* of the social is the achievement of *eudaimonia* by each of its members, the *eudaimonia* of each of the members of a given social group implicates the *eudaimonia* of the group at large. I do in fact believe that individual *eudaimonia* depends on collective *eudaimonia*, but this is not something that follows from what has been said thus far. I shall defend this thesis below.

12   For a discussion on Aristotle's doctrine of natural slavery see his *P* I, 4–13.

13   Nussbaum, *The Fragility of Goodness*, *op.cit.*, n. 1, p. 355.

14   *P* I, 4.

15   *P* 1254a 15–6.

16   When discussing *psyche* we saw that, according to Aristotle, one's organs exist for the sake of our psychological world (organs are not human goods but, rather, they are means for a greater end – instruments of psychological life one could say). Indeed, organs do not seem to have a value independently of the roles they play in securing the life of a subject, understood as a creature with a psychological world – a rational creature. This is perhaps most clearly evidenced by the value we place on the body of someone who is no longer able to have a psychological life (I am particularly thinking here of cases such as those of comatose individuals who have no chance of coming back to life). When someone leaves us in this manner, we consider the person to have left (quite independently of the fact that the body continues to live on). Almost literally, we consider a living body without a mind to be a living corpse.

17   Even though he never makes this claim explicitly, it seems that Aristotle thinks that the aristocratic class of Athens is the substantial form of the city-state.

18   We have reached the conclusion that a good community must be a pluralistic one yet again – using an alternative route.

19   For a thought-provoking account of how generalist theories tend to privilege the 'moral paradigms' within which they are written, and at least implicitly dismiss other such paradigms, see Margaret Walker's, *Moral Understandings: A Feminist Study in Ethics*, New York: Routledge, 1998.

20   *EN* 1155a 23.

21   These claims might initially seem to contradict my charge against Aristotle that his ethics is too parochial because it is fundamentally an ethic of *philia*. But note that viewing the social as a network of friends does not necessarily – and in Aristotle's case does not, or at least does not clearly and systematically – involve the view that one must care and be concerned for those one does not know (or those one only knows superficially).

22   Nussbaum agrees that *philia* is not perfectly translatable as friendship and the reason she provides is that *philia* is a much wider concept than friendship. Bonds of *philia* are relationships such as the love of the mother towards a child, family relations, and so on. Nussbaum believes that what is common to all bonds of *philia* is that they are relationships involving genuine love for a person. For this reason she thinks *philia* is

better translated as 'love'. But this translation is also imperfect, Nussbaum argues, because love, more than *philia*, can be understood asymmetrically – it can be understood as a relationship between the one who loves and the one who is being loved. For more details on the difficulties in translating *philia* see her *The Fragility of Goodness, op.cit.*, n. 1, p. 354.

I will use both 'love' and 'friendship' to refer to *philia*, and I ask the reader to bear in mind that these terms must be understood in the context of the present qualifications. This said about the nature of *philia*, it is also worth mentioning that I will primarily be focusing on friendships amongst equals, or, more specifically, friendships amongst *eudaimon* subjects because I believe, for reasons that will become plain below, that it is from this type of *philia* that one is able to learn and exercise complete virtue most fully. And it is this skill – the skill that defines the *eudaimon* subject as such – that will allow us to establish the dependency of healthy social affiliations generally on *philia*. The primary sort of *philia*, to use a passage quoted by Sherman (although she uses a slightly different translation from the one presented below in her *Fabric of Character, op.cit.*, n. 7, p. 131), is defined as follows by Aristotle:

> But if active loving is a mutual choice with pleasure in each other's acquaintance, it is clear that in general the primary friendship is a reciprocal choice of the absolutely good and pleasant because it is good and pleasant; and friendship itself is the habit from which such choice springs. (*EE* 1237a 30–34)

23  Not all bonds of *philia*, as Aristotle notes, involve reciprocity. Aristotle is thinking here of cases such as the love 'of father to son and in general of elder to younger, that of man to wife and in general that of ruler to subject' (*EN* 1158a 13–14). Nonetheless, to repeat, we shall see that, paradigmatically, bonds of *philia* are symmetrical with regard to the exchange of care and concern.

24  There are other secondary sorts of *philia* that cannot properly be described as instrumental. These are relationships of the sort a mother has towards her child, and other such kinds of asymmetrical relationships involving genuine care and concern, but which cannot properly be described as solely instrumental or advantage-based friendships.

25  Aristotle distinguishes between the two forms of instrumental *philia* in *EN* 1156a 7–22. Also, Sherman offers a good sketch of Aristotle's classification of the different types of *philia*:

> To begin with, we must set down some definitional points. Friendship (*philia*), Aristotle stipulates, is the mutually acknowledged and reciprocal exchange of goodwill and affection that exists among individuals who share an interest in each other on the basis of virtue, pleasure, or utility ([*EN*] ... VIII. 2). In addition to voluntary associations of this sort, Aristotle includes among friendships the non-chosen relations of affection and care that exist among family members and fellow citizens (cf. [*EN*] VIII. 9, VIII. 12, IX. 6). (Sherman, *The Fabric of Character, op.cit.*, n. 7, p. 124).

26  Nussbaum, *The Fragility of Goodness, op.cit.*, n. 1, pp. 355–6.
27  John Cooper, 'Aristotle on Friendship', in A. Rorty (ed.), *Essays on Aristotle's Ethics*, Berkeley: University of California Press, 1980, p. 337.
28  *EN* 1155b 31–2.
29  *EE* 1237b 1.
30  The similarities between our relationships with artefacts and purely commercial relationships will also become apparent, but my main interest here is to compare our relationships with objects to instrumental *philia*.
31  *EN* 1156a 10–18.

32 It is worth noting here that I am not fully satisfied with Aristotle's division of instrumental engagements given that relationships that are for the sake of pleasure are a kind of relationship for the sake of utility, since pleasure, in relationships that are for-the-sake-of pleasure, is a kind of utility.

33 In Aristotle's words, '... each pleasure is bound up with the activity it completes' (*EN* 1175a 29–30).

34 Sherman, *The Fabric of Character*, *op.cit.*, n. 7, p. 129. Sherman cites *EN* 1156a 18-b 24 in support of her claims.

35 However, as discussed above, I disagree with the strong distinction Aristotle makes between instrumental *philia* and *philia* that is for the sake of pleasure, but my disagreement here is minor.

36 For this reason, it is appropriate to refer to the primary sort of *philia* as virtue friendship. I shall from now on use 'primary *philia*' and 'virtue friendship' interchangeably. Other ways of describing this sort of friendship, which help bring out different aspects of these sorts of relationship are 'perfect friendship' (Ross's translation of *EN*) and 'character friendship' (Cooper's rendition in 'Aristotle on Friendship', *op.cit.*, n. 27, pp. 307–8). Sherman makes some brief comments in support of Cooper's rendition in *The Fabric of Character*, *op.cit.*, n. 7, pp. 124–5.

37 *EN* 1156b 7–13.

38 *EN* 1156a 23–4.

39 I think it is exaggerated to claim that our interests always change. We typically commit ourselves to lifelong projects.

40 Of course, one must bear in mind the distinction I have already discussed above between instrumental friendships and outright exploitative relationships, or purely commercial ones. In an instrumental friendship there is interest in the person as such who has what is of interest to his or her friend, whilst in an exploitative or purely commercial relationship there is only concern for utility and nothing more.

41 A *eudaimon* subject might not enjoy the company of his or her good friend if the conditions are bad enough – if, for instance, one's friend is suffering some incurable and crippling disease. But, even if this were the case, a virtue friend would find the company of his or her friend desirable because of the appreciation a virtue friend has of his or her companion's character (even though he or she might not get any pleasure out of such a relationship for a considerable length of time).

42 N. Sherman, 'Character, Planning, and Choice', *Review of Metaphysics*, **39**, 1985, p. 104.

43 *EN* 1172a 10–14.

44 Sherman, 'Character, Planning, and Choice', *op.cit.*, n. 42, pp. 103–4.

45 Sherman, *The Fabric of Character*, *op.cit.*, n. 7, pp. 127–8. Sherman cites *EN* 1169b 10, 1154a 4, 1155a 5–6 and 1169b 16–17 in support of her claims.

46 J. Annas, *The Morality of Happiness*, New York: Oxford University Press, 1993, pp. 251–2.

47 Cooper, 'Aristotle on Friendship', *op.cit.*, n. 27, pp. 301–40.

48 I am aware of the controversy regarding whether Aristotle is the author of *Magna Moralia*. However, this is not the place to engage in this discussion. What I think is clear, and what I think is important for the purposes of this particular investigation, is that the passage I shall quote is written in the spirit of Aristotle's *Ethics*. So, for the purposes of this investigation, I shall simply assume that the *Magna Moralia* is Aristotle's.

49 Aristotle, *Magna Moralia*, ed. D. Ross, Oxford: Clarendon Press, 1966.

50 For a short discussion on Aristotle's conception of self-sufficiency, see Jonathan Lear's, *Aristotle: The Desire to Understand*, Cambridge: Cambridge University Press, 1988, p. 201. See also Sherman, *The Fabric of Character*, *op.cit.*, n. 7, pp. 128–30.

51 On this topic see Marilyn Friedman's, *What are Friends For? Feminist Perspectives on Personal Relationships and Moral Theory*, Ithaca, New York: Cornell University Press, 1993, where she emphasizes the role that difference plays in friendships. In her words:

Other relationships, as well, inform us of experiences that test various moral guidelines. Nevertheless, friendship, that is, a relationship of some degree of mutual intimacy, benevolence, interest, and concern, strongly promotes trust and the sharing of perspectives, a kind of mutuality that, in turn, fosters vicarious participation in the very experience of moral alternatives. (p. 199)

52 *EN* 1170a 4–11.
53 Certainly, some individuals who promote the general good, and Gandhi is reportedly a case in point, are not terribly competent at the level of sustaining intimate relationships. But, the case I am now considering is not just the case of individuals who are incompetent friends. I am presently considering the more extreme case of an individual who has no intimate relationships whatsoever.
54 To love, of course, cannot be reduced to merely claiming that one loves. Indeed, it is conceivable that a given individual might never make a claim of this sort and yet love.
55 The present discussion highlights the stark limits of ethics understood as a theoretical discipline. The limit is imposed because the theoretical medium is not the primary medium in which the ethical is played out. By now we know that the primary mode of ethical understanding is a practical mode – a mode that is constituted by actions more than by judgement. The mode of the ethical is the mode of being in the world – the mode of understanding which expresses the fact that we are embodied creatures bent on the idea of meaningfully coming to terms in action with the world we inhabit. I do not understand the extent to which evil is being done unless I act in ways that reflect my understanding. There are limits, of course, imposed by the fact of our finiteness. As one cannot love everyone, neither can one reach out to help everyone. It is equally clear, though, that most people, myself included, do far less than ought to be done, and this has to do with the fact that our relevant mode of understanding – the practical mode – is more often than not underdeveloped.
56 The ignorance at issue here is not just any sort of ignorance. Rather, it is primarily the sort of ignorance we could, mirroring the notion of practical understanding, characterize as practical ignorance – ignorance of the sort that impairs appropriate action and affect.
57 In making these claims I seem to be aligning myself more closely with Plato than Aristotle even though I do think that there are aspects of Aristotle's thought, as we are now seeing, that could lead to this conclusion. But, this said, it is not at all clear that Aristotle would endorse the present Platonic conclusions.
58 The case of an ignorant entrepreneur just presented is slightly misleading given that it does not clearly separate the issue of practical understanding, which mainly interests us here, from the issue of intellectual understanding. So, it is worth adding here that the reasoning I have attributed to my fictitious entrepreneur is meant to be reasoning that expresses practical beliefs.
   It might also be worth adding here that cases of *akrasia* (weakness of will) also seem to count as instances of practical ignorance insofar as, when in such states, one is not committed to acting in accordance with the conclusions reached by one's best all-considered judgements. One is (temporarily) blind to, or practically ignorant of, the importance of following the basic principles that guide action. The notion of *akrasia* I am considering here is Davidson's. Davidson holds that a given action comes as a consequence of *akrasia* if it goes against what he terms the Principle of Continence – the basic principle of practical reasoning – which states that one ought to 'perform the action judged best on the basis of all available relevant reasons': D. Davidson, 'How is Weakness of Will Possible', *Essays on Actions and Events*, Oxford: Clarendon Press, 1980, p. 41. An action that violates this principle is an action in which:

   ... the akratic agent has what it takes to be reasons both for and against a course of action. He judges, on the basis of all his reasons, that one course of action is best, yet opts for another; he has acted 'contrary to his own best judgement'. ('Deception and

Division', in J. Elster (ed.), *The Multiple Self*, Cambridge: Cambridge University Press, 1987, p. 80).

To repeat, the blindness occurs insofar as the *akratic* agent does not properly understand the basic principles that guide action.

59 I do not want to suggest here that a practically wise individual will get along with anyone. I merely want to highlight the fact that empathy is a necessary requirement for ethical engagements with others. I might add here something that I consider to be obvious – namely, that there are many ways of getting along with those one dislikes (some good and some bad). So, one could say, an ethic ideally informs the ways in which one engages with those one dislikes.

60 Nussbaum, *The Fragility of Goodness*, op.cit., n. 1, p. 362.

61 *EN* 1172a 8–14.

62 Cf. M. Friedman, *What are Friends For?*, op.cit., n. 51, pp. 195–203. I quote a passage from Friedman that is relevant to the present claim in note 51 *supra*.

63 In Chapter 2.

64 I do not want to give the impression that all continuous relationships are good ones. All I am defending here is that the best sorts of relationship cannot be fleeting ones. Obviously it takes quite a long time to come to know someone (probably years rather than months), and perhaps it even takes a longer time to develop a common intertwined history, which seems to be the mark of a good friendship. But, on second thoughts, I am not sure that separating the issue of coming to know someone from having a common history is really such a good idea given that it seems to me that sharing a history involves participating in the development of one's friend's character.

65 *EE* 1240b 1–3.

66 Although it is clear that the general impression one gets from Aristotle's account of friendship is one that is paradigmatically represented by homogenous group of male citizens. Indeed, I think this is a problem with Aristotle's account of friendship, but I also think it would altogether be a grave mistake simply to dismiss his account on these grounds. It seems to me that the issue of friendship, and its relationship to the good (ethical) life, has never been more successfully dealt with in the long history of Western philosophy than in Aristotle's *Ethics*. And, I think the relative lack of interest in the issue of friendship since Aristotle has adversely affected our subsequent accounts of the ethical. This relative lack of interest, I think, has among other things, helped established the now prevalent divide between ethical matters and the day-to-day living of our lives.

67 Sherman, *The Fabric of Character*, op.cit., n. 7, p. 132.

68 *EE* 1241a 16–18.

69 Sherman indicates that Aristotle refers to this type of consensus as *homonoia*. See *The Fabric of Character*, op.cit., n. 7, p. 132.

70 Ibid., p. 1.

71 P. Bowden, *Caring: Gender-Sensitive Ethics*, London: Routledge, 1997, p. 150.

72 *EN* 1129b 17–19.

73 In general, by 'community' I simply mean a human group that is linked together by dialogical bonds, in the broadest sense of 'dialogical'. But more specifically, when referring to communities in this section I will be referring not to a specific subset of a wider community, but to the widest sort of community at a given time. In our time the relevant community is the global one. But, given that my intention here is to establish some a-historical facts about our communal nature, I do not intend my claims to refer exclusively to our contemporary global community. There have been many communities across the span of history and, indeed, many synchronic communities existed in times when no dialogical links existed between some civilizations (American and European civilizations before the discovery of the Americas to give one example).

I might also mention that I am aware that my broad characterization of community does not accord with our more parochial commonplace conception of community. In this section I intend to show why the emphasis placed on more localized communities is not wholly warranted. This is particularly the case in relation to the issue of justice.

74 *EN* 1129a 7–10.

75 Although this is not the place to engage in a detailed account of the contemporary justice/virtue debate, it is nonetheless worth mentioning that the account of justice I will now be defending – namely, an account that holds that justice flows from virtue – is in frank opposition to much of the current debate on these matters. Current debate tends to present justice and virtue in opposition to one another. It might also be worth mentioning here that, even though I commence this section with an account of justice that is not the sort of conception that prevails in contemporary debates on the matter, it should become clear later on why I think this initial conception is the primary one – the conception of justice upon which all other conceptions are rendered fully intelligible. For a thought-provoking discussion on the contemporary polarization of the justice/virtue debate, and a defence of a compatibilist account, see Onora O'Neil's, *Toward Justice and Virtue: A Constructive Account of Practical Reasoning*, Cambridge: Cambridge University Press, 1996.

76 *EN* 1129b 25–9.

77 For a thought-provoking discussion of how the size of a given community has a direct effect on the possibilities of achieving a given communal ideal (in this instance the ideal of participative democracies) see Jane Mansbridge's, 'The Limits of Friendship', in R. Pennock and J. Chapman (eds), *Participation in Politics*, New York: Lieber-Atherton, 1975, pp. 246–75.

78 This claim is not incompatible with my anti-foundationalist stance as it might at first seem. What I am claiming here is simply that laws cannot be taken for granted on face value. Rather, what gives the laws their *raison d'être* has to do with the ethical ideal that informs our lives – namely, the ethical ideal of living in accordance with complete virtue and how complete virtue is constitutive of *eudaimonia*.

79 I do not want to claim that, if the ideal social conditions obtain, each member of our global community will, in fact, flourish, because it is clear that there are other conditions for flourishing that a community, no matter how good, cannot provide.

80 The concept of care is very pertinent here, given that it is a concept that involves ethical directedness toward others but which does not necessarily involve intimacy of the sort we have in our primary relationships (although, of course, our primary relationships are to a greater or lesser degree relationships of care). I do think that there are different levels of caring, and it is important to realize that these levels exist. There are levels of caring in which the care for a given individual is specifically directed towards that individual, such that the caring admits of no substitutions. The caring relationship I have with a specific friend is defined as such by my caring for that *specific* individual. But I think that there are other, broader caring relationships that do admit of substitution. Consider relationships such as the relationship between a nurse and his or her patient or the caring of an aid worker directed toward those in need of aid. For a thought-provoking alternative view on what is involved in caring see Bowden's *Caring, op. cit.*, n. 71.

81 P. Levi, *The Drowned and the Saved*, London: Abacus, 1999, pp. 100–101.

82 MacIntyre, *After Virtue, op.cit.*, n. 2, p. 32.

83 For an alternative critique of the Modern self – one that engages with Rawls and Habermas – see Ross Poole's, 'Liberalism and Nihilism', *Morality and Modernity*, London: Routledge, 1991, pp. 65–89.

84 MacIntyre, *After Virtue, op.cit.*, n. 2, p. 12.

85 There is another relevant parallel between the immortal life discussed above and our current concerns with the paradigmatic contemporary subject. Remember that, in order to avoid a total collapse of the relevant orderings that were sustaining his or her life, the immortal we discussed was forced to undertake the ultimately self-defeating task of

constructing a stable environment within which to dwell – an environment that was fully under his or her control. Such an environment, we saw, was not conducive towards having a meaningful existence. It seems that one of the fundamental goals of the contemporary Western subject, and the society he or she fosters, is the goal of control – of perfect stability. We insure ourselves, worry about health, about having a stable abode, and a permanent job, and so on. Many of these concerns are, of course, valuable ones. The problem is the motivations behind these concerns, as well as the fact that, as we have seen, a radically controlled environment is one where the relevant ordering for good living cannot obtain. Risk is necessary for well-being.

86   J.P. Sartre, *Being and Nothingness*, New York: Washington Square Press, 1992, p. 567.
87   I shall return to the issue of the actor below when dealing with Nietzsche.
88   MacIntyre, *After Virtue, op.cit.*, n. 2, particularly pp. 113–14 and 256–9.
89   F. Nietzsche, 'On the Uses and Disadvantages of History for Life', *Untimely Meditations*, Cambridge: Cambridge University Press, 1997, pp. 59–123.
90   Ibid., p. 122.
91   Ibid., p. 60–61.
92   Ibid., p. 63.
93   P. Patton, 'Nietzsche and the Problem of the Actor', in A. Schrift (ed.), *Why Nietzsche Still? Reflections on Drama, Culture, and Politics*, Berkeley: University of California Press, 2000, pp. 170–83.
94   Patton takes the idea of inhabiting a role from Ishiguro's novel *The Remains of the Day*.
95   I do not agree with Nietzsche's account that history reveals only the impermanent, fleeting, and meaningless. There is, as this investigation has shown, a universal element in us that exists across time, and which defines us as persons. Another way of making much the same point is that the history that is relevant here is the history of persons.
96   For a concise, yet informative, discussion on the purported dichotomy between the liberal ideal of individuality and the communitarian ideal of interconnectedness see Moira Gatens' and Genevieve Lloyd's, *Collective Immaginings: Spinoza, Past and Present*, London: Routledge, 1999, pp. 132–35. I might also mention that Taylor has an interesting discussion on the confusions that have made the liberal/communitarian distinction appear as a dichotomy in his 'Cross-Purposes: The Liberal-Communitarian Debate', in N. Rossenblum (ed.), *Liberalism and the Moral Life*, Cambridge, Massachusetts: Harvard University Press, 1989, pp. 159–82.
97   R. Malan, *My Traitor's Heart*, London: Vintage Books, 1991.
98   You could, of course, feel this way because you fear for your life. But this is not the sort of fear that is relevant at present. The fear at issue is the sort of fear that comes with a yearning for one's lost place of belonging.
99   My claims here assume that the individual who has materialized in the forest has come from somewhere, and that he or she has a sense that the place where he or she has come from is home – he or she feels that he or she has a place of belonging. By contrast, an individual who has lived in an oppressed and alienating environment may well feel relatively relaxed about being taken away from this oppressive situation (think of the first pilgrims who migrated to North America). Such an individual is, in an important sense, homeless. He or she is looking for home, and may well consider a pristine forest to be an ideal place to settle down. Indeed, I am assuming here that if one does not have a place of belonging, one will be looking for such a place. This need for a place of belonging, I suggest, is a fundamental fact about our condition as persons. But, importantly, the sort of individual I am considering in the above example is the one who is not homeless – the one who has mysteriously been taken away from where he or she belongs.
100  One could speculate here, and probably fairly accurately, that the pressures of modern Western life undermine the possibility of establishing enduring and deeply intimate relationships, and perhaps this aspect of contemporary life plays a large role in producing the overarching feeling of alienation, unhappiness and distrust that seems to permeate our contemporary Western culture.

101 In making this claim I am explicitly aligning myself with Taylor and against what he identifies as the atomism that pervades our contemporary modes of thought regarding the relationship of an individual to his or her community. Taylor argues that this atomism, which is pervasive in contemporary political modes of thought, is largely due to a tradition that draws its inspiration from Locke (and, I might add, Hobbes) whose theories presuppose the possibility of a moral subject existing in isolation from a community. Taylor further argues, and rightly so, that this tradition is in direct opposition to Aristotelian communitarianism which, as we have seen, conceives of persons as existing only amongst others – only as *zoon politikon*. In Taylor's words:

> A social view of the human good, by contrast, holds that an essential constitutive condition of the search for it is bound up with being in society. Thus if I argue that an individual cannot even be a moral subject, and thus a candidate for the realization of the human good, outside of a community of language and mutual discourse about the good and bad, just and unjust, I am rejecting the atomist view, since what a person derives from society is not some aid in realizing his or her good but the very possibility of being an agent seeking that good. (The Aristotelian resonances in the above sentence are, of course, not coincidental.) (C. Taylor, 'Distributive Justice', in R. Solomon and M. Murphy (eds), *What is Justice? Classic and Contemporary Readings*, New York: Oxford University Press, 1990, p. 337).

# Select Bibliography

Annas, J. (1993), *The Morality of Happiness*, New York: Oxford University Press.

Aquinas, T. (1984), 'The Principles of Nature', *Selected Writings of St Thomas Aquinas*, trans. R. Goodwin, Indianapolis: Bobs-Merrill Educational Publishing, pp. 7–14.

Aquinas, T. (1994), *Commentary on Aristotle's De Anima*, trans. K. Foster and S. Humphries, Notre Dame: Dumb Ox Books.

Arendt, H. (1974), *The Human Condition*, Chicago: University of Chicago Press.

Aristotle (1966), *Ethica Eudemia*, ed. D. Ross Oxford: Clarendon Press.

Aristotle (1966), *Ethica Nichomachea*, ed. D. Ross, Oxford: Clarendon Press.

Aristotle (1966), *Magna Moralia*, ed. D. Ross, Oxford: Clarendon Press.

Aristotle (1966), *Politica*, ed. D. Ross, Oxford: Clarendon Press.

Aristotle (1968), *De Anima*, ed. D. Ross, Oxford: Clarendon Press.

Aristotle (1970), *Physica*, ed. D. Ross, Oxford: Clarendon Press.

Aristotle (1989), *Metaphysica*, ed. G. Goold, Cambridge, Massachusetts: Harvard University Press.

Aristotle (1990), *A New Aristotle Reader*, ed. J. Ackrill, Oxford: Clarendon Press.

Aristotle (1994), *Ethica Nichomachea*, trans. H. Rackham, Cambridge, Massachusetts: Harvard University Press.

Borges, J. L. (2000), 'The Immortal', in D. Yates and J. Irby (eds), *Labyrinths: Selected Stories and Other Writings*, London: Penguin Books, pp. 135–49.

Bowden, P. (1997), *Caring: Gender Sensitive Ethics*, London: Routledge.

Cavell, M. (1993), *The Psychoanalytic Mind: From Freud to Philosophy*, Cambridge, Massachusetts: Harvard University Press.

Cherniak, C. (1986), *Minimal Rationality*, Cambridge, Massachusetts: MIT Press.

Cooper, J. (1975), *Reason and Human Good in Aristotle*, Cambridge, Massachusetts: Harvard University Press.

Cooper, J. (1980), 'Aristotle on Friendship', in A. Rorty (ed.), *Essays on Aristotle's Ethics*, Berkeley: University of California Press, pp. 301–40.

Davidson, D. (1980), 'How is Weakness of Will Possible', *Essays on Actions and Events*, Oxford: Clarendon Press, pp. 21–42.

Davidson, D. (1980), 'Psychology as Philosophy', *Essays on Actions and Events*, Oxford: Clarendon Press, pp. 229–44.

Davidson, D. (1984), 'Thought and Talk', *Inquiries into Truth and Interpretation*, Oxford: Clarendon Press, pp. 155–70.

Davidson, D. (1985), 'Incoherence and Irrationality', *Dialectica*, **39** (4), pp. 345–54.

Davidson, D. (1985), 'Rational Animals', in E. LePore and B. McLaughlin (eds), *Actions and Events: Perspectives on the Philosophy of Donald Davidson*, Oxford: Basil Blackwell, pp. 473–80.

Davidson, D. (1986), 'Radical Interpretation', *Inquiries into Truth and Interpretation*, Oxford: Oxford University Press, pp. 125–39.

Davidson, D. (1987), 'Deception and Division', in J. Elster (ed.), *The Multiple Self*, Cambridge: Cambridge University Press, pp. 79–92.

Davidson, D. (1991), 'Three Varieties of Knowledge', in A. Phillips Grifiths (ed.), *A.J. Ayer: Memorial Essays*, Cambridge: Cambridge University Press, pp. 153–66.

Davidson, D. (1992), 'The Second Person', *Midwest Studies in Philosophy*, **17**, pp. 255–67.

Davidson, D. (1994), 'The Problem of Objectivity', *Proceedings from the Francqui Chair Lectures given at the Institute of Philosophy at the Catholic University of Leuven*, October-December, pp. 203–20.

Davidson, D. (1999), 'Reply to Dagfinn Føllesdal', in L. Hahn (ed.), *The Philosophy of Donald Davidsion*, Chicago: Open Court, pp. 729–32.

Davidson, D. (1999), 'Reply to W. V. Quine', in L. Hahn (ed.), *The Philosophy of Donald Davidson*, Chicago: Open Court, pp. 80–86.

Dreyfus, H. (1980), 'Holism and Hermeneutics', *Review of Metaphysics*, **34**, September, pp. 3–23.

Dreyfus, H. (1996), 'What is Moral Maturity? A Phenomenological Account of the Development of Ethical Expertise', paper presented at Murdoch University.

Fodor, J. and LePore, E. (1996), *Holism: A Shopper's Guide*, Oxford: Blackwell.

Føllesdal, D. (1999), 'Triangulation', in L. Hahn (ed.), *The Philosophy of Donald Davidson*, Chicago: Open Court, pp. 719–26.

Friedman, M. (1993), *What are Friends For? Feminist Perspectives on Personal Relationships and Moral Theory*, Ithaca, New York: Cornell University Press.

Gadamer, H. G. (1986), 'Composition and Interpretation', *The Relevance of the Beautiful and Other Essays*, Cambridge: Cambridge University Press, pp. 66–73.

Gatens, M. and Lloyd, G. (1999), *Collective Imaginings: Spinoza, Past and Present*, London: Routledge.

Hartman, E. (1977), *Substance, Body, and Soul: Aristotelian Investigations*, Princeton, New Jersey: Princeton University Press.

Heidegger, M. (1993), 'The Origin of the Work of Art', in D. F. Krell (ed.), *Basic Writings: From Being and Time (1927) to the Task of Thinking (1964)*, New York: Harper San Francisco, pp. 139–203.

Heidegger, M. (1993), 'The Question Concerning Technology', in D. F. Krell (ed.), *Basic Writings: From Being and Time (1927) to The Task of Thinking (1964)*, New York: Harper San Francisco, pp. 307–41.

Heidegger, M. (1995), *Aristotle's Metaphysics Θ 1–3: On the Essence and Actuality of Force*, Bloomington: Indiana University Press.

Heil, J. (1992), *The Nature of True Minds*, Cambridge: Cambridge University Press.

Hume, D. (1990), *Enquiries Concerning the Principles of Morals*, Oxford: Clarendon Press.

Kertesz, I. (1992), *Fateless*, Evanston, Illinois: Northwestern University Press.

Lear, J. (1988), *Aristotle; The Desire to Understand*, Cambridge: Cambridge University Press.

Levi, P. (1999), *The Drowned and the Saved*, London: Abacus.

McDowell, J. (1998), 'Virtue and Reason', in N. Sherman (ed.), *Aristotle's Ethics: Critical Essays*, Lanham, Maryland: Rowman & Littlefield, pp. 121-43.

MacIntyre, A. (1984), *After Virtue: A Study in Moral Philosophy*, Notre Dame, Indiana: Notre Dame University Press.

Malan, R. (1991), *My Traitor's Heart*, London: Vintage Books.

Malpas, J. (1990), '*Kategoriai* and the Unity of Being', *Journal of Speculative Philosophy*, **4**, 13–36.

Malpas, J. (1992), *Donald Davidson and the Mirror of Meaning: Holism, Truth, Interpretation*, Cambridge: Cambridge University Press.

Malpas, J. (1994), 'Self-knowledge and Skepticism', *Erkenntnis*, **40**, pp. 165–84.

Malpas, J. (1998), 'Death and the Unity of a Life', in J. Malpas and R. Solomon (eds), *Death and Philosophy,* London: Routledge, pp. 120–34.

Malpas, J. (1999), *Place and Experience: A Philosophical Topography*, Cambridge: Cambridge University Press, pp. 138–56.

Malpas, J. and Wickham, G. (1995), 'Governance and Failure: On the Limits of Sociology', *Journal of Sociology*, **31** (3), November, pp. 37–50.

Malpas, J. and Wickham, G. (1997), 'Governance and the World: From Joe Dimaggio to Michael Foucault', *The UTS Review: Cultural Studies and New Writing*, **3** (2), November, pp. 91–108.

Mansbridge, J. (1975), 'The Limits of Friendship', in J. R. Pennock and J. W. Chapman (eds), *Participation in Politics*, New York: Lieber-Atherton, pp. 246–75.

Millett, S. (1996), *Autopoiesis an Immanent Teleology: Toward and Aristotelian Environmental Ethic*, unpublished PhD dissertation, Murdoch University.

Nagel, T. (1986), *The View from Nowhere*, Oxford: Oxford University Press.

Nietzsche, F. (1967), *The Birth of Tragedy and The Wagner Case*, New York: Vintage Books.

Nietzsche, F. (1997), *Untimely Meditations*, in D. Breazeale (ed.), Cambridge: Cambridge University Press.

Nussbaum, M. C. (1994), *The Fragility of Goodness; Luck and Ethics in Greek Tragedy and Philosophy*, Cambridge: Cambridge University Press.

Nussbaum, M. C. (1995), 'Aristotle on Human Nature and the Foundations of Ethics', in J. E. J. Altham and R. Harrison (eds), *World, Mind, and Ethics: Essays on the Ethical Philosophy of Bernard Williams*, New York: Cambridge University Press, p. 86–131.

Nussbaum, M. C. (1998), 'The Discernment of Perception: An Aristotelian Conception of Private and Public Rationality', in N. Sherman (ed.), *Aristotle's Ethics: Critical Essays*, Lanham, Maryland: Rowman & Littlefield, pp. 145–81.

Oakley, J. (1992), *Morality and the Emotions*, London: Routledge.

O'Neill, O. (1996), *Toward Justice and Virtue: A Constructive Account of Practical Reasoning*, Cambridge: Cambridge University Press.

Orwell, G. (1984), *Nineteen Eighty-Four*, Harmondsworth: Penguin Books Ltd.

Owens, J. (1981), *Aristotle: The Collected Papers of Joseph Owens*, ed. J. R. Catan, Albany, New York: State University of New York Press.

Patton, P. (2000), 'Nietzsche and the Problem of the Actor', in A. Schrift (ed.), *Why Nietzsche Still? Reflections on Drama, Culture, and Politics*, Berkeley: University of California Press, pp. 170–83.

Peters, F. E. (1967), *Greek Philosophical Terms: A Historical Lexicon*, New York: New York University Press.

Quine, W. V. O. (1960), *Word and Object*, Cambridge, Massachusetts: MIT Press.

Quine, W. V. O. (1969), 'Ontological Relativity', *Ontological Relativity and Other Essays*, New York: Columbia University Press, pp. 26–58.

Quine, W. V. O. (1999), 'Where Do We Disagree?', in L. Hahn (ed.), *The Philosophy of Donald Davidson*, Chicago and La Salle: Open Court, pp. 73–9.

Ricoeur, P. (1992), *Oneself as Another*, Chicago: University of Chicago Press.

Sartre, J.-P. (1992), *Being and Nothingness*, New York: Washington Square Press.

Sherman, N. (1985), 'Character, Planning, and Choice', *Review of Metaphysics*, **39**, pp. 83–106.

Sherman, N. (1989), *The Fabric of Character: Aristotle's Theory of Virtue*, Oxford: Clarendon Press.

Sophocles (1994), *Philoctetes*, ed. H. Lloyd-Jones, Cambridge, Massachusetts: Harvard University Press.

Taylor, C. (1989), 'Cross-Purposes: The Liberal-Communitarian Debate', in N. L. Rossenblum (ed.), *Liberalism and the Moral Life*, Cambridge, Massachusetts: Harvard University Press, pp. 159–82.

Taylor, C. (1989), *Sources of the Self*, Cambridge, Massachusetts: Harvard University Press.

Taylor, C. (1990), 'Distributive Justice', in R. C. Solomon and M. C. Murphy (eds), *What is Justice? Classic and Contemporary Readings*, New York: Oxford University Press, pp. 335–9.

Taylor, C. (1995), 'Explanation and Practical Reason', in M. C. Nussbaum and A. Sen (eds), *The Quality of Life*, Oxford: Clarendon Press, pp. 208–41.

Taylor, C. (1999), *Philosophy and the Human Sciences: Philosophical Papers 2*, Cambridge: Cambridge University Press.

Telfer, E. (1989–90), 'The Unity of Moral Virtues', *Proceedings From the Aristotelian Society*, **90** (1), pp. 35–48.

Walker, M. (1998), *Moral Understandings: A Feminist Study in Ethics*, New York: Routledge.

Williams, B. (1973), 'The Makropulos Case: Reflections on the Tedium of Immortality', *Problems of Self: Philosophical Papers 1956–1972*, London: Cambridge University Press, pp. 82–100.

Williams, B. (1985), *Ethics and the Limits of Philosophy*, Cambridge, Massachusetts: Harvard University Press.

Williams, B. (1986), 'Hylomorphism', in J. Annas (ed.), *Oxford Studies in Ancient Philosophy*, Vol. 4, Oxford: Clarendon Press, pp. 189–99.

Woodfield's, A. (1976), *Teleology*, Cambridge: Cambridge University Press.

# Index